D1760220

COSMOPOLITAN STYLE

Rebecca L. Walkowitz

COSMOPOLITAN STYLE

MODERNISM BEYOND THE NATION

Columbia University Press   New York

Columbia University Press
Publishers Since 1893
New York   Chichester, West Sussex
Copyright © 2006 Columbia University Press

Columbia University Press wishes to express its appreciation
for assistance given by the Mosse/Weinstein Center for Jewish Studies
at the University of Wisconsin–Madison for the publication of this work.

Library of Congress Cataloging-in-Publication Data
Walkowitz, Rebecca L., 1970–
Cosmopolitan style : modernism beyond the nation / Rebecca L. Walkowitz.
p. cm.
Includes bibliographical references and index.
ISBN 0-231-13750-8 (cloth : alk. paper) — ISBN 0-231-51053-5 (electronic)
1. English fiction—20th century—History and criticism. 2. Modernism (Literature)—
Great Britian. 3. Cosmopolitanism—Great Britain. I. Title

PR888.M63W35   2006
823'.9109112—dc22   2005054818

Columbia University Press books are printed
on permanent and durable acid-free paper.

Printed in the United States of America
c 10 9 8 7 6 5 4 3 2 1

For my parents, Daniel Walkowitz and Judith Walkowitz

In short, it is a matter of knowing what one wants to write about, whether butterflies or the condition of the Jews. And when one knows, then it remains to decide how one will write about it.

—JEAN-PAUL SARTRE, "WHAT IS LITERATURE?"

I hope you will like my "trivial" play. It is written by a butterfly for butterflies.

—OSCAR WILDE, LETTER TO ARTHUR L. HUMPHREYS

CONTENTS

ACKNOWLEDGMENTS

THIS BOOK ABOUT cosmopolitanism got its start and was completed in four provincial centers: Brighton, Cambridge, Manhattan, and Madison. Most of the initial thinking and much of the writing took place at Harvard University, where I was challenged and nourished by an extraordinary group of colleagues and by mentors who supported me generously from the beginning. I am especially indebted to Philip Fisher, Marjorie Garber, Barbara Johnson, and D. A. Miller. Philip Fisher offered wise advice on every chapter and introduced me to several of the novels that are featured in this study. Marjorie Garber's readings made me want to write, and her warm encouragement of this project and of all of my other projects has been unstinting. Barbara Johnson taught me to think about the conflict between politics and desire, and her comments on several chapters of my dissertation changed the way I understand critique. D. A. Miller, in whose vibrant classroom I spent two semesters as an undergraduate, inspired me to apply to graduate school. Other teachers at Harvard and at the University of Sussex, where I spent two stimulating years between 1992 and [1994], influenced the work I have done here: my thanks to Homi K. Bhabha, Michael Fried, Henry Louis Gates Jr., and Jann Matlock for their provocations and kindness. My peers at Harvard were my first readers and have continued to be valued friends. I am very grateful for the keen intelligence and good humor of Aviva Briefel, Dan Chiasson, Amanda Claybaugh, Nick LoLordo, Mun-Hou Lo, Monica Miller, Sianne Ngai, Patrick O'Malley, Martin Puchner, and Catherine Toal.

Jennifer Crewe at Columbia University Press has been a wonderful editor, and I am grateful for her professionalism and her lively interest in this study.

My thanks to Juree Sondker and Michael Haskell for their work in preparing the book for publication and to Christopher Schmitt, Sara Phillips, Aarthi Vadde, Thomas Dancer, and Taryn Okuma for their research support. I am very pleased to acknowledge the financial assistance of the Graduate School of Arts and Sciences at Harvard University, the Mrs. Giles Whiting Foundation, the U.S. Department of Education, the American Council of Learned Societies, and, at UW-Madison, the Institute for Research in the Humanities, the Graduate School of Letters and Science, the Center for European Studies, the Language Institute, and the Department of English. Early versions of the chapters in this book were presented at Harvard University, Columbia University, the UW-Madison Institute for Research in the Humanities, the UW-Madison Cosmopolitan Cultures seminar, the Chicago Literature and Society Seminar, the Psychoanalysis and Colonialism conference, the Modernist Studies Association conference, the Narrative conference, the Midwest Modern Language Association conference, the Modern Language Association conference, and the American Comparative Literature Association conference. I would like to thank my hosts and the audiences on all of those occasions. Parts of several chapters have appeared in other forms: "Virginia Woolf's Evasion: Critical Cosmopolitanism and British Modernism," in *Bad Modernisms*, ed. Douglas Mao and Rebecca L. Walkowitz (Durham: Duke University Press, 2006), 119–44; "Conrad's Adaptation," *Modern Drama* 44, no. 3 (Fall 2001): 318–36; "Narrative Theatricality: Joseph Conrad's Drama of the Page," in *Against Theatre: Creative Destructions on the Modernist Stage*, ed. Alan Ackerman and Martin Puchner (London: Palgrave, forthcoming); and "Ishiguro's Floating Worlds," *ELH* 68, no. 4 (Winter 2001): 1037–64. My thanks to Duke University Press, the University of Toronto Press, Palgrave, and the Johns Hopkins University Press for permission to include portions of these essays here.

Many interlocutors have helped me to imagine what a book about "cosmopolitan style" could look like. For their conversations about this project, my warm thanks to Richard Begam, Michael Bernard-Donals, Antoinette Burton, Christopher Castiglia, Guillermina De Ferrari, Aparna Dharwadker, Vinay Dharwadker, Betsy Draine, Sara Guyer, Jonathan Gil Harris, Eric Hayot, Deborah Jenson, Louise Keely, John Kerkering, Jacques Lezra, Lucienne Loh, Venkat Mani, Nancy Rose Marshall, Jon McKenzie, David McWhirter, Madhavi Menon, Mary Ann O'Farrell, Mario Ortiz-Robles, Cyrena Pondrom, Leah Price, Thomas Schaub, Scott Straus, Harriet Turner, Richard Walker, Carl Wennerlind, and Jesse Wolfe. Several friends and colleagues read portions of the book. I am grateful to Amanda Anderson, Michèle Barrett, Susan Stanford Friedman, Theresa Kelley, Michael LeMahieu, Douglas Mao, Rob Nixon, Bruce Robbins, and John Tiedemann for their many superb comments. Some people are important to the production of a book because they help you to keep working.

Others are important because they help you to stop working. A rare few help with both. Amanda Claybaugh, Lee Edelman, Caroline Levine, Joseph Litvak, and Martin Puchner have been extraordinary readers, listeners, and comrades; Susanne Wofford has been a wonderful mentor and friend. All have provided warmth and wit in equal measure, and I am deeply grateful to each of them.

My parents, to whom this book is dedicated, introduced me to the pleasures and the politics of cosmopolitanism. They have lived with this endeavor longer and more fully than they may care to recall and have enabled me intellectually, emotionally, and financially. I am delighted to thank them on this occasion.

Every day I am grateful for the love and enthusiasm of Henry Turner, who has shared my life in all four of the cities in which this book was conceived. His company has been a delight; his generosity has made my work possible; and his intelligence has made it better.

COSMOPOLITAN STYLE

INTRODUCTION

CRITICAL COSMOPOLITANISM AND MODERNIST NARRATIVE

*I sat at a table near the open terrace door, my papers and notes spread out around
me, drawing connections between events that lay far apart but which seemed to
me to be of the same order.*

—W. G. SEBALD, *VERTIGO*

WHAT DOES IT mean, today, to be a British novelist, or even an English writer? At the beginning of the twenty-first century, someone who wins a prize for British fiction may have been born outside Great Britain, may be a citizen of Great Britain who lives elsewhere, or may live in Great Britain while remaining a foreign national;[1] a writer may win a prize for English fiction but English may not have been the language in which the award-winning book was first composed; a writer who wins an English fiction prize may also win, in England, a foreign literature prize as well. The late novelist W. G. Sebald, who was emerging as a major figure in British letters when he died in a car accident in December 2001, fit many of these characteristics: he was born in Germany in 1944, he settled permanently in England in 1970, he wrote each of his four novels originally in German before they were translated into English, and yet in the few years before his death his novels were celebrated as some of the most significant new works of contemporary British fiction. In 2001, Sebald published *Austerlitz*, for which he was posthumously awarded the National Book Critics Circle Award in the United States, the Foreign Fiction prize from the London *Independent*, and the Koret prize for Jewish literature, though Sebald was not Jewish; in addition, the novel was short-listed for the prestigious W. H. Smith literary prize, which in forty years of competition has never gone to a contemporary work composed in a language other than English.

That some of these awards seem mutually exclusive may suggest that readers are now more willing to overlook literary classifications than they have been in the past or that they are less concerned, in an age of globalization and near-immediate translation, about the original language of a text.[2] Yet the importance and visibility of immigration as a principle, topic, and condition of Sebald's writing should not be underestimated: shuttling among several nations and among memories of several nations, Sebald's narrators draw "connections" among experiences separated by time, place, and tone. He is willing, even eager, to assemble cultural and ethical points of view that seem inconsistent or incommensurate. Sebald does not transcend the categories of British, English, foreign, German, and Jewish writing. But he unsettles the differences among them. His novels disorient the conventions of national literature and cultural distinctiveness by adding new experiences, such as the *kindertransport* and Chinese silk production, to narratives of British culture, while also embedding these experiences in places other than Britain. Sebald thus enhances and also disables local points of view: enhances, because he shows the global networks in which even the most local experiences participate, and disables, because he suggests that those networks change what local experiences are.

In this double gesture, Sebald's writing participates in a tradition of British literary modernism that includes the novels of Joseph Conrad, James Joyce, and Virginia Woolf at the beginning of the twentieth century, as well as those of Salman Rushdie and Kazuo Ishiguro at the end. I argue that these writers have used the salient features of modernist narrative, including wandering consciousness, paratactic syntax, recursive plotting, collage, and portmanteau language, to develop a critical cosmopolitanism. This has meant thinking beyond the nation but also comparing, distinguishing, and judging among different versions of transnational thought; testing moral and political norms, including the norms of critical thinking; and valuing informal as well as transient models of community.[3] While my book focuses on *literary* style, I will be arguing that the concept of style more broadly conceived—as attitude, stance, posture, and consciousness—is crucial to many of the other, nonliterary practices of cosmopolitanism whose study has transformed disciplines such as history, anthropology, sociology, transnational cultural studies, and media studies.

By speaking of *critical* cosmopolitanism, I mean to designate a type of international engagement that can be distinguished from "planetary humanism" by two principal characteristics:[4] an aversion to heroic tones of appropriation and progress, and a suspicion of epistemological privilege, views from above or from the center that assume a consistent distinction between who is seeing and what is seen. When added to an ideal or a method in cultural theory, the adjective "critical"—as in "critical cosmopolitanism," "critical heroism," "critical internationalism," and "critical globalization," to name just a few recent examples—tends to imply double consciousness, comparison, negation, and persistent self-reflection: an "unwillingness to rest," the attempt to operate "in the world . . . [while] preserving a posture of resistance," the entanglement of "domestic and international perspectives," and the "self-reflexive repositioning of the self in the global sphere."[5] Yet the case of "critical cosmopolitanism" is somewhat different from the others, since the philosophical tradition of cosmopolitanism has long involved both reflection and demystification: in a "cosmopolitan society," Immanuel Kant wrote in his 1784 essay on Enlightenment, a person should be "completely free as well as obliged to impart to the public all his carefully considered, well-intentioned thoughts."[6] Kant argues that one is free as well as obliged to question the coercive guidance of church and state, to cultivate unauthorized thought, and to understand "a violation of rights in *one* part of the world" as a violation "felt *everywhere*."[7]

Critical cosmopolitanism, as I am using it in this study and as it has been articulated in related ways by a variety of theorists,[8] implies a new reflection about reflection. It involves two gestures of critique that supplement and in some ways contest Kant's model: one corresponds to Max Horkheimer's distinction between "traditional" and "critical" theory; the other involves what I call the critique of critique, which I identify in the work of several modernist writers and which scholars of the novel and other theorists are now formulating in their efforts to historicize and challenge the protocols of "critical reading."[9] In Horkheimer's distinction, "critical theory" involves the effort—an effort that is something of an injunction—to position knowledge in history, to investigate the social uses of knowledge, and to evaluate the political interests that knowledge has served. Critical theory rejects the idea of "neutral" categories and "the insistence that thinking is a fixed vocation, a self-enclosed realm within society as a whole" (232, 243). Horkheimer's theory is committed to social progress, as Kant's is, and to the belief that social progress will depend on demystification and enlightenment. But the critique of critique often departs from Horkheimer's program. It extends the investigation of categories that seem to be neutral to the affective conditions (rationality, purpose, coherence, detachment) that have seemed to make argument or engagement possible. This involves questioning the "faith in exposure" and "method" that have been central to the tradition of critical theory.[10] The critique of critique includes Theodor W. Adorno's suspicion of instrumental action and "responsible" theory in his essays of the late 1960s and Stuart Hall's emphasis in the 1990s on a cultural politics that is rooted in differentiation rather than in negation.[11]

More recently, the critique of critique has led scholars to analyze the history of critical dispositions and to associate critique with a greater range of social dynamics and embodied affects: Michael Warner speaks of "reverence" as a critical idiom, for example, and Jordana Rosenberg of "enthrallment."[12] And writing of "ugly feelings," Sianne Ngai argues that twentieth-century artists have developed "models of subjectivity, collectivity, and agency not entirely foreseen by past theorists of the commonwealth."[13] Of course, it is difficult to think of "reverence" as a critical disposition, since Enlightenment ideas of critique so much depend on the value of autonomous thinking and the freedom from religious or political authority. But Warner asks to us to consider that the "apparent abnegation of agency" can create opportunities for new reflection, reasoning, and self-cultivation (18), just as Ngai proposes that thinking about powerlessness can generate new opportunities for intellectual inquiry (14). And, indeed, the willingness to relinquish physical or psychological control, to become temporarily and purposefully inattentive, or "disconcerted" as Ngai puts it, is central to early-twentieth-century conceptions of self-knowledge and of the limits of self-knowledge.

This study focuses on novels that develop and examine new attitudes of cosmopolitanism and do so in the service of a kind of critique. To be sure, modernist narrative strategies can be adapted for various political enterprises, as can critical attitudes. *Cosmopolitan Style* is concerned with writers who have used naturalness, triviality, evasion, mix-ups, treason, and vertigo to generate specific projects of democratic individualism, on the one hand, and of antifascism or anti-imperialism, on the other. A new distrust of civilizing processes, and of the role of art in these processes, leads these writers to develop forms of critical cosmopolitanism that reflect both a desire for and an ambivalence about collective social projects. Cosmopolitan attitudes of mix-up and evasion disrupt neutral models of purpose, evaluation, and detachment not only by resisting them but also by transforming or amending them: with flirtation, Salman Rushdie adds playfulness and confusion to a politics of antiracism that has relied on tolerance and distinction; with evasion, Virginia Woolf suggests that autonomous thinking sometimes involves the refusal to think purposefully. As a tradition of political affiliation and philosophical thought, cosmopolitanism has always involved a negotiation between distance and proximity. But twentieth- and twenty-first-century writers emphasize conditions of limited or suspended agency, and they ask us to consider how conceptions of belonging are bound up in the production, classification, and reception of literary narratives.[14]

Critical cosmopolitanism thus means reflecting on the history, uses, and interests of cosmopolitanism in the past—how, for example, cosmopolitanism has been used to support or to tolerate imperialism.[15] And it also means reflecting on analytic postures, the history, uses, and interests of "the critical"—how, for example, a commitment to collective agency may be a style rather than an index of transnational politics. One can see this double emphasis in a sentence from the opening paragraph of *Cosmopolitanism*, a collection of essays that first appeared in *Public Culture* in 2000. The editors are explaining that they will not define their eponymous term because, they contend, "specifying cosmopolitanism positively and definitively is an uncosmopolitan thing to do."[16] One might imagine that the authors of this sentence, Carol Breckenridge, Sheldon Pollock, Homi K. Bhabha, and Dipesh Chakrabarty, are making an unserious claim: one that is, as Oscar Wilde might say, "perfectly phrased" but not exactly useful. Yet the claim, in all its unseriousness, captures the overlapping, somewhat contradictory projects of traditional and critical cosmopolitanism:[17] it combines the useful cosmopolitanism of belonging beyond the polis or the nation, and the "perfectly phrased" cosmopolitanism of dissenting individualism and decadent refusal. In this sentence, cosmopolitanism refers to a philosophical project and also to an attitude (refusing to specify positively and definitively). By insisting that there has not been only one cosmopolitanism, Breckenridge, Pollock, et al. are articulating a critical theory in Horkheimer's sense, and by insisting that cosmopolitanism might involve thinking and feeling in nonexclusive, nondefinitive ways, the editors are invoking, instead of judgment and progress, an ethos of uncertainty, hesitation, and even wit that is sometimes at odds with political action and with the interventionist paradigms of critical theory.

At the beginning of the twentieth century, modernist writers sought to measure various experiences of thinking and feeling globally, especially in the contexts of imperialism, patriotism, and world war. But it is in their additional reflection on the relationships between narrative and political ideas of progress, aesthetic and social demands for literalism, and sexual and conceptual decorousness, that Conrad, Woolf, and Joyce make their most significant contributions to the analytic project of critical cosmopolitanism. Writing against xenophobia and against nativist conceptions of community, Ishiguro, Rushdie, and Sebald have revived efforts to question the definitions and uses of naturalness, argument, utility, attentiveness, reasonableness, and explicitness. In this book, I will be referring to a specific repertoire of literary strategies that were developed by writers at the beginning of the twentieth century and later transformed by writers at the end; two of the novelists I discuss, Ishiguro and Rushdie, are still publishing today. This project, therefore, focuses on two distinct periods in literary history: in the first part of the book, most of the work I consider was published between 1899 and 1940; in the second part, most was published between 1982 and 2001. As this structure should suggest, I am not restricting modernist practices to a single historical period (the early twentieth century) or to a single global orientation ("Europe" or "the West"), though I will be focusing on works of literature produced in the twentieth century by writers who are situated, at least in part and not always happily, within Great Britain and Ireland.[18] I am calling these writers British because they are British citizens, have lived in Britain, or have worked within a British literary tradition, even if all have worked within other (English, Irish, Indian, German, Polish, Japanese) traditions as well. All with the exception of Joyce lived or first published in England, but I speak of Britain in order to emphasize global contexts of citizenship, world war, empire, and decolonization, and to examine rather than obscure the many different experiences, local and transnational, that inform British culture today.[19]

The writers I examine in this study generate cosmopolitan styles not simply because they *are* cosmopolitan but because, in the simplest terms, they imagine that conditions of national and transnational affiliation depend on narrative patterns of attentiveness, relevance, perception, and recognition. Moreover, they assert the often-invisible connections between personal and international experiences.[20] Formal patterns of relevance and recognition, these writers propose, are crucial to the politics of cosmopolitanism: in *The Secret Agent*, Conrad shows how social processes of classification create the physical characteristics of foreigners; in *Mrs. Dalloway*, Woolf asks us to see the social and literary conventions of patriotism that determine where and when war happens; and in *The Rings of Saturn*, Sebald suggests that those who focus only on the present and the proximate will fail to notice that the lavish architecture of a train station in Belgium was funded by the profits of colonialism in Africa.

Modernism involves strategies that respond to and engage with the experience of modernity, a condition of industrialization and "spirit of critique," as Dilip Parameshwar Gaonkar puts it, that scholars now associate not only with the past and with the West but also with emergent practices of "non-Western people everywhere."[21] Michel Foucault provides a definition of modernism that I will use to describe the projects of all of the novelists I consider in this study. He writes of "an attitude" or "consciousness" of modernity: "a type of philosophical interrogation—one that simultaneously problematizes man's relation to the present, man's historical mode of being, and the constitution of the self as an autonomous subject."[22] Two more recent theorists also emphasize attitude and consciousness but extend Foucault's model to non-European contexts: Susan Stanford Friedman presents modernism "as the structural principle of radical rupture—wherever, whenever, and in whatever forms it might occur," and Dipesh Chakrabarty, describing modernist practices in early-twentieth-century Calcutta, writes of "the struggle to make capitalist modernity comfortable for oneself," which includes "cultivating a certain style of being in the eyes of others."[23]

Cosmopolitan Style diverges from traditional accounts of international modernism by treating literary style politically, as a supple and disputed concept within twentieth-century British culture, and by replacing static models of modernist exile with more flexible, more dynamic models of migration, entanglement, and mix-up. Whereas critics from Terry Eagleton to Caren Kaplan have argued that early-twentieth-century writers used metaphors of exile to represent various experiences of displacement, I argue instead that modernist writers troubled the distinction between local and global that most conceptions of exile have presupposed.[24] This book returns to the subject of modernism and internationalism, as recent books by Pericles Lewis, Jessica Berman, and Jed Esty have done, but it uses the resources of late-twentieth-century fiction and cultural theory to offer a new analytic vocabulary both for the earlier period and for the writing that follows. I examine the late-twentieth-century "internationalization of English literature," to use Bruce King's phrase, not only as an expansion of places, actors, and even languages but also as an extension of modernist impulses and practices.[25] By shifting from the concept of "international modernism" to the concept of "critical cosmopolitanism," I am emphasizing intellectual projects more than intellectual conditions, though I will in the chapters that follow often consider the social and historical circumstances of world war or migration that gave these projects their specific opportunities, limits, and motivations. In the past, international modernism has referred to the experience of artists who moved from one European city to the next or to the mingling of national languages and cultural materials within works of art.[26] Even today, the category tends to invoke communities of artists or artists who travel instead of analytic interventions or ideas of community. Many works of modernism are international in their themes and traditions and origins, but they may not be cosmopolitan in the several senses I've been describing. T. S. Eliot's *Waste Land* is a prime example—perhaps the preeminent example—of a modernist text that is certainly cosmopolitan in its posture of worldliness, in its collage of national traditions, and in its resistance to the moral niceties of modern culture, but it is not especially interested in representing patterns or fictions of affiliation, in rejecting fixed conceptions of the local, or in comparing the uses and histories of global thinking.[27]

The writers I discuss in this study have been concerned with the need both to transform and to disable social categories: with what ought to be described, on the one hand, and with the social conditions and political consequences of description, on the other. Arguing that patterns of description and recognition are a central concern of modernist narrative, I follow Virginia Woolf, who asserts in her essays that novelists need to discard the "custom" and "convention" that keep them from representing "what is commonly thought small," such as the "dark places of psychology" and the daily experience of women.[28] Later novelists focus on the inadequacy and indispensability of representing minority experiences in the contexts of racism and imperialism: Ishiguro examines the political consequences of narrative strategies that seem to imitate the characteristics of specific cultures, and Rushdie suggests that it is better to mix up nativist readers than to correct them.[29] It is this concern with description—the uses of imitation and parody, the determination of what is describable or worthy of description, the novel's status as a cause or an effect of national culture, the processes and political contexts of knowing and recognizing—that modernist narrative brings to the tradition of cosmopolitanism and to the development of its current "critical" forms.

Before examining how "style" is a crucial aspect of "cosmopolitanism," I will consider, first, what the meanings of cosmopolitanism are and, second, how the project of cosmopolitanism, which tends to conjure a vision of ethics, community, politics, and new interdisciplinary paradigms, is related to the project of style, which can seem trivial, idiosyncratic, apolitical, and anachronistically literary. Recent studies by Jessica Berman and Amanda Anderson have offered comprehensive accounts of the philosophical traditions of cosmopolitanism within nineteenth- and early-twentieth-century literature. *Cosmopolitan Style* emphasizes the tradition of cosmopolitan posture or attitude and explores how developments in modernist literary style coincide with new ways of thinking about political critique. At the same time, this study argues for the persistence of modernist concerns and techniques in late-twentieth-century writing. The terms I introduce highlight personal affects or mannerisms that are less than affirmative: naturalness carries the suggestion of pretense, and triviality the sense of pettiness, while mix-up and vertigo imply a lack of agency or efficacy; evasion and treason suggest downright negligence and even intentional bad faith. With these terms, I foreground and to some extent value the artful idiosyncrasies and political ambiguities of critical cosmopolitanism.

THE MEANINGS OF COSMOPOLITANISM

The novelists I consider share a common skepticism about the generalizations of collective agency, about political commitments defined by national culture, and about efforts to specify and fix national characteristics. And they have provoked substantial criticism from a variety of groups, including British writers opposing German militarism, Irish writers opposing British rule, socialist writers suspicious of rootlessness, fascist writers suspicious of individualism, and postcolonial writers suspicious of non-Europeans who address European audiences. In climates of insurgent nationalism and resurgent nativism, some early-twentieth-century critics dismissed Conrad, Joyce, and Woolf as indecent, evasive, or opportunistic, while later critics have called Rushdie and other international writers blasphemous and inauthentic. To be sure, these writers have engaged in "thinking and acting beyond the local,"[30] have imagined collective affinities in retreat from the nation, or have conceived of the center from the perspective of the margins, to name just a few of the cultural practices that the term "cosmopolitan" has come to designate. Yet they do not reject all local affiliations or collective endeavors: they are attached to nations and cultural groups through acts of citizenship and custom, and several have participated, sometimes loosely and sometimes actively, in social, cultural, and political organizations, such as the Irish National Theatre (Joyce), the 1917 Club and the Hogarth Press (Woolf), and PEN, the international association of writers (Rushdie).

Late-twentieth-century theories of cosmopolitanism rely on three, somewhat different traditions of thought: a philosophical tradition that promotes allegiance to a transnational or global community, emphasizing *detachment* from local cultures and the interests of the nation; a more recent anthropological tradition that emphasizes multiple or flexible *attachments* to more than one nation or community, resisting conceptions of allegiance that presuppose consistency and uncritical enthusiasm; and a vernacular or popular tradition that values the risks of social deviance and the resources of consumer culture and urban mobility. In Europe, vernacular cosmopolitanism has included such practices as *flânerie*, dance hall entertainment, department store shopping, and cultural exhibitions.[31] While the philosophical tradition has often involved elements of attachment—an attachment to all of humanity or a commitment to intercultural understanding—changes in the study of culture in the late nineteenth century altered the *meaning* of attachment in important ways, and the anthropological tradition reflects that alteration.[32]

The various strands of cosmopolitanism differ not only in their ideal of allegiance, whether it needs to transcend the local, but also in their understanding of how the local is defined. Whereas the philosophical tradition derives its view from Enlightenment theories of culture, which assumed distinctiveness and coherence, the anthropological and vernacular traditions have been shaped by modernist theories and practices, which began to treat culture as a process rather than an essence. In *The Predicament of Culture*, published in 1988, James Clifford argues that late-nineteenth-century and early-twentieth-century ethnographers, among whom he includes Friedrich Nietzsche and Joseph Conrad as well as Franz Boas and Bronislaw Malinowski, "inaugurated an interconnected set of assumptions that are now in the last quarter of the twentieth century just becoming visible."[33] It is possible to understand syncretism and transience as qualities of a local community, Clifford asserts, because early-twentieth-century writers began to define cultures not as natural or coherent objects but as "constructs" and "achieved fictions" (95). Today, when advocates of cosmopolitanism combine the political energies of the philosophical tradition with the cultural strategies of the anthropological and vernacular traditions, they tend to imagine a more transient, more changeable idea of the nation than the one implied by the philosophical model. Clifford describes local cultures as practices of "dwelling *and* travel," and Homi K. Bhabha seeks recognition for "the ambivalence that exists within any site of identification and enunciation."[34] Similarly, Bruce Robbins calls for a diverse "cosmopolitics" that is geographically and sometimes nationally "situated."[35] In paradoxical formulations, Clifford, Bhabha, and Robbins convey their political and intellectual resistance to versions of cultural attachment that subsume either too much or too little. Bhabha and Robbins imagine neither a cosmopolitanism everyone would share, as in the Kantian ideal championed by Martha Nussbaum, nor a cosmopolitanism that shares in nothing, having no national or cultural properties at all. They imagine new theories of sharing, which value the partial allegiances and unassimilated communities that for many constitute home.

This shift in the definition of culture helps to explain why Victorian images of cosmopolitanism promote detachment from a definitive nation or community, as Amanda Anderson has shown, whereas modernist images, from Conrad's calculated naturalness to Rushdie's immigrant mix-up, assume more integration among cultures and less uniformity within them.[36] *Cosmopolitan Style* focuses on persistent efforts to reimagine the center in terms of peripheries, within and without, by writers in the first and last decades of the century. My emphasis on the margins of the century and of Britain in some ways complements Jed Esty's recent book on modernism and imperialism, which focuses on the middle of the twentieth century and on those writers—Virginia Woolf, E. M. Forster, and T. S. Eliot in their late phases, proponents of cultural studies in its early phase, and postwar immigrants such as Doris Lessing and George Lamming—who imagined England as "a center without a periphery."[37] However, while Esty distinguishes between what he sees as the expansive, privileged, and outward-looking perspectives of high modernism and the bounded, limited, and inward-looking perspectives generated by late modernism (the 1930s and after), I argue that communal aspirations, urban patterns of participant observation, and ethnographic self-consciousness were important components of modernism in its earliest stages. Modernist writers influenced by the traditions of aestheticism and decadence sought to redefine the scope of international experience (by focusing on the personal, the intimate, and the artificial) and to resist the affects of heroic nationalism (by developing and analyzing marginal groups within metropolitan culture).[38] For example, I see Virginia Woolf's turn to the renovation of English values, in *Three Guineas* (1938) and in her late essay "Thoughts on Peace in an Air War" (1940), as a way of newly articulating rather than rejecting internationalism.

The novels I examine approach large-scale international events, such as world war and immigration, by focusing on the trivial or transient episodes of everyday life. One way to view these novels is to say that in focusing on the trivial and the transient, they are little occupied with political or international conditions. But one might observe, instead, that these novels are testing and redefining what can count as international politics: they may emphasize incidents that seem to be trivial in order to reject wartime values of order and proportion, or they may emphasize what seem to be only personal experiences in order to expand what we know of global processes. Recent work on modernist art and literature has begun to advocate the latter view, arguing that many early-twentieth-century intellectuals, influenced by Walter Pater and Oscar Wilde, understood individualism as a social and political cause.[39] *Cosmopolitan Style* joins these efforts to disaggregate the various internationalisms of British modernism and to consider how public debates about privacy, intimacy, immigration, sexuality, education, and marriage influenced modernist thinking about national boundaries and affiliations.[40] It expands the analysis of international modernism by including those narratives that seem to address domestic or private themes but without assuming that (a) such narratives simply underwrite a celebration of ritualized English communalism or (b) that they are oblivious to colonizing practices abroad.

Part of the task for new work on individualism and politics has been to introduce a new understanding of what modernism was. Another, less explicit part has been to correct past conceptions of modernism by highlighting a greater range of social actors and political affects. In this second gesture, scholars of modernism are emphasizing the relationship of "the political" to "politics," to follow Chantal Mouffe's distinction, where "the political" designates "antagonism that can take many forms and emerge in different types of social relations," whereas "politics" refers to "the ensemble of practices, discourses, and institutions which . . . are affected by the dimension of 'the political.'"[41] Writing of Virginia Woolf's engagement with "the dilemmas of the urban and of modernity," including the dilemmas of market economies, Jennifer Wicke suggests that "the obliquity of Woolf's approach" is advantageous rather than troublesome because it allows the novelist to show, to use Mouffe's terms, how the "politics" of markets affects "the political" of everyday life—how, for example, European economies function on a "miniature scale" (14–15).

Like contemporary feminists who have sought to undo the "public/private divide" that long characterized studies of modernism and modernity, Woolf and writers after her have sought to demonstrate that ideas about gender shape conditions of patriotism as well as conditions of political dissent.[42] In addition, these writers demonstrate that what we can know about gender and patriotism is circumscribed by narrative practices. This means that one must focus critical attention not only on war, state policy, and even military uniforms (as Woolf does in *Three Guineas*) but also on conventions of writing, which determine how arguments are made, how words can be used, and even which comparisons are relevant and which irrelevant or impertinent. My study understands Woolf's "obliquity" as a strategic evasion of heroic culture and wartime patriotism; in addition, I argue that Conrad and Joyce, as well as later writers, demonstrate forcefully that "the political" infuses small-scale decisions about sexuality, childrearing, marriage, shopping, education, art, and social decorum. Woolf, Ishiguro, and Sebald suggest in discussions of shell shock, femininity, militarism, and homosexuality that state policies often reflect assumptions about gender and sexuality that are largely invisible or unexamined. Woolf's analysis of this issue is both direct and indirect. Directly, she will announce in *Three Guineas*, "as a woman, I have no country," and will show powerfully how the politics of gender in England is related to the politics of fascism in Germany.[43] Indirectly, in "The Mark on the Wall" and in *Mrs. Dalloway* (as I discuss in chapter 3), she will propose that British imperialism and wartime masculinity are generated by narratives that require euphemism and hypotaxis.

The claim that literary norms operate politically has been crucial tenet not only of feminist writing by Woolf and later scholars but also of postcolonial fiction and criticism by Ngugi wa Thiong'o, Chinua Achebe, Frantz Fanon, Edward Said, and Gauri Viswanathan. The continuity among these efforts suggests that there is a strain of "postmodernism" that links Woolf and other early-twentieth-century writers to contemporary postcolonial and cosmopolitan novelists: both groups aim to analyze and invent new "rules and categories" of art, which Jean-François Lyotard has called the postmodern condition within modernity.[44] Among postcolonial writers, analysis and invention have focused on the use of the English language in anticolonial literature, the implication of culture in imperialism, and the relevance of culture to the politics of national liberation. Ishiguro, Rushdie, and Sebald address these issues directly: in *An Artist of the Floating World*, Ishiguro considers whether national allegiance and social responsibility depend on the use of specific literary and visual styles (realist, impressionist, allegorical, and so forth); in his story "Good Advice is Rarer Than Rubies," Rushdie proposes that the vernacular culture of proverbs can be used to mix up and resist the clichés of imperialist culture; and in *The Rings of Saturn*, Sebald oscillates among different historical periods to show that the architectural history of England is bound up with the violent pasts of Europe, Asia, and Africa. Feminist and postcolonial theorists, like these contemporary writers, have worked to expand and politicize areas of social and cultural life that have seemed apolitical in the past. These efforts have diversified the theory and practice of critical cosmopolitanism.

I argue that the syncretic but less-than-national tradition of cosmopolitanism, which is often associated with aestheticism, dandyism, and *flânerie* at the fin de siècle, helped to establish a new analysis of perception and alternative tones of political consciousness among early modernist writers. I want to retain the association between cosmopolitanism and the late-Victorian tradition of aesthetic decadence, a repertoire of excessive and purposefully deviant cultural strategies whose values include pleasure, consumption, syncretism, and perversity.[45] The decadent tradition is important to British modernism because it amplifies the place of transience and artificiality within models of national culture and transnational mobility. Of course, Oscar Wilde and other decadent artists have influenced many writers in the twentieth century.[46] However, this influence has been largely ignored in accounts of international modernism, which have tended to emphasize the outward-looking nature of cosmopolitanism and to associate the avant-garde, as the military metaphor implies, only with tones of antagonism, timeliness, and heroic certainty.[47] Some critics have sought to develop more capacious, less exclusive brands of cosmopolitanism by refusing to assume that only people who travel are able to know and touch the world: offering anecdotes as well as detailed histories, Mica Nava, Monica L. Miller, Arjun Appadurai, and Amitava Kumar argue for the inclusion of consumption, imagination, longing, and fantasy among cosmopolitan practices in the twentieth century.[48] Nava would have us notice, for example, that while the consumption of exotic clothing by middle-class English women is not a form of "politics"—it does not act within or on political institutions—it is part of "the political," in that it shapes social relations of gender, bodily display, urban mobility, and transnational fantasy.

This book treats cosmopolitanism not simply as a model of community but as a model of perversity, in the senses of obstinacy, indirection, immorality, and attitude; this approach allows me to consider the relationship between gestures of idiosyncratic contact or distance and those of sympathetic association. A perverse cosmopolitanism is especially visible in the work of Rushdie, who advocates incorrectness and flirtation as strategies of antiracism, or Sebald, who suggests that transnational sympathies may be nurtured by vertiginous points of view: Sebald writes of Roger Casement, who managed British colonies while criticizing the exploitation of colonized peoples, received a knighthood but was later executed for treason, and was celebrated as a patriot but later reviled as a homosexual. Rushdie's and Sebald's examples of cosmopolitanism include acts of antagonism and individualism as well as acts of community or group affiliation. It will be important for my argument that cosmopolitanism in the early twentieth century can refer not only to practices and affiliations that seem to exceed national collectivity but also to those that seem to preclude, pervert, or abjure national collectivity or civic culture: these can include domestic or intimate practices that seem, perhaps by design, exceptional or eccentric, or they can include manners or behaviors, such as those attributed to Jewish immigrants, that seem naturally to lack any trait whatsoever.

Throughout the twentieth century, as many critics have argued, there has never been a single or coherent "national culture" of Britain, but there have been various efforts to define it: some involve privileging one or more spaces (England, the United Kingdom) over others (Scotland, Wales, the colonies); some involve identifying those practices and people that do not belong by virtue of race, location, or behavior; others involve identifying alternative or more local collectivities in the context of antiracism or of anticolonial projects of national liberation. For the writers in this study, who have tried to resist one or more of these efforts, willful perversity and posture are not accidental or expendable elements of critical cosmopolitanism. On the contrary, these writers suggest, new conceptions of national culture and international belonging require new social attitudes about authenticity, patriotism, and moral correctness. This is why, for example, Joyce focuses his critique of British colonialism and Irish nativism on a system of manners that requires "acquiescence" and "cheerful decorum." These social attitudes, Joyce argues, have helped to keep Irish culture in place. Joyce rejects cheerful decorum by inventing a literary style that purposefully gives offense: he refuses to separate trivial details from serious politics and in fact suggests that anticolonialist art needs to cultivate a promiscuous style of attention.[49]

MODERNIST COSMOPOLITANISM

Some scholars have sought to extricate the international aesthetics of early-twentieth-century modernism from the international politics of late-twentieth-century anticolonialism, multiculturalism, and migration. In *Cosmopolitan Geographies*, Vinay Dharwadker reports approvingly that the new theory and practice of cosmopolitanism "has been freighted with politics rather than with aesthetics."[50] He attributes this emphasis to transformations in the latter quarter of the twentieth century—the consolidation of new types of nationalism, the empowerment of new immigrant communities, the accelerated globalization of capital—and to concerns with "urgent practical problems" (1–2). Similarly, in a survey of the new paradigms, Samuel Scheffler isolates the "common parlance" of cosmopolitanism from other "specialized" meanings presently in circulation.[51] Putting to one side the "posture of worldly sophistication" suggested by colloquial usage, Scheffler divides his remaining subject into two "doctrines": a "doctrine about justice" and a "doctrine about culture" (255–57). His definition implies that the doctrines are part of a political sphere fundamentally separate from acts of self-fashioning and "posture." For her part, Martha Nussbaum eschews European decadence by invoking Rabindranath Tagore's novel *The Home and the World*.[52] With this invocation, Nussbaum attaches her "worldwide community of human beings" to colonized India, conventional narrative practices, and the critique of "superficial" love.[53]

It is understandable that scholars as different as Nussbaum and Dharwadker would want to reject values that seem wholly frivolous or Eurocentric (or both), given the problems of exploitation and inequality that they want an ideal of cosmopolitanism to correct, and it is certainly true that the decadent tradition of aestheticism, dandyism, and flirtation has involved gestures of Eurocentrism and frivolity. However, practices of *bricolage*, aestheticism, and syncretism, which are mainstays of the decadent repertoire, are nevertheless visible in

Dharwadker's examples of anticolonial cosmopolitanism (as in his account of the strategically "ruralized" cosmopolitanism of Mahatma Gandhi) and even, though perhaps accidentally, in Nussbaum's renovated universalism (her example of the cosmopolitan ideal is not only Tagore's novel but also Satyajit Ray's film of that novel, in which cosmopolitanism, characterized by the belief in universal right but also by the desire to learn French and read English poetry, is presented as an alternative to the strident pragmatism that the narrative associates with anticolonialist nationalism).[54] That there are echoes of modernism in contemporary versions of cosmopolitanism does not (or not necessarily) mean that modernism is more committed to ethical action than we thought it was or that cosmopolitan theorists have learned more than they know from modernist culture. I want to suggest, rather, that contemporary versions of cosmopolitanism have included, in their ambivalence about modernization, a persistent effort to reassess the definition and temporality of progress.[55]

Yet some contemporary theorists of cosmopolitanism have been reluctant to associate the new project of critical cosmopolitanism, which emphasizes adverse or quotidian experiences of transnational contact, with modernism, which they argue emphasizes rarified and exceptional experiences. This is the view of modernism that Bruce Robbins offers in *Feeling Global*, when he criticizes Susan Sontag by linking her shrill demands for unconflicted self-sacrifice to "the modernist aim of disorientation, defamiliarization, making strange." Sontag's international project is "like modernism," Robbins continues, in that it "is open to the very few, and it takes its aesthetic value—in part at least—from that very inaccessibility, that critical remoteness from the habits of the benumbed multitude."[56] I argue, on the contrary, that the literary and cultural tradition of modernism reflects a conflict about the content and constituency of international experience and an effort to display relationships between everyday, private activities and public, international ones; in addition, I argue that the idiosyncratic vision of modernism is congruent to and necessary for the *critical* aspect of today's critical cosmopolitanism. In a sense, I think that Robbins is right about modernism but wrong about the analytic conditions of the brand of "cosmopolitics" he advocates.[57] In my view, what Scheffler calls "posture"—that is, a purposeful affect or stance—makes new conceptions of attachment, culture, and affiliation possible. Robbins's cosmopolitanism is "like modernism" not because it is open only to the very few but because it does involve "estrangement" and "hesitation," a term that Robbins will invoke and admire in a later essay.[58] His critique of "modernist" cosmopolitanism notwithstanding, Robbins has been perhaps the strongest advocate of a theory of cosmopolitanism that requires rather than rejects aesthetic experience, "strategic acquiescing," and models of conscience that are "rooted in routine duties and pleasures as well as in once-in-a-lifetime renunciations."[59] Indeed, one might say that he is more concerned with the democratization of actors (read: anyone can think globally or act strategically) than he is with the democratization of affects (read: all global thinking is "cosmopolitical").

In this project, I argue that "discrepant" and "critical" models of cosmopolitanism, which have focused attention on the contested histories of globalization and on a new range of international actors, not only retain but also deploy modernist narrative strategies.[60] For example, while Walter Mignolo limits his model of critical cosmopolitanism to actors who emerge "from the various spatial and historical locations of the colonial difference" (179), he identifies as its principal "tool" something he calls "border thinking," which involves various techniques of *bricolage*: not the invention of new vocabularies but the tactical use of dominant vocabularies (180), "the critique of all possible fundamentalism" (181), and other acts of "appropriating and transforming" (183). Not simply in Mignolo's work but in the work of many other theorists of cosmopolitanism as well there is an oscillation between a project that is defined by located bodies and experiences (for example, people who live on or between state borders) and a project that is defined by analytic perspective, experimentation, and self-consciousness (for example, "border thinking"). Although the editors of the anthology *Cosmopolitanism*—where Mignolo's essay is collected—will not specify their eponymous term positively or definitely, as I've discussed, they do offer two possible meanings: on the one hand, it is a "critique of modernity that minoritarian cosmopolitans *embody*" (6, emphasis added), and, on the other hand, it is a kind of "thinking" (10), for which "minoritarian" experience is a "source" (13). While the editors are indeed arguing that there are "plural . . . cosmopolitanisms" (8) because intellectual formations will differ according to time and place, they are less self-conscious in their move between an emphasis on new voices and an emphasis on the critique of voice—a tension or an oscillation that I have associated with the project of literary modernism and that Foucault, Chakrabarty, and others have associated with the experience of "modernity" more generally.

Most theorists argue that cosmopolitan practices are made possible by a located experience, but most argue also that these practices depend on—do not exist without—an analysis of self and location. "Being cosmopolitan," for texts and for people, means engaging in an intellectual program rather than inhabiting a cultural position. That said, being a cosmopolitan *flâneur*, to take one example, is a rather different experience for those who have full access to the city than it is for those—women, migrants, colonial subjects—who do not, not only because some observers can move and observe more easily than others but also because some are themselves the objects of intense or hostile scrutiny.[61] But the self-conscious project of looking and in some cases appropriating is significant in each case, even as the risks, resources, and outcomes of urban observation will vary. Melba Cuddy-Keane has argued forcefully, speaking of "cultural globalization" in terms that are very similar to those I use to describe critical cosmopolitanism, that "not every cultural encounter should be taken as a form of cultural globalization. Fundamentally, what is at issue is not a prescribed feature of a text but a distinctive form of consciousness."[62] Chakrabarty's account of *adda*—"the practice of friends getting together for long, informal, and unrigorous conversations," which was common in early-twentieth-century Calcutta—offers a prime (nonliterary) example of cultural globalization: as Chakrabarty describes it, *adda* was an effort to resist "capitalist modernity" or to make it "comfortable for oneself" (*Provincializing Europe*, 180). While *adda* was a Bengali practice and is now often described by nationalists as "peculiarly Bengali" (183), Chakrabarty explains, it was also a cosmopolitan practice in several senses: it was a space for reading and discussing books from South Asia as well as from Europe and the United States (198); it was a space where "a democratic and cosmopolitan vision of the world could be nurtured and sustained" (199); and it "provided for many a site for self-presentation, of cultivating a certain style of being in the eyes of others" (187).

Like *flânerie* and dandyism, Charkrabarty emphasizes, *adda* was not a utopian activity: it was a bourgeois space predicated on the separation of the sexes and on an escape, largely for men, from domestic responsibility; its unrigorous conversations were "opposed to the idea of achieving any definite outcome" (204).[63] In Chakrabarty's account, *adda* was neither an ideal nor an experience; rather, it was an activity that involved using the materials of Anglo-Irish and U.S. literary modernism to create new "mannerisms." It was, Chakrabarty writes, "an arena where one could develop new techniques of presenting oneself as a character—from Wilde or Shaw or Joyce or Faulkner—through the development of certain mannerisms (meant for the enjoyment of others), habits of speech, and gestures" (206). In this account of Calcutta "modernism" (182), Anglo-Irish and U.S. modernist texts are not models but tools; using Wilde, Shaw, Joyce, and Faulker, Bengalis created their own attitude of modernity.

As I see it, my extended account of critical and alternative cosmopolitanisms has two important consequences: first, it suggests that cultural strategies of posture have a significant role in even those cosmopolitan paradigms that involve actors who are not social elites or whose position in the world is not in all ways privileged; second, and more tendentiously, it suggests that paradigms that emphasize ethical or political commitments may contain antiheroic or aleatory impulses, whose influence can be seen in the articulation of more narrow kinds of efficacy or in the strategic refusal of aspects of modernization, instrumentality, attentiveness, and historicism. Rather than rejecting cosmopolitanism outright or attempting to "dissociate" cosmopolitanism from the lineaments of "class, hierarchy, and affluence," as some theorists have proposed, it may be more useful, politically as well as intellectually, to acknowledge the analytic complexities of the cosmopolitan tradition.[64] It is not my aim simply to expand the definition of critical cosmopolitanism to include modernist practices. Rather, I suggest (a) that there is no critical cosmopolitanism without modernist practices and (b) that the implication of modernist practices in critical cosmopolitanism must change what we claim about the relationship between idiosyncratic expressions of culture and the conditions of international sympathy or reparation.

COSMOPOLITAN MODERNISM

The tradition of writing that I describe in this project is not always ethical. Those literary strategies I call "cosmopolitan styles" often privilege the ability to see and think mistakenly, irreverently, trivially, and momentarily over the necessity to see and think correctly or judgmentally. In Conrad's and Rushdie's novels, thinking irreverently is in some ways ethical or subversive because it extends perception, makes it more various, and because it can provide an alternative to what Stefan Collini has called "those more instrumental, pragmatic, aggregative processes which are nonetheless wholly necessary for running the world and getting its business done."[65] For Woolf, Joyce, and Ishiguro, modernist innovation can involve confronting, analyzing, and diversifying the language of political commitment. As a response to the politics of euphemism, Woolf's evasion is not efficient, as explicitness would be, but it offers an alternative to the brutal instrumentality she attributes to wartime patriotism.

The analysis of perception and its provocations has been important to formal accounts of modernist experimentation as well as to cultural, political, and geographic accounts of urban experience and empire. These accounts of literary and political seeing come together in the phrase "metropolitan perception," which Raymond Williams uses to mean both the affirming experience of "privileges and opportunities" in the imperial center and the disorienting, sometimes liberating experience of urban crowds and urban isolation.[66] Most striking in Williams's account of modernist development is his argument that "immigration to the metropolis"—and it is significant that Williams speaks of "immigration," which connotes popular or economic aspirations as opposed to "travel" or "exile"—was "the most important general element in the innovations in form" (45). For the immigrants who became writers, like Joseph Conrad, for the writers who became immigrants, like James Joyce, and for the so-called natives, like Virginia Woolf, immigration, Williams asserts, "forced certain productive kinds of strangeness and distance: a new consciousness of conventions and thus of changeable, because now open, conventions" (47). Thinking of modernism's conditions in terms of immigration helps to explain why late-twentieth-century writers such as Rushdie, Ishiguro, and Sebald would make use of critical strategies developed by early-twentieth-century writers such as Conrad, Joyce, and Woolf.

Cosmopolitan Style shares Williams's sense that the themes and formal innovations of modernism respond to the conditions of the metropolis, that they are in some sense products of European imperialism, but this does not mean, either for Williams's argument or for mine, that modernism is a mirror of imperialism or that the experience of the metropolis was uniform or uniformly experienced even within the city center. The idea of "metropolitan perception," while registering the influence of increasing mobility, social diversity, and consumer culture on modernist ideas of consciousness and perspective, should not lead us to imagine that modernist writers as different as Woolf and Conrad shared the same experience of centrality, or that Joyce's Dublin was, to follow Williams's distinction, an "imperial and capitalist metropolis" rather than a "deprived hinterland" (47). In an influential essay, Fredric Jameson proposes that metropolitan texts do not ignore or exclude "the imperialist situation" but rather distort it because they display the failure of perception (the fact of an unseen colonized world) rather than "colonized daily life": that is, instead of perceiving the experience of colonized peoples, readers perceive the limitations of their perception.[67] Jameson's argument is useful because it challenges our sense that modernism is detached from social problems and political situations and because it helps to enlarge what a modernist account of international conditions, including the conditions of imperialism, could look like.[68] His argument is predicated, however, on a definition of the political and on a distinction between spectatorial and transfiguring practices that is somewhat narrower than the one I have employed.[69]

In my reading of Woolf, I argue that the ethical pitfalls and aesthetic opportunities of diverting or withholding attention are central topics for modernist art, and thus I see inattentiveness as an effect of innovation rather than of ignorance. I examine the modernist encounter with European "otherness," which for Jameson merely occludes a lack of encounter with what he calls the "more radical otherness" of colonized peoples (49), as it prepares the way for initial practices of self-reflection and for later practices of immigrant mixing and antiracist critique.[70] Indeed, modernists themselves were less certain than Jameson that anger, regret, and judgment are the only ways to inspire critical thinking and critical action, especially given that Bloomsbury writers like Forster were focused, as Jameson acknowledges, on the dangers of militarism and heroic masculinity in Europe.[71] It should be said that I do not claim to find or to describe a consistent tradition of anti-imperialism in British modernism: as many scholars have shown, Conrad in some ways admired British imperialism even as he criticized Belgian policies; Woolf's emphasis on England, while it brought attention to private and domestic experiences, can seem to ignore the experiences of empire. All the same, I propose that late-twentieth-century theories of cosmopolitanism, including those that are focused on the critique of imperialism, often build on the experimental tones and analytic strategies of modernist narrative.

IDIOSYNCRASY OF STYLE

All of the writers I consider promote two kinds of entanglement: the literal knotting together of cultures and experiences that seem to be disparate, such as British censorship and Irish nationalism (Joyce), Chinese silk and English urns (Sebald), Japanese militarism and U.S. democracy (Ishiguro), a party in the evening and a suicide in the afternoon (Woolf); and the effect of ethical discomfort or embarrassment that is generated by incommensurate or unconventional associations. Since a new understanding of description is central to the project of modernism, a cosmopolitan style is also a modernist style: it registers the limits of perception and the waning of a confident epistemology, the conflict between the exhaustive and the ineffable, the appeal of the trivial, the political consequences of uniformity and variousness in meaning, the fragmentation of perspectives, and the disruption of social categories. Conrad, Joyce, and Woolf ask how national experiences can or should be represented, but the contemporary writers Rushdie, Ishiguro, and Sebald ask as well how novels might function as effects or symptoms of a national culture. Like Rushdie and Ishiguro, Sebald prompts his readers to imagine that British literature might reflect more than one national or cultural tradition; that the national location of a given work is no longer unique or consistent; that fiction and journalism are proximate ventures. Just as Ishiguro proposes that British novels can have Japanese narrators and even seem like novels in translation, Sebald suggests that novels about German narrators, which are in fact composed in German, can respond and contribute to the tradition of British writing. The effect of vertigo is specific to Sebald's quite disorienting work, as I discuss in chapter 6, but the trope of connections among geographically and ethically disparate events pervades the literary and cultural projects of cosmopolitanism in the twentieth century.

Recent attacks on cosmopolitan decadence—disparaged as "cultural inventiveness," "self-indulgence," or "unbelonging"—have a long history in debates about modernism and modernist cultural practices, including practices of writing.[72] Early-twentieth-century critics of cosmopolitanism presumed that cultural artifacts, as a matter of course, should articulate and maintain existing cultures. These critics argued that literature should conform to a writer's "experience," by which they meant a coherent national tradition that was neither changeable nor uncertain. More than this, readers assumed that they knew, before reading a text, what a writer's experience—English, Polish, German, Japanese—was. The assumption that a novel will express a writer's nationality, that the novel functions metonymically, rests on a conception of literary style that is not only antimodernist but anterior to modernism; moreover, it is continuous with theories of culture that modernists often sought to challenge.[73]

In early-twentieth-century Britain, a well-known champion of expressive literature was the critic and editor J. Middleton Murry, who presented his definition of "style" to an audience at Oxford University in 1921. Murry was no fan of the "calculated subtleties" he found in the writing of many of his contemporaries; in 1926, he would remark that "ten years hence no one will take the trouble" to read either *Jacob's Room* or *The Waste Land*, both of which he condemns as "failures."[74] He finds the writing of Woolf and Eliot "over-intellectualized" where it should be "instinctive" and full of "spontaneity" (591). In his lectures on "The Problem of Style," Murry classifies the new trend as a "hypertrophy of style" because it disfigures and exceeds the realities of nature.[75] Literature, Murry writes, should reflect "an author's success in compelling language to conform to his mode of experience," and "false" writing is "produced when the vital reference of language to this mode of experience" is lost (23). The hypertrophic style is doubly false, Murry insists, because it fails to convey nature and then conceals this failure by creating an artificial, eccentric form of life. "Instead of being obviously hollow and lifeless," Murry explains, "a barren idiosyncrasy of style . . . may present the appearance of luxuriant growth"; it has, he adds, "the vitality of a weed or mushroom, a vitality that we cannot call precisely spurious, but that we certainly cannot call real" (22). In excess of expression, Murry argues, literature deviates from its purpose.

Murry's view, that there is cultural perfidy implicit in literary deviation, corresponded to many other, more popular views of cosmopolitan identity and art. Murry's attack demonstrates, however, not a consistent anticosmopolitanism but rather an inconsistent nativism: he was married to Katherine Mansfield, who was born in New Zealand; he published in magazines alongside Bloomsbury artists; and he attended parties and social gatherings with many experimental writers, including those (Woolf, Eliot) he criticizes in his lecture. In this period, one could be a patron of international art and a supporter of international artists while also embracing nationalist and sometimes nativist theories of culture: as I discuss in chapter 1, even Edward Garnett, who recommended Joseph Conrad's first story for publication and whose wife, Constance Garnett, was an important translator of Russian novelists, would speak of the "secrets of Slav thought" that Conrad brought to "our [English] tongue."[76] This combination of nativist theory and international practice links Murry to other major figures, such as Arthur Symons and the art historian Selwyn Image, and also to less-major journalists and popular writers. In a debate about "Cosmopolitan Art," published in *The Art Journal* in 1902, Image argued that cosmopolitans, who abandon their own national traditions, can inhabit other traditions only artificially and insubstantially.[77]

Image's article matches a review of Conrad that was published by the Irish writer Robert Lynd in 1908. Lynd finds Conrad's work shallow, and he sees this failing as an index—an effect that is also a sign—of "cosmopolitan" identity.[78] In particular, he disparages Conrad for his ability and willingness to write in a chosen rather than a given language.[79] Without a given language, Lynd asserts, Conrad's texts fail to achieve a natural expression. In the early twentieth century, the term "cosmopolitan" was attributed to artists who seemed to invent identities rather than inhabit them and to work that dramatized this process of invention. The critics claim to know an artist's rootlessness from the material he or she produces, even as they imagine that the life and not the craft is responsible for this effect. To imagine anything else, of course, would be to suggest that the artist could generate a self, rather than merely reveal it.

Two decades later, in very similar terms, the critic W. J. Turner argued in *The New Statesmen* that Igor Stravinsky had "become so cosmopolitan" playing for audiences in London and Paris that his work seemed "artificial" and "empty."[80] Turner is not suggesting that Stravinsky has intercultural or transcultural sympathies but rather that his work displays an unnatural or theatrical attitude towards national as well as musical traditions. Because he is distanced from his "roots," Turner asserts, Stravinsky is "too consciously clever," where he might be more "instinctive" and emotional. By this argument, artifice of mind, attributed to cosmopolitan living, leads to work whose superficial fashion indicates a lack of substance: "there is a curious affinity between Stravinsky's music and the smart hats and frocks of society." Turner implies that Stravinsky's music has no content, it is equivalent to "smart hats and frocks," and also that it has no value, since those who give importance to fashion will have little taste for serious music. The problem of style is posed as a problem of artificial nationality: Turner focuses not so much on the natural affiliation Stravinsky has lost as on the unnatural affiliation he has sought to cultivate. One can see in the critiques of Stravinsky and Conrad that the work of art is said to lack content in the same way that the affiliations of the artists are said to lack content, and indeed the latter condition is blamed for the former predicament. I argue that Conrad promotes this connection between strategies of affiliation and styles of art; his work suggests that identities are affirmed by social practices of recognition and that art can intervene in the ways of thinking that make recognition possible. Stravinsky's critic asserts, with tongue-in-cheek approval, that the composer "has managed to avoid expressing anything at all with wonderful skill" (475).

The problem with Conrad, Lynd likewise explains, is that he has lost the "concentration and intensity of vision" that one's "own language" confers (210).

If styles of writing can affirm cultural norms, Woolf will propose, they can also help to change them. Readers are wary of change, as Theodor W. Adorno later argues in an aphorism called "Morality and Style," because what is recognizable or familiar is often mistaken for what is relevant and responsible.[81] The socialization of writing is one of the international conditions that modernist novelists seek to represent and often to resist. One can see this resistance in the purposeful triviality of Joyce's fiction, in Woolf's narrative evasions, and in Ishiguro's treasonous syntax. For those who believe that literature best achieves "morality" by refusing its ready protocols, being bad becomes the only way to make good.

BUTTERFLIES AND JEWS

Early-twentieth-century concerns about the unnaturalness of modernist art became, at midcentury, a more explicit debate about the politics of literary style. It is well known that Jean-Paul Sartre, Georg Lukács, Theodor W. Adorno, George Orwell, and others were focused in this period on the political efficacy of modernist art. It is less noticed, however, that this focus was motivated by questions of cosmopolitanism.[82] How can writers change international conditions? In times of international crisis, are some literary styles more useful or more responsible than others? What are the topics appropriate to committed literature? Do the unsettling methods of cosmopolitan art serve to resist the adverse realities of cosmopolitan culture? Or do they facilitate them?

The midcentury debate about modernism and international politics is in some ways old-fashioned, especially in its Cold War distinctions between First and Third World. However, the debate remains significant and influential in its efforts to think about modernism globally and to consider whether the aesthetic strategies of literary modernism are relevant to projects of antiracism and decolonization. In "What Is Literature?" (1947), an essay composed in the wake of the Second World War, Jean-Paul Sartre argues that "committed literature" is the necessary and strategic response to the international problems of the postwar era. Among these problems, Sartre identifies "the present machinations of the Soviet government . . . American anti-Semitism and Negrophobia, our own [French] colonialism and the attitude of the [allied] powers in regard to Franco."[83] To uproot totalitarianism, racism, colonialism, and fascism, Sartre argues, writers need to adopt a literary style that is transparent and descriptive: they need to display the conditions they seek to resist, bear witness to them, directly and exclusively (36–37). "The function of the writer," Sartre proposes, "is to act in such a way that nobody can be ignorant of the world and that nobody may say that he is innocent of what it's all about" (36). Because the prose writer only "*makes use* of words" (34, emphasis in text), Sartre contends, his style "should pass unnoticed" (39). As Sartre defines it, committed writing depends not on the perfection of one's style but on the correctness of one's topic, whose relevance to international affairs and other matters of political urgency should be obvious and compelling. "In short," he argues, "it is a matter of knowing what one wants to write about, whether butterflies or the condition of the Jews" (40). For Sartre, committed writing is cosmopolitan writing, and the proper subjects of cosmopolitan literature are Jews, but not butterflies; social facts, but not fleeting consciousness; political identities, but not trivial experiences.

Adorno responded to Sartre's volley in 1962, in the wake of two subsequent international events: the German translation of Sartre's essay and the construction of the Berlin Wall. Calling his essay "Commitment," Adorno invokes Sartre's theory only to replace it with a commitment of his own. Adorno argues that literary styles not only transmit but also shape social circumstances, and thus, he contends, "Sartre's conception of commitment strikes at the cause to which Sartre is committed."[84] Adorno's contention is this: Sartre's argument, by dismissing so-called trivial or decadent themes, reinforces the moral distinctions that make racism possible. Adorno rejects Sartre's image of "alternatives"—butterflies or Jews, communication or silence—as an accommodation to predetermined choices and the rigidity of social thought (80). Committed literature, he argues, should produce discomfort rather than certainty because "the course of the world" will be altered only by the encounter with ideas "that cannot be admitted at any cost" (78). Adorno calls for art that is purposefully "strange or upsetting" (78–79), that ruptures boundaries of taste and convention, that generates experiences that are not "officially approved" (88). He concludes that there is a profound compatibility between Sartre's demand for useful, utilitarian writing and the fascist rejection of "what is said to be unnatural, overly intellectual, unhealthy, and decadent" (78). Refusing to think about butterflies, Adorno implies, may only hurt the Jews.

In this exchange, Sartre seems to be arguing that writers need to describe social conditions in order to change them, while Adorno is arguing that writers best change social conditions by resisting the conventions of description. The distinction between Sartre and Adorno is sharpest when they are speaking about "committed literature" in the abstract; however, when Sartre considers that literature has served to *produce* colonialism, for example, his argument takes a different course. In "Black Orpheus," an essay about Afro-French poetry and the négritude movement, Sartre acknowledges that writers aiming to resist or change the norms of national culture will need to "notice" literary style. Looking back at "What Is Literature?" from the perspective of "Black Orpheus," one can see that Sartre's initial conception of "committed writing" had assumed a shared community of readers and writers; it had assumed that authors are always at home in the language they are using.[85] "Black Orpheus" affirms that literature may be one of the social institutions that a writer is seeking to change, and it recognizes that Afro-French writers may have a different approach to communication, in French, than French writers do.

Négritude poetry helped Sartre to see that literary modernism informs the project of anticolonialism. Ironically, it is Sartre, rather than Adorno, who provides a nascent theory of cosmopolitan style. Sartre argues in "Black Orpheus" that modernist poetry, rather than realist prose, generates the most effective resistance to French colonialism: négritude poetry allows African and West Indian writers not only to redescribe Afro-French identity and to reject racist descriptions, but also to alter descriptive methods, which are embedded in the French language of the past.[86] Négritude poetry is revolutionary, Sartre argues, both because it replaces colonialist descriptions of "Africans" with African descriptions and because it redirects the analytic gaze from colony to metropolis: when the French read négritude poetry, Sartre asserts, "suddenly France seems exotic in our own eyes" (292). Furthermore, Sartre contends, if Afro-French writers were to ignore the relationship between aesthetic traditions and national cultures, they might reproduce or fail to resist the conditions of racism. "When the Negro declares in French that he rejects French culture," Sartre explains, "he accepts with one hand what he rejects with the other" (301). Instead, négritude writers take a different tack: "since the oppressor is present in the very language they speak," Sartre concludes, "they will speak this language in order to destroy it"; the négritude poet aims to "de-Frenchify" French words by "break[ing] their usual associations" and "violently" bringing them together with unfamiliar images and topics (303). Sartre argues that Césaire and other Afro-French poets have given a "rigorously defined function" to modernist literary strategies: they have shown their political and cultural use (312).

The tactic of breaking "usual associations" and creating new, sometimes "violent" connections serves to de-Frenchify French culture much as Sebald's entanglements serve to de-British British. These efforts do not simply offer alternatives to national affiliation; they attempt to make national culture less homogenous. It is important to observe that writers such as Ishiguro and Sebald are developing new models of the nation: Sebald may propose that butterflies and the condition of the Jews are, surprisingly, of "the same order,"[87] but he does this to assert only a tentative contiguity rather than a new coherence. Indeed, once Sartre begins to question the norms of collectivity, he begins to question in turn the priorities of sympathetic attentiveness that he took for granted in "What Is Literature?" For all his concern about literary decadence in the earlier essay, Sartre later celebrates decadent strategies in "Black Orpheus." Those strategies include violent correspondences, perversity of subject matter, indecorous allusions, experimental rhythms, and erotic sensuality.[88] Sartre's claim that antiracist poetry needs to reject habitual Frenchness leads him to value heterogeneous impressions, much as Walter Pater valued "any stirring of the senses, strange dyes, strange colors, and curious odors, or work of the artist's hands, or the face of one's friend."[89] To be certain, Pater disavows the claims of social or political commitment, but he prefigures Sartre's contention that aesthetic constraints, including hierarchies of subject matter, reinforce social rigidity.

The project of de-Frenchifying French that Sartre attributes to négritude poetry exemplifies the tactic of "assimilation"—really, a kind of unassimilation—that the sociologist Michel de Certeau later includes among his practices of countercultural *bricolage*.[90] In *The Practice of Everyday Life*, de Certeau describes "tactics" as makeshift cultural maneuvers that bring moments of innovation into rigid social disciplines. The affinity between de Certeau's tactics and the literary strategies of modernism is legible, for example, in Amanda Anderson's discussion of Oscar Wilde, whose style of detachment she describes as

> a certain punctuation of the aesthetic mode: it is not so much living for every moment, as Pater would have us do, but rather seizing the moment which the drama of life only occasionally or intermittently presents to us. To seize the moment requires simultaneously an ethical finesse and an artful capacity; it is entirely outside of the sphere of conventional morality or virtue and in fact often flies in the face of such morality.[91]

The paradigmatic tactician in de Certeau's theory is the itinerant and unplaced consumer, whom he describes variously as an immigrant, an apartment renter, a nomad, a traveler, and a poacher (ix–xxiv). De Certeau borrows his metaphors from the late twentieth century, but he could have included early-twentieth-century figures such as female shoppers in Oxford Street, Jewish advertising canvassers in Dublin, and secret agents in Soho. The paradigmatic tactic in de Certeau's theory is assimilation, though not as it is usually defined. There is, de Certeau argues, a "misunderstanding" about assimilation: "This misunderstanding assumes that 'assimilating' necessarily means 'becoming similar to' what one absorbs, and not 'making something similar' to what one is, making it one's own, appropriating or re-appropriating it" (166). De Certeau uses the term "misunderstanding" generously: he suggests that the interpreters of assimilation are unable rather than unwilling to see more than one definition of the term. He does not add that these interpreters may not wish to acknowledge assimilation's mix-up: that immigrants add themselves to national cultures, which are then transformed in the process.

My contention in this book, that the modernist strategies of cosmopolitan writing have served to test and expand the critical methods of international thinking, has been shaped by the work of Adorno and de Certeau. Readers may notice Adorno's imprint on my claims about the politics of style and de Certeau's in my emphasis on the connections between private acts or opportunities and institutional systems. It is perhaps more common to associate Adorno with "resignation," the title of one of his late essays, than with interventions or tactics, but I argue throughout this book that Adorno presents dissenting thought, including his own, as a precondition for social change.[92] Adorno's conviction that social norms are embedded in traditions of literary style and that literary style is embedded in the politics of national culture makes his work particularly significant for theories of culture and cosmopolitan fiction. Adorno asserts that the homogenization of writing—at the level of narrative structure, diction, and syntax—is responsible for and reinforces the homogenization of culture, which he associates with fascism. He aims to reject familiar habits of thought by refusing their styles of expression.

De Certeau is important for my study because, unlike Adorno, his work helps to show how avant-garde strategies function in popular culture and in the culture of everyday life. If Adorno imagines a world of art that resists everyday culture, de Certeau rejects this distinction and proposes that everyday activities accommodate strategies of art. De Certeau submits that shopping, reading, and walking, for example, offer moments of imaginative resistance within the space of dominant culture. De Certeau's examples of "resistance" are ephemeral and poetic: he does not propose that reading or walking or even shopping will change the urban environment or government policy.[93] In addition, most of his examples involve unselfconscious acts: everyday habits rather than critical practices. My use of "tactics" is somewhat different than de Certeau's because writers are producers as well as consumers: British modernists have used new critical attitudes to circulate and provoke new conceptions of self and community.

TACTICS

Each of the following chapters examines a "tactic" or "attitude" of critical cosmopolitanism as it is developed in the work of a twentieth-century novelist and in theories of modernism and international culture: Joseph Conrad's "naturalness," James Joyce's "triviality," Virginia Woolf's "evasion," Salman Rushdie's "mix-up," Kazuo Ishiguro's "treason," and W. G. Sebald's "vertigo." I call these tactics "cosmopolitan styles" to emphasize the importance of affect, manner, and self-consciousness in all practices of critical cosmopolitanism and to identify the use of new narrative strategies in the cosmopolitan literary practices of the twentieth century. A cosmopolitan style is not an alternative to or replacement for a cosmopolitan politics or what Bruce Robbins and others have called "cosmopolitics."[94] Rather, it describes an analytic feature of critical cosmopolitanism, which has been used politically by writers such as Joyce, Woolf, and Ishiguro. In addition, a focus on styles of cosmopolitanism is meant to value what Jane Gallop has called "alternative ways of theorizing," versions of cosmopolitan theory that pay attention to the "narrative forms" in which theory is produced.[95] It is for this reason that my introduction has examined closely the aesthetic strategies of contemporary cosmopolitan theory; the chapters will examine in turn how twentieth-century writers have used the innovations of modernist narrative to generate cosmopolitan interventions. I have been proposing that cosmopolitan theory is more literary and more modernist than its practitioners have previously acknowledged. I will be arguing, further, that modernist fiction produces a cosmopolitan theory that emphasizes the analytic (new ways of thinking and feeling) as well as the thematic (new objects of thinking and feeling) and that brings together several gestures of critique—the progress of knowledge, the analysis of progress in history, the resistance to some forms of progress, and the dilation of knowing into feeling, partial knowing, knowingness, and refusing to know.

The first half of *Cosmopolitan Style* focuses on Conrad, Woolf, and Joyce, each of whom has been hailed, for different reasons, as the exemplary British novelist of the twentieth century. This exemplarity is telling both about the critical history of British fiction and about changing definitions of national culture in Britain. The second half of the book focuses on Ishiguro, Rushdie, and Sebald, whom I have chosen in part to reflect a range of "new ethnicities" in late-twentieth-century Britain—the different internationalisms of Japanese, Indian, and German immigration—and in part to provide what I take to be the most striking recent examples of literary cosmopolitanism.[96] By introducing this study with Conrad and concluding with Sebald, I aim to reemphasize the place of Europe within early- and late-twentieth-century British writing. I am suggesting that it is important, once again, to consider Britain's status as a European nation and to consider how Britain's relationship to Europe complicates the oppositions between empire and metropolis, East and West, and Europe and America that have dominated recent scholarship in British studies. Scholars who teach and write about literature in English often make a distinction between British and world literature, where "British" refers to literature in English produced in the British Isles and "world" to literature in English produced in the former British colonies (except the United States).[97] My point in writing about "the British novel" is to privilege texts that seem to be testing the protocols and boundaries of British culture. For this reason, it has seemed right to me to include Joyce and Rushdie in this project, even though each also participates in other national and diasporic traditions. And I have included Sebald, even though his work was not written originally in English. Whether the texts I consider *are* "British" is less significant to me than the tension they articulate, what I see as a modernist tension, between enhancing and disabling that term.[98]

My emphasis on analytic strategies has led me to privilege different postures of cosmopolitanism, such as naturalness and evasion, rather than different experiences of cosmopolitanism, such as travel and migration. In this emphasis, I have sought to focus attention on the critical models that writers use to present and interpret experiences, while continuing to acknowledge the new range of experiences that shape the materials and circumstances of writing. The tactics I identify reflect this double gesture: on the one hand, they describe specific practices of cosmopolitan culture, such as the mixing or mixing-up of different cultural traditions within a single literary text; on the other hand, they serve as analytic paradigms that show, for example, how the purposeful mix-up of languages opposes the aggressive rhetoric of the "immigrant's mistake."[99] I have chosen terms that have both a local and general relevance: local because they operate in one or more examples of cosmopolitan writing; and general because they operate conceptually within theories of cosmopolitan practice. I have looked for words that function, often tacitly or unremarkably, within debates about modernism, political strategies of writing, and cosmopolitanism.

My own tactics are comparative in several senses: broadly, I have compared projects of critical cosmopolitanism with projects of modernist narrative, in an effort to revise what "international modernism" is and to argue that early-twentieth-century literary strategies continue to shape cosmopolitan practices at the end of the twentieth century; more narrowly, I have brought together the novels of contemporary immigrant writers, which focus on the global, non-Western entanglements of British culture, with those of European modernists, which focus primarily on the experiences of British-born characters and on entanglements closer to home. In the later period, I have treated writers of European descent alongside writers of non-European descent; in the earlier period, I have treated a writer born in England alongside writers born in Ireland and Poland. A comparative methodology offers risks and opportunities: on the risk side, it may seem insufficiently attentive to the distinctive histories of postcolonial, immigrant, or non-Western peoples and insufficiently resistant to an old, universalizing tradition of British fiction; on the opportunity side, it may introduce alternatives to the prevailing oppositions between postcolonial and British, East and West, margin and center, non-European and European.

While my aim has been to examine boundaries without stepping over them, it is true that I have tended to assemble rather than separate a variety of cosmopolitan projects.[100] As Carolyn Dever has argued about the role of theory in feminist activism, comparison or abstraction allows for the presentation of "a systemic justification, definition, explanation, or hypothesis," even though, by virtue of its sweep and selectivity, it "represents the failure to account for all the material claims and challenges local evidence presents."[101] By comparing different kinds of British, English, modernist, and cosmopolitan writing from two different periods, several places, and two languages, I have sought to analyze and suspend national distinctions. This allows for new, alternative distinctions to emerge—collectivities defined by culture rather than by place; by place rather than by language; by town or region rather than by country; by contestation rather than by consensus; or by values and pleasures rather than by history and law. Cosmopolitan writers allow us to see that an effective politics may need to be specific and purposeful, but it need not be local.

To establish the cosmopolitan project of modernist fiction, the first chapter of this book turns to Joseph Conrad, whose work is concerned with patterns of attentiveness, relevance, perception, and recognition. In his novels and prefaces, Conrad develops a style of *naturalness*—a manner that passes for nature—to show how these patterns shape conditions of national and international affiliation. Emphasizing naturalness, I approach Conrad as an inheritor not of Kipling but of Wilde: I argue that Oscar Wilde's social paradoxes prefigure, at the level of epigram, the cultural artifice that Conrad represents at the level of narrative. The chapter looks closely at *The Secret Agent* (1907), the "domestic" fiction that generated Conrad's reputation as a cosmopolitan writer. I argue that Conrad makes naturalness both a topic and a characteristic of his fiction: he makes his texts British not by excluding international characteristics but by displaying them. Treating British culture as a paradigm of manners rather than of instincts, Conrad presents his quintessentially British novels as "effects" (his word) of cosmopolitan production.

The second chapter focuses on James Joyce, whose cosmopolitanism is motivated not by a desire to seem British, as in Conrad's case, but by the competing urgencies of anti-British nationalism, aesthetic individualism, and antiracism. Valuing the *trivial* for its taint of pettiness and impermanence, Joyce promotes two, somewhat different models of national culture: a fixed culture that can be described through the collection of minor details; and a transient culture for which minor details mark the principle of inexhaustible, proliferating characteristics. Sustaining the tension between these two models, Joyce's triviality is committed both to describing Ireland and also to changing it. Reading among several of Joyce's texts, including "Two Gallants," *A Portrait of the Artist as a Young Man*, and the "Wandering Rocks" and "Cyclops" episodes of *Ulysses*, I argue that Joyce cultivates triviality as an alternative to the false decorum of British imperialism, Irish anti-Semitism, and Catholic evangelism.

In the third chapter, I examine modernist efforts to replace a heroic model of political engagement with new political affects such as evasion and agitation. A style of *evasion* allows Virginia Woolf to analyze the generalizations of British culture and to notice, for example, that many British citizens have European origins, that metropolitan art is international art, and that London's landmarks memorialize the itinerary of imperial conquest. Whereas Woolf is often seen as an emphatically English writer, I argue that her analysis of heroism and her emphasis on the political nature of intimacy are crucial to later cosmopolitan fiction. Woolf does not focus on scenes of colonialism or immigration, as Joyce and Conrad do, but she shows how colonizing policies have shaped what it means to be an honorable man (to follow Cynthia Enloe's example) and how these policies in fact *rely* on ideas of honor and masculinity that are supposedly private and domestic.[102]

To establish the revival of modernist cosmopolitanism at the end of the century, the fourth chapter examines the novels of Kazuo Ishiguro, who embraces *treason*—the refusal to tell a consistent story about politics, about oneself, or about the past—as a tactic of immigrant writing and antifascist dissent. Ishiguro conceives of treason in people, nations, and art as more reliable and sometimes more responsible than absolute or merely dutiful allegiance. Like Woolf, Ishiguro rejects national triumphalism, whether British imperialism, German anti-Semitism, or Japanese militarism, and he situates his analysis within a tradition of novelistic manners: his narratives about immigration or world war are also narratives about marriage, problems between parents and children, unconsummated romantic attractions, and the details of professional housekeeping. Ishiguro offers a cosmopolitan approach to international topics, arguing, for example, that free speech and militarism are rooted in intimate disputes about social achievement, education, and childrearing. Showing that a politics of individualism can lead to a politics of collectivity, he proposes that global action cannot (indeed, does not) ignore the microintimacies of domesticity.

Tactics of *mix-up*, nicknaming, collage, assimilation, and flirtation are the subjects of the fifth chapter, which focuses on Salman Rushdie's critique of racist aphorism and xenophobic name-calling in *The Satanic Verses*, several stories from *East, West*, and his novel about New York, *Fury*. Like Michel de Certeau, who moves among the metropolises of London, New York, and Paris, Rushdie is an itinerant ethnographer, though of London, New York, and Bombay. In his writing of the 1990s, he embraces the literary and cultural mix-up, arguing that correctness in naming and social description does not constitute a practical or even ethical model for antiracist literature. In his later work, Rushdie distinguishes among different versions of cosmopolitanism: he suggests in *Fury* that the mix-up of national traditions is a common strategy not only of twenty-first-century British fiction, such as his own, but also of multinational capitalism.

All of the authors I consider in this study write about adverse social conditions—fascism, world war, colonialism, displacement—but also about useless details, trivial sensations, exquisite moments, transient beauty, playful nicknames, and decorative objects. This diversity of topics generates a dizzying uncertainty of place and perspective that Sebald addresses directly in his novels. Making connections among high and low culture, among disparate anecdotes, narrators, and settings, Sebald's palimpsest of memories and nations introduces *vertigo* as an ethics of cosmopolitan culture. My final chapter turns to Sebald, who unassimilates the British novel by emphasizing the foreign entanglements of his own endeavor and of those past endeavors, such as Conrad's, whose example he follows and reimagines. Naturalness, triviality, evasion, treason, mix-up, and vertigo: these styles of cosmopolitanism are the subject of this book.

COSMOPOLITAN MODERNISM

PART 1

CONRAD'S NATURALNESS

There was nothing foreign in his accent, except that he seemed in his slow enunciation to be taking pains with it. And Mrs Verloc, in her varied experience, had come to the conclusion that some foreigners could speak better English than the natives.

—JOSEPH CONRAD, *THE SECRET AGENT*

THAT ONE MIGHT belong to a culture by choice rather than by nature was commonly vilified, in the early twentieth century, as a principle of cosmopolitan "adaptability."[1] An insult with a double edge, adaptability implied a lack of positive identity, on the one hand, and a surfeit of abject identity, often Jewishness, on the other. It described, as historian Deborah Cohen has argued, a characteristic of unmarked "invaders," whose versatility with language and manners helped them to live abroad without detection.[2] As a skill of individuals, adaptability meant that people could belong to more than one culture, or they could operate within cultures that were not, or not yet, their own. As a concept, adaptability meant something more: inclusion in a culture might depend not on the expression of innate attributes but on the performance of learned codes and habitual gestures. In Britain, nativist writers were disturbed to think that foreigners were passing as locals, but they were even more disturbed to imagine that foreigners might *become* locals, by learning to be natural or by changing the conditions of nature.

This chapter examines the naturalness of Joseph Conrad, whose choice of English as a language of composition and whose focus on global systems of trade, imperialism, and espionage have made him, among critics in his own time and throughout the twentieth century, at once the most British and the most cosmopolitan of novelists. For some, Conrad's choice made him exceptionally foreign: writing all of his fiction in a language he had to learn, Conrad became not simply a stranger in England but one whose fiction is nowhere at home. For others, Conrad's foreignness made him the most English of writers, as F. R. Leavis claims in his canonical account of the English novel. Only because he was foreign, Leavis argued in 1948, could Conrad choose English and thus inaugurate "the great tradition" that precedes him: Jane Austen, George Eliot, and Henry James. Allowing origin to follow imitation, Leavis's narrative is typically Conradian: by virtue of his choice, Leavis proposes, the novelist affirmed the coherence and value of English literature.[3] Aiming to describe a distinctly national tradition, Leavis emphasizes preference and patriotism, but he minimizes agency and self-consciousness, which would imply cosmopolitanism. Leavis proposes that Conrad does not belong to English culture voluntarily, as a cosmopolitan would, but rather he belongs "in the full sense," by *nature* (18). Leavis describes Conrad's choice as a compulsion that follows not the pleasures of cultural mixing or even the necessities of social circumstance but the imperatives of art. Claiming that Conrad's "themes and interests demanded the concreteness and action—the dramatic energy—of English" (17–18), Leavis uses the international Conrad to create a natural national tradition: a literary and cultural lineage that is both coherent and continuous.

Today, in many critical accounts, Conrad is the exemplary figure of British modernism. He is exemplary, critics propose, because his foreignness was more extreme than the exile of his contemporaries: not only did he leave his native country for reasons of personal safety, the argument goes, but he left behind his native language as well.[4] Critics often attribute the innovations of Conrad's style to his history of literal and metaphorical displacement.[5] In this chapter, I make a related but in some ways opposite claim: Conrad becomes legible as a foreigner in his life because he displays adaptability, or naturalness, in his work. I do not mean to deny that Conrad was a foreigner in England; nor do I mean to underestimate the difficult conditions of immigration and transience in which Conrad's writing developed. Rather, I propose that Conrad's reputation comes to shape his history. I suggest that Conrad's analysis of display and perception in his novels, what is often called his "impressionism," should be understood both as a philosophical critique of social categories and as an urbane practice of ethnographic self-fashioning.[6] To measure the aesthetic and political implications of Conrad's writing, we need to see the relationship between two strains of cosmopolitanism in his work: the geographic cosmopolitanism of immigration, international travel, and colonialism, which the novels describe, and the aesthetic cosmopolitanism of literary impressionism and decadence, whose values the novels reproduce and whose urban meanderings and ambiguous poses are crucial to his later texts. By disaggregating the several aspects of cosmopolitanism in this period, I will show that Conrad brought to his work diverse, sometimes conflicting strategies of national and international affiliation.

In Conrad's novels, themes of deracination and cultural mixing meet practices of experimentation and promotion. Fredric Jameson's account of the oscillation between realism and romance in Conrad's writing provides one very useful way to describe this encounter.[7] However, I would associate Conrad's mixing of genres less with "schizophrenic writing" (219), as Jameson does, than with a kind of critical dandyism: the tactical deployment of rhetoric and social detail, which allows Conrad to reproduce and also to manipulate the norms of British culture.[8] Conrad's preoccupation with art, perhaps the chief characteristic of literary decadence, extends from his well-known interest in the medium of writing to his corollary interests in the media of everyday culture: if Conrad establishes an analogy between the representation of storytelling and a novel's telling of its story, as Edward Said and others have shown, he also comes to connect the novel's art of presentation to more quotidian, more pervasive, and less visible practices of artful presentation, such as physical gesture, sartorial and bodily display, and the design of shop windows and street signs.[9] Like Walter Pater, Conrad is interested in the reader's perception of perception, the recognition of habit and the process of defamiliarization; like Oscar Wilde, he is interested in the social processes that make norms seem natural.[10] Conrad's narratives may extend the terrain of Rudyard Kipling and Rider Haggard, but they also follow the path of Wilde: in international settings, colonial and metropolitan, Conrad brings everyday culture to many of Wilde's precepts, allowing that "facts" are made rather than found, that description creates rather than reflects social categories, that art lends coherence to "nations and individuals," that foreign styles are the effects of British fiction.[11] I will suggest at the end of this chapter that Wilde's social paradoxes prefigure at the level of epigram the cultural artifice that Conrad represents at the level of narrative.[12]

As many scholars have shown, Conrad is critical of norms in some cases and reproduces nature in others: his novels present racism as an arbitrary science and an instrument of exploitation, but they also invoke racist stereotypes. Patrick Brantlinger contends persuasively that Conrad may be more interested in reputation, stereotype, and "propaganda" (Brantlinger's term) than he is in actual people or in the project of replacing racist stereotypes with antiracist identities.[13] One might say that Conrad resists, above all, the "fact" of identity, both in his own life and in the description of his characters. In the colonial context, resisting the fact of identity may seem to ignore, or even support, one of the principal strategies of European imperialism: the process of reducing individuals to abstract, dehumanized groups. However, in the European context, where the rhetoric of individuality is used to justify imperialism, resisting the fact of identity allows Conrad to show how nature is produced. Conrad does not imagine more inclusive or more flexible paradigms of belonging, but neither does he allow the old paradigm to function as it did, invisibly and timelessly. Rather, he presents belonging as a social process, introducing naturalness—the purposeful imitation of what passes for nature—as a literary tactic that later novelists, such as Kazuo Ishiguro and W.G. Sebald, will use both to reorient and to diversify British points of view.

I argue that Conrad is exemplary as a British writer in the early twentieth century not because he is the most foreign but because he is the least natural. His novels emphasize strategies of promotion: how social gestures, including the gestures of writing, become legible as necessary and defining characteristics. Conrad's work attests to an emerging conflict between naturalness and nature, between a model of identity based on manners and a model based on instinct or race. Conrad addresses this conflict directly in his texts: he shows how social processes make details into facts, behaviors into characteristics, persons into categories. By attributing cultural distinctions to an interpretive history, Conrad links national identities to conditions of visibility, how people are perceived, rather than to conditions of existence, what people really are. Deflecting charges of adaptability in his life while depicting adaptability in his novels, Conrad develops naturalness as a characteristic of British culture and as a tactic of critical cosmopolitanism.

✳✳✳

This chapter focuses on *The Secret Agent*, the novel about national reputations that helped to shape Conrad's cosmopolitan reputation among early readers. The case of *The Secret Agent* is striking: reviewers attributed the novel, a tale of anarchists and foreigners in London, to Conrad's cosmopolitan nature, even while the novel attributes such characteristics to the fiction of rhetorical display. I will begin by describing Conrad's efforts, in prefaces and letters, to refute or manipulate the characteristics that readers assigned to him. I will then turn to *The Secret Agent*, in which Conrad teaches readers to distrust both apparent identities and "established reputations."[14] Scenes of display may be pervasive in Conrad's work, but *The Secret Agent* is unique among the novels because it assigns these scenes to a specific cultural milieu: bohemian Soho and its cast of immigrants, foreigners, and other indeterminate residents. In *The Secret Agent*, Conrad presents the skillful manipulation of social details and local manners as a norm of cosmopolitan London.

Eager to differentiate naturalness from nature, early-twentieth-century reviewers emphasized Conrad's foreign origins while they praised his fluent use of the English language. One is reminded that to call someone "a natural" is to notice how effortless his or her actions appear; it is to notice not nature but the appearance of nature. Whereas naturalness is culturally and historically specific because it depends on a projected impression, nature lays claim to timelessness, to a world apart from representation and recognition. Conrad understood this distinction. In a letter to his French translator Hugh-Durand Davray, he argues that his novels cannot function in any language other than English. The work, Conrad explains to Davray, "is written for the English—from the point of view of the effect it will have on an English reader."[15] Contrasting his interests with those of Rudyard Kipling, his most acclaimed predecessor in the English literature of empire, Conrad argues,

> A *national* writer like Kipling, for example, translates easily. His interest is in the *subject*: the interest of my work is in the *effect* it produces. He talks about *his compatriots*. I write *for them*.
>
> (29; ORIGINAL EMPHASIS)

Making English novels of "effects," Conrad asserts the reality that writing creates against the locations and national origins that situate writing. Rather than talking "about" the English, transmitting experiences and characteristics that precede literature, Conrad writes "*for*" them, expressing nothing so much as the conditions of reception.

While the difference between nature and naturalness was central to Conrad's literary project, his work was produced in the context of a literary culture devoted to categories of national distinctiveness and authenticity. For this reason, one observes in Conrad's public writings a very different set of claims than those he offers in private letters, such as the one to his translator. In his public comments, Conrad claimed to write not for effect but for transparency. He made these claims in response to early critics and reviewers who described him in published reports as a foreigner playing the role of an Englishman; to his readers, the better he played this role, the more foreign and decadent he seemed. Reviews of *The Secret Agent* attributed the novel's dark view of London to the fact that its author was a foreigner to England and to English culture. These reviews often claimed that Conrad's novel was nothing more than the natural expression of his foreign self. His choice of English as a literary language was thought to confirm this fact, as it emphasized the artifice of Conrad's endeavor. Through the rhetoric of choice, Conrad's contemporaries registered his imposture; through the accusation of artifice, early-twentieth-century critics sought to differentiate Conrad's impersonation of Englishness from the nature of Englishness and other national cultures.

The Irish critic Robert Lynd, reviewing Conrad's writing in a London newspaper in 1908, argued that literature should follow and invigorate national traditions: one should only want or choose what one has been given, and everyone is given, he asserts, something specific and distinct. Lynd writes,

> Mr. Conrad, as everybody knows, is a Pole, who writes in English by choice, as it were, rather than by nature. According to most people, this choice is a good thing, especially for English literature. To some of us, on the other hand, it seems a very regrettable thing, even from the point of view of English literature.[16]

The phrase "choice, as it were" reflects Lynd's belief that language cannot be chosen at all. Lynd regrets not Conrad's failure to be English but his failure to be Polish, the nationality to which "everybody knows" Conrad belongs. Lynd is concerned less about Conrad's actions (giving up the Polish language, electing to write in English) than about the implication of these actions for the distinctiveness of national cultures; Conrad's choice suggests that national culture is a matter of self-identification and practice rather than a matter of race or nativity. The logic of Lynd's critique follows the logic of adaptability: only because Conrad is "cosmopolitan" and "homeless," Lynd argues, does he choose to write in English; writing by "choice" rather than by "nature," however, Conrad *becomes* cosmopolitan, the kind of person who chooses. Behind Lynd's critique of Conrad is his conviction that all literature should express a particular national culture whose circulation and continuity it serves to maintain. For Conrad, on the contrary, literature is the medium through which culture is perceived and in some measure produced.

Many reviewers of *The Secret Agent* saw the novel as a turning point in Conrad's career: with *The Secret Agent*, Hugh Walpole wrote in 1916, "a new attitude was most plainly visible."[17] Even those reviewers who sought to defend Conrad from the cosmopolitanism of whimsical, denationalized writing supported him much as Lynd attacked: by locating in his work the manifestation of an "alien . . . genius."[18] Everywhere, critics imposed the same language of inevitability: for Lynd, Conrad should not write in English because he is Polish; for others, Conrad's choice of English was irrelevant because the writing betrays its author's Polishness all the same. Edward Garnett, who recommended Conrad's first novel for publication, later wrote in the *Nation* that the author of *The Secret Agent* had brought the "secrets of Slav thought" to "our [English] tongue";[19] a reviewer in the *Glasgow News* found it "not an irrelevant reflection upon *The Secret Agent* that its author, Joseph Conrad, is of Polish birth";[20] and Arthur Symons, whose magazine accepted Conrad's first published short story in 1896, celebrated the novelist as a man of "inexplicable mind" who "does not always think in English" even when he uses English words.[21] The reviewers are eager to keep the actual apart from the observed.

Rather than dispute the logic of these comments, Conrad spent much of his career, in prefaces and in biographical essays, insisting that his art was a product of natural inclination. This may sound like a direct contradiction of Conrad's sensibility as he described it to his translator, and in some ways it is. However, this insistence allowed Conrad to refute the personal implications of adaptability (a foreign nature) while also embracing the professional implications of naturalness (success in art). In a 1919 introduction to *A Personal Record*, first published in 1912, Conrad refutes "certain statements" in the press, that he had "exercised a choice" to write in English and that his work, in its sensibility and themes, reflects its author's "Sclavonism."[22] Conrad's refutation seems clear enough:

> The first object of this note is to disclaim any merit there might have been in an act of deliberate volition. The impression of my having exercised a choice between the two languages, French and English, both foreign to me, has got abroad somehow. That impression is erroneous. . . . English was for me neither a matter of choice nor adoption.
>
> (III–V)

Conrad does not deny a specific interest in English so much as he denies an indulgent one, where his choice of English would suggest that he could have chosen, indifferently, another language altogether. He objects to the values associated with the ability to choose and to the notion that he might be "able to do freakish things intentionally, and, as it were, from mere vanity" (iii).

For Conrad, denying choice and adoption becomes the only way to deny the natural foreignness ("Sclavonism") and insincerity ("vanity") that intention has come to designate. The accusation of indulgence leads Conrad to claim imperatives. He proposes that English is natural to his writing because, through English, through a language and culture that he has had to learn, he has found the subject of his work. His encounter with English, he argues, inspired him to write:

> All I can claim after all those years of devoted practice, with the accumulated anguish of its doubts, imperfections, and falterings in my heart, is the right to be believed when I say that if I had not written in English I would not have written at all.
>
> (VI)

Conrad conforms to the rhetoric of necessity because the alternative—choice—would seem to affirm a frivolous cosmopolitanism. Once choice is deemed an attribute both of foreigners and of dandies, it can no longer characterize the deliberate work of a respectable English writer.

It is in this context that one should read Conrad's "Author's Note" to *The Secret Agent*, which he published in 1920, some thirteen years after the novel first appeared. Claiming to have begun *The Secret Agent* "impulsively" and without intention, Conrad explains:

> It's obvious that I need not have written that book. I was under no necessity to deal with that subject. . . . [Having finished *Nostromo* and *The Mirror of the Sea*], I gave myself up to a not unhappy pause. Then, while I was yet standing still, as it were, and certainly not thinking of going out of my way to look for anything ugly,

the subject of *The Secret Agent*—I mean the tale—came to me in the shape of a few words uttered by a friend in a casual conversation about anarchists or rather anarchist activities; how brought about I don't remember now.

(THE SECRET AGENT, 37–39)

Conrad is denying a fatal attraction to his topic: he did not intend to write the novel, but, then again, the novel was not intrinsic to him either. The shock that the novel caused, Conrad goes on to suggest, is a shock contained and produced by the narrative whose "tale" arrived from elsewhere. The author is not an agent, he proposes, but an instrument.

The "Author's Note" begins by explaining that "the origin of *The Secret Agent*" resides in a "reaction" to *Nostromo*, the novel Conrad had published three years earlier. Whereas the "far-off Latin-American atmosphere" of *Nostromo* required effort, Conrad explains, the London of *The Secret Agent* was not a matter of purpose but of chance and convenience. Conrad denies having any curiosity, a quality he values in *The Secret Agent* because it leads to the questioning of facts and the distrust of reputations. In the "Author's Note," Conrad wants to disavow interest in "gratuitous" pleasures or literary adventure (43). Instead, he claims that the anarchist story *came to him*: the conversation that produced the tale was so "casual," Conrad reports, that he can no longer recall how it began. Conrad presents *The Secret Agent* as a narrative of uncertain origins. By claiming that his topic reflected no choice of his own, Conrad segregates the subject of the novel, the contamination of London, from his "purely artistic purpose" (41).[23]

Conrad may be criticized as a "cosmopolitan" or commended as a "foreigner," but either way these nominations assumed that qualities of belonging reflect attributes that cannot be chosen: they cannot be adopted, nor can they be relinquished. Moreover, critics suggest, the novelist's attributes are expressed in his writing, where—as Garnett puts it—Conrad has translated foreign thoughts into English and into "London." Garnett suggests that Conrad has made English and England cosmopolitan, but it may be rather that *The Secret Agent* projects, more than the novels before it, the syncretic and artificial conditions of English culture. Whereas Walpole finds in *The Secret Agent* a "new attitude," I would suggest that the novel's subject (cosmopolitan London) brings to light an attitude (naturalness) that persists throughout Conrad's work. *The Secret Agent*, a novel set in London without a single character who is English or English only, may seem all the more "foreign" because it finds the deliberate effects of Englishness in the heart of domestic space. The novel's title character, we are told, is "thoroughly domesticated," as if comfort or familiarity must be created from the start (47). Conrad's novel includes a range of experiences that one expects to find familiar: marriage, habits of perception, government institutions, and landmarks of local color, such as restaurants, shops, and city streets. Yet Conrad suggests that domestic culture is full of foreign activities, such as colonialism and European politics, as well as foreign people, those immigrants and cosmopolitans who make their home in the city. In *The Secret Agent*, Conrad attributes the characteristics of British culture to artful display and tactical promotion. His novel seeks to consider how inherent attributes are strategically produced and how national identities are shaped by conditions of collective expectation.

✳✳✳

Conrad's characters often proclaim, "things do not stand being looked into."[24] This phrase constitutes a warning, but it is a warning that Conrad generally disregards: he knows that looking will disrupt social organization, and he is willing, even eager to take the risk. Marlow famously explains, in *Heart of Darkness*, that imperialism thrives on the activities and expressions that go without seeing: "The conquest of the earth, which mostly means the taking it away from those who have a different complexion or slightly flatter noses than ourselves, is not a pretty thing when you look into it too much."[25] Looking closely at "the conquest of the earth," one sees not only the manifest ugliness of European imperialism but also the practiced indifference that allows hypocrisy to function; indifference is disrupted, Conrad suggests, by the critical pressure of excessive examination. Marlow is pointing not simply to racial discrimination and appropriations of land but to the heroic rhetoric ("the conquest of the earth") that transforms ignoble acts into noble gestures. Conrad suggests that only by looking "too much," only by looking more avidly than is necessary or required, can one assess or even discern the conditions of political complacence. In Marlow's example, the excessive act of looking at rhetoric makes the more usual act of looking at bodies less normal and more arbitrary.

In general, excessive looking allows readers to notice the acts of merely sufficient perception in which they can no longer simply participate. Looking "too much" creates alternatives to socialized vision, as it does for the imagined worker in Conrad's well-known credo, from the preface to *The Nigger of the "Narcissus"*: "To arrest, for the space of a breath, the hands busy about the work of the earth, and compel men entranced by the sight of distant goals to glance for a moment at the surrounding vision of form and colour, of sunshine and shadows; to make them pause for a look, for a sigh, for a smile—such is the aim."[26] Conrad hopes to make distracted observers out of "entranced" workers. In his novels, those who engage in excessive or unproductive looking are able to see, unlike those who are absorbed by habit, that perception is a social process rather than an automatic or natural response. The knowledge of social process allows characters to manipulate perception by making use of display and by recognizing the strategies of promotion employed by others.

In some ways, *The Secret Agent* shares with Conrad's other novels a concern with verbal propaganda—one thinks of phrases such as "the conquest of the earth" in *Heart of Darkness*, the "one of us" refrain in *Lord Jim*, or the belief in "material interests" in *Nostromo*.[27] Yet *The Secret Agent* expands the repertoire of social persuasion, adding, to the verbal propaganda introduced by characters and by the narrator, the visual propaganda of the city: shop windows, fashioned bodies, and even a literal signpost. Conrad establishes an analogy between the self-conscious displays of secret agents, pornography shops, and Soho street signs and the novel's display of facts, such as racial and social characteristics or the nature of family relations. Because Conrad equates his own strategies with the strategies of assimilation deployed by London criminals and detectives of indeterminate origin, *The Secret Agent* seems to express decadent values as well as to describe them. The novel suggests that some foreigners can pass as natives because, like Conrad, they know how to manipulate perception. Conrad's foreigners assimilate not by becoming homogeneously English but by fitting their own mixed characteristics into the cosmopolitanism of London. *The Secret Agent* makes readers see national belonging as a performance of requisite effects, and it presents characters as everyday artists, whose skills of political manipulation rely on their knowledge of spectators rather than of life.[28]

At the center of the novel is a plot to alter the perception of facts: an official of an unnamed foreign embassy plans an attack on the Greenwich Observatory because he wants to stimulate a crackdown on English liberty; the bombing will stimulate police action, the provocateur expects, by creating something to be policed. The aim of the bombing is simply the impression it will produce: the fear of crime and the sense that "science" is at risk (67). The bombing is a ruse, whose structure of pretense Conrad introduces in the first paragraph of the novel. *The Secret Agent* opens with a description of the Soho pornography shop owned by Adolf Verloc, a spy to the foreign embassy and the "secret agent" assigned to carry out the bombing:

> Mr Verloc, going out in the morning, left his shop nominally in charge of his brother-in-law. It could be done, because there was very little business at any time, and practically none at all before the evening. Mr Verloc cared but little about his ostensible business. And, moreover, his wife was in charge of his brother in law.
>
> (45)

The words "nominally" and "ostensible" convey the duplicity of the narrative's world: Mr. Verloc has deputized his brother-in-law only in name; his shop is a business only in appearance. The opening paragraph yields several conditional statements, some of which seem to contradict the others: the shop is not really left in charge of the brother-in-law; the shop can be left in charge of the brother-in-law because there are very few customers; even when there are customers, practically none come when the brother-in-law is in charge; even if customers come when the brother-in-law is in charge, it does not matter because Mr. Verloc does not care about the shop, which is not his real business; and even if the shop were his real business and he did care about it and he did have customers and the customers did come during the day, it is not the brother-in-law but Mrs. Verloc who is in charge.

One learns at the beginning of the novel that pretense governs the arrangements of Verloc's family and business. One learns later that the pretense of family is inseparable from the pretense of foreign crime: Mrs. Verloc, known as Winnie, marries to provide security for her "half-idiot" brother, Stevie; she encourages Verloc to involve Stevie in his business so that Verloc will want to keep him in the household; Verloc does not perceive the real cause of Winnie's interest, just as Winnie does not perceive Verloc's real business; finding Stevie at hand, Verloc uses him to transport the Greenwich bomb; however, Stevie drops the bomb accidentally, destroying not "science" but himself. One kind of domestic catastrophe replaces another, and the private affair leads to the discovery of the political debacle.

The novel begins with an account of verbal propaganda: Verloc may say that his brother-in-law is in charge of his business, but the family arrangement as well as the business are social fictions whose veneer of normalcy serves to keep less conventional arrangements from view. Unlike most of the characters, the reader can see the fictions because Conrad invokes the language of presentation, gesturing to less ostensible, less nominal details that he has not yet described. Elsewhere, in the voice of the Assistant Commissioner, Conrad offers an explicit analogy between the novel's art and everyday social artifice. Like Conrad, the Assistant Commissioner knows that what counts as a meaningful fact depends one's manner of speaking. Conversing with his supervisor, who wants information "only no details," the Assistant Commissioner decides to adopt a "parenthetical manner" (143). In this way, he explains, "every little fact—that is, every detail—fitted with delightful ease." Instead of subtracting details, as he was asked, or making details more important, the Assistant Commissioner speaks trivially, so that no detail seems trivial (less significant) in the least. For the novel, any designation of importance or irrelevance is not to be trusted because significance is a matter of presentation.

This is an insight that Conrad extends to the constituents of metropolitan London, where not only narratives but also places, people, and objects achieve social meaning through strategic display. Indeed, the narrative ruse in the opening paragraph seems, retrospectively, to echo the visual tricks that pervade the English scene. In the third paragraph of the novel, Conrad describes Verloc's shop window, where strategic display is natural both to the genre of the window and to the genre of pornography:

> The window contained photographs of more or less undressed dancing girls; nondescript packages in wrappers like patent medicines; closed yellow paper envelopes, very flimsy, and marked two and six in heavy black figures; a few numbers of ancient French comic publications hung across a string as if to dry; a dingy blue china bowl, a casket of black wood, bottles of marking ink, and rubber stamps; a few books, with titles hinting at impropriety; a few apparently old copies of obscure newspapers, badly printed, with titles like *the Torch, the Gong*—rousing titles. And the two gas jets inside the panes were always turned low, either for economy's sake or for the sake of the customers.
>
> (45)

The pornography shop provides camouflage for Verloc's anarchist activities by making the appearance of strange, disheveled men seem normal. The shop is convenient for Verloc in many ways: it allows him to pretend to his colleagues that he is a fellow anarchist (in fact, he is a spy of a foreign embassy); it allows him to pretend to the foreign embassy that he is a spy (in fact, he is a police informer); it allows him to pretend to his wife and mother-in-law that he has a business (in fact, he is lazy and does very little). Like cosmopolitan London, as Conrad will come to describe it, the pornography shop is made of diverse, contradictory parts, such as the assorted paraphernalia that it sells: "photographs of more or less undressed dancing girls," "a few numbers of ancient French comic publications," and "a soiled volume in paper covers with a promising title" as well as "bottles of marking ink" and "rubber stamps" (45–46). We might say that these are similar objects: the exotic origins of the first three items can be equated to the imperial origins of the "marking ink" (known also as "Indian ink," made in China or Japan) and the "rubber stamps," whose primary material is a natural product of empire. For most, however, the last two items are legible only as English conveniences—those everyday objects that aid and obscure the sale of eccentric goods. Indian ink and colonial rubber, central to global trade, are the products that make up England.

The marking ink and the stamps are useful because they allow customers to pretend, at any given moment, that they have come to purchase common objects rather than foreign magazines. However, since Verloc is not in fact trying to sell pornography, the ink and the stamps are useful in another way: they make the shop look authentic by projecting a pretense of respectability; that pretense is crucial to the genre of the shop. The low light in the window and the nondescript packages lend the shop a coyness that makes its other ruse—it is a meeting place for anarchists—less visible. Roland Barthes would call the ink and the stamps "useless details" because they serve to affirm Verloc's reputation as a shopkeeper: they have no denotative content; rather, they convey the reality of the shop.[29] But Verloc understands the usefulness of so-called useless details.[30] Pretending to run a pornography shop requires the knowledge of pornography (what the shop sells) as well as the knowledge of how pornography is concealed (what the shop must claim to sell). To look naturally foreign, Conrad suggests, the pornography shop must display a deliberate Englishness.

The most striking example of this point comes in Conrad's display of people. Over the course of the novel, the Assistant Commissioner poses as an anarchist and a "stranger" by speaking English all too well (187). Conrad suggests, as his reviewers do, that the deliberate choice of English is a defining characteristic of foreigners, yet, unlike his reviewers, Conrad suggests also that foreignness is a manner that anyone can adopt. The Assistant Commissioner transforms himself into a foreigner by stepping into a caricature that the narrative has generated. Assuming attributes he and we have learned to call "foreign," the Assistant Commissioner investigates the source of the Greenwich bombing by fitting into its milieu. This investigation takes him to Verloc's shop.

Conrad's text provides an account of the "customers" who typically call at the shop and whose appearance and gestures the novel configures as the manner the Assistant Commissioner will appropriate. The customers are of two main types: "either very young men" or "men of a more mature age." Of the latter group, it is said, they "had the collars of their overcoats turned right up to their moustaches, and traces of mud on the bottom of their nether garments" (45). The reader encounters the physical description two chapters before being told who these older men are, before being told that, in fact, they are not customers at all. The physical description quickly becomes an apposition, a defining characteristic: "the evening visitors—the men with collars turned up and soft hats rammed down"—nod "familiarly" when they enter the shop (46). Once the "visitors" are named as "anarchists," the apposition becomes the evidence for an identity that it has helped to create. *The Secret Agent* produces the conditions that make identities recognizable, imagining social roles by creating their characteristics.

The Assistant Commissioner becomes "foreign" because unremarkable aspects of his person become newly meaningful as specific attributes. He alters his appearance just as he altered his speech, changing not the details but the style; he refuses to call this strategy "a disguise" (148). With a "short jacket" and "low, round hat," the Assistant Commissioner emphasizes "the length of his grave, brown face"; he gives himself "the sunken eyes of a dark enthusiast and a very deliberate manner" (150). While the jacket and hat give new emphasis to the Assistant Commissioner's features, his face and eyes in fact remain the same. Conrad suggests that there is pleasure in this process: the necessary physical traits are said to be "brought out wonderfully" by the strategic choice of clothing. The Assistant Commissioner's "deliberate manner," better than a "disguise," suits him to his task: he is transformed into one of many "queer foreign fish"; he fits in among strangeness by looking as conspicuous as possible (150–51). The Assistant Commissioner becomes noticeable by taking notice, for the more closely he considers his activities, the more "unplaced" he feels (152). Checking his image in a sheet of glass, the police supervisor is "struck by his foreign appearance" (151) and then adopts the details the novel has attributed to anarchists and strangers. Deliberateness makes the Assistant Commissioner feel foreign, so much so that the characteristics of foreigners, invented as "characteristics" by the novel, become natural to him.

In the language of chance and opportunism—the very language that he uses to describe his own writing process in the later "Author's Note"—Conrad renders the Assistant Commissioner's "inspiration":

> He contemplated his own image with a melancholy and inquisitive gaze, then by sudden inspiration raised the collar of his jacket. This arrangement appeared to him commendable, and he completed it by giving an upward twist to the ends of his black moustache. He was satisfied by the subtle modification of his personal aspect caused by these small changes. "That'll do very well," he thought. "I'll get a little wet, a little splashed—"
>
> (151–52)

The "subtle modification," intentional but inspired, affirms the recognition (the "foreign appearance") that had provoked it. Some thirty pages later, at the shop, the Assistant Commissioner is taken for the foreigner he has become. Winnie Verloc, tending the front counter, notices that "he . . . wore his moustaches twisted up. In fact, he gave the sharp points a twist just then. His long, bony face rose out of a turned-up collar. He was a little splashed, a little wet. A dark man, with the ridge of the cheek-bone well defined under the slightly hollow temple. A complete stranger" (187). To Winnie, the Assistant Commissioner not only looks foreign but sounds foreign as well: "There was nothing foreign in his accent, except that he seemed in his slow enunciation to be taking pains with it. And Mrs Verloc, in her varied experience, had come to the conclusion that some foreigners could speak better English than the natives" (187). A deliberate and precise English, combined with a "turned-up collar" and purposefully sharpened moustache, allows Winnie Verloc to recognize, as it were, that the stranger has come "from the Continent" (187). The Assistant Commissioner has performed foreignness by sounding as "English" as possible. Speaking deliberately is not a sign that the Assistant Commissioner knows his English well so much as a sign that he knows his signs: he knows that conveying foreignness has more to do with reputed truths than with actual ones.

The Assistant Commissioner has acquired this knowledge, the novel suggests, not by wandering through London but by working in the colonies: living as a foreigner abroad has made him something of a foreigner, and an anarchist, in England. His subordinates fear that he will "disorganize the whole system of supervision" (197). Like the Assistant Commissioner, Verloc, too, is not quite a local: he is "a foreign political spy" (208) and also "a natural-born British subject" (59). He is, Conrad tells us, "cosmopolitan enough," which means he knows his way around London. Verloc's experience of the world has taught him not to be fooled by apparent nominations: seeing that "No. 1 Chesham Square" is marked on a wall at least sixty yards away from the area it designates, Verloc is without "surprise or indignation" (53), for London's "topographical mysteries," the novel suggests, match his own. Both Verloc and the Assistant Commissioner possess a "mistrust of established reputations" (129).

The peculiar foreignness of Verloc, the Assistant Commissioner, and the pornography shop is echoed in the novel by two other artifacts: the Foreign Embassy, which sponsors the novel's bombing incident, and "the little Italian restaurant round the corner," where the Assistant Commissioner goes to polish his "strange" appearance. The Embassy is defined by a foreignness it cannot occupy: it must reside within the geographic boundaries of one country even as it remains the representative, by metonymy, of the other country it serves. Similarly, the Italian restaurant is a "peculiarly British institution" (152), whose "fraudulent cookery" could exist, would exist, nowhere in Italy. This fraudulence causes the patrons to lose "all their national and private characteristics," the Assistant Commissioner observes. The people before him "seemed created for the Italian restaurant," as if the place, in its artifice, attracts a fitting clientele or as if it makes its patrons fit by compromising the social categories that usually define them. The local authenticities of London—the turned-up collar, the twisted moustache, the Embassy, the Italian restaurant—are the products of cosmopolitan artifice. What is most foreign in Conrad's novel is a strangeness invented at home, which is strange above all to those for whom things English are most familiar.

***

Conrad suggests in his novel that interpretation is limited by the meanings that characters and readers are able to recognize. For this reason, the novel presents "curiosity" as a crucial attribute both of spies and of detectives. For Conrad, the way people look—in what manner and with what preconceptions looking takes place—tells us most about them. It is thus, for example, that Verloc will attribute his wife's "unreadable face" at the end of the novel not to his failed vision (and insensitivity) but to hers: "Curiosity being one of the forms of self-revelation, a systematically incurious person remains always partly mysterious" (216). Conrad describes Winnie's "air of unfathomable indifference" (46), which he later attributes to her "philosophical, almost disdainful incuriosity" (216). Unlike the Assistant Commissioner, Winnie Verloc holds to an "uninquiring acceptance of facts" (155). Her sense that "things do not stand much looking into" repeats throughout the novel (172). Without looking into "facts," Winnie accepts things as they seem and is unable to see the prejudices, stereotypes, and ruses that direct her vision. Curiosity, for Conrad, requires the deliberate perception both of objects and of history: one must notice that reputations are established in the space and time of narrative.

By alternating between omniscient narrative and free indirect discourse, often several times in a single paragraph, Conrad conflates the practice of the novel with practices of social perception, such that the reader's knowledge is shaped by the way that characters read. Conrad's characters assign the individuals they meet to cultural types they have observed or imagined in the past; they make these assignments by naming incidental details as significant characteristics and by conforming these characteristics to the types they have already imagined. Like Winnie, who thinks that the Assistant Commissioner sounds strange after she has already decided that he is a stranger, Mr. Vladimir of the Foreign Embassy fits Verloc's appearance to the behavior he has diagnosed:

> Mr Vladimir formulated in his mind a series of disparaging remarks concerning Mr Verloc's face and figure. The fellow was unexpectedly vulgar, heavy, and impudently unintelligent. He looked uncommonly like a master plumber come to present his bill. The First Secretary of the Embassy, from his occasional excursions into the field of American humour, had formed a special notion of that class of mechanic as the embodiment of fraudulent laziness and incompetency.
>
> (62–63)

Vladimir, who thinks from the start that Verloc is lazy, incompetent, and fraudulent, confirms his judgment by finding in Verloc physical and mental characteristics that imply these behaviors. Although the passage begins with these characteristics, it is clear that Vladimir has noticed only those that will correspond to the stereotype he names in conclusion. The stereotype is the perspective that directs Vladimir's judgment; it is what Barthes calls a "view," a habit of description that organizes details into well-established frames.[31] In Conrad's work, the stereotype precedes the characteristics that seem to justify its invocation. Vladimir's observation is ultimately both fixed and unmoored by its definitive origin: Verloc is said to be "fraudulent," but the caricature that justifies this assessment is also something of a fiction, derived from the "American humour" Vladimir has taken seriously. Verloc embodies a falseness that is as false as the stereotype that confirms it.

Vladimir's strategies of observation are comparable to those used by Verloc's anarchist colleague, Comrade Ossipon, who relies on a theory of criminality devised by Cesare Lombroso. Lombroso's theory, which was fashionable in the 1880s (when the novel is set), argued that criminals could be identified by visible marks on their bodies, such as large ears or poor eyesight. Ossipon, it is said, "was free from the trammels of conventional morality—but he submitted to the rule of science" (*The Secret Agent*, 259). After Winnie has killed Verloc, Ossipon looks at her with new eyes: "He gazed at her, and invoked Lombroso, as an Italian peasant recommends himself to his favourite saint. He gazed scientifically. He gazed at her cheeks, at her nose, at her eyes, at her ears . . . Bad! . . . Fatal! [. . .] Not a doubt remained . . . a murdering type" (259). Ossipon had planned to seduce and marry Winnie for her inheritance, but his assessment of her as a "murdering type" leads him to steal the money and abandon her on a boat bound for the Continent. Ossipon's judgment is instrumental in his actions: transforming Winnie's body into a type, he transforms his act into an imperative. As Vladimir looks at Verloc, so Ossipon looks at Winnie: in each case, the perception imposed reflects not curiosity but conformity; Vladimir and Ossipon see what they expect or want to find.

Both of these examples complicate Ian Watt's famous account of "delayed decoding," a method of description he ascribes to Conrad's work. The method functions, Watt explains, by combining "the forward temporal progression of the mind, as it receives messages from the outside world, with the much slower reflexive process of making out their meaning" (175). *The Secret Agent* does offer many examples that correspond to Watt's account, but I want to suggest a different lesson. Take, for example, Verloc's perception of Privy Councillor Wurmt, who becomes a "person" over the course of several sentences. For Verloc, everything at the embassy initially seems strange:

> Another door opened noiselessly, and Mr Verloc immobilizing his glance in that direction saw at first only black clothes. The bald top of a head, and a drooping dark grey whisker on each side of a pair of wrinkled hands. The person who had entered was holding a batch of papers before his eyes and walked up to the table with a rather mincing step, turning the papers over the while. Privy Councillor Wurmt, Chancelier d'Ambassade, was rather short-sighted.
>
> (54)

The effect of the unfolding is to delay recognition for the reader, much as it is delayed for Verloc, and also to force the reader to participate in the

assembly of an identity produced in the collection of details. The reader is given time—and literal space on the page—to notice and join in this process. While the delay between the "black clothes" and the "person" can be attributed in part to Verloc's "decoding," it is also caused by a more physical impediment: the Privy Councillor has covered his face with papers. There are really two "delays" here, and the second makes a joke of the first. While it appears at first that Verloc's recognition is delayed by his perception, the reader sees at the end of the passage that it is not Verloc's sight but the Privy Councillor's vision that is most to blame. In this passage, perception is a way of seeing and also a characteristic that informs and differentiates persons who are seen. Conrad will take this idea further in the later examples involving Vladimir and Ossipon, whose perception is constituted by details they have already learned to look for. "Decoding" in these cases follows a different progression: the "meaning" that characters seek to "make out" generates the "messages" that they interpret. The messages are thus never entirely "outside" perspective. Cultural types are affirmed, even constituted, in the process of recognition.[32]

At the end of *The Secret Agent*, one sees that characters, like Conrad's readers, are reluctant to embrace their role in the novel's fictions. For this reason, they transform individual acts into passive constructions. Verloc calls Stevie's death a "pure accident" because Stevie did not mean to trip and because Verloc did not mean for him to die (230); a detective describes "the casual manner" in which Stevie's address "had come into his possession," even though he has surreptitiously ripped it from the clothes among Stevie's remains (109). Even Winnie's mother makes inevitable those facts whose intentions might bring discomfort, telling herself that Winnie married Verloc as a matter of "providence" rather than sacrifice (72). Finally, when Winnie commits suicide, her death is reported in a newspaper as "an impenetrable mystery" because neither she nor the cause of her distress can be identified (266). The last lines of the newspaper article repeat throughout the last chapter of the novel. They are lines that the anarchist Comrade Ossipon has memorized: "*An impenetrable mystery seems destined to hang for ever over this act of madness or despair*" (original emphasis). Ossipon, who had imagined a world governed by inevitable truths, is haunted by the "destiny" for which he is responsible. He sees that he is the (secret) agent of the "impenetrable mystery."

In Conrad's vision of English life, domestic ease exists only through the efforts of cultivated naturalness. Winnie Verloc is noted for "the masterly achievement of instinctive tact" (172) and her husband for "calculated indiscretions" (183). Winnie's "tact" is like the other deliberate characteristics produced throughout the novel, but it condenses in a phrase the structure of description that Conrad elsewhere illustrates in a paragraph or in several chapters: Winnie's tact is a characteristic that is formative as soon as it is formulated. It is best achieved without achievement because it is, like other local truths, a mastery that depends on the invisibility of effort. These kinds of artifacts are beneath notice because they lack noticeable history. To make this history visible, Conrad represents English culture as a *social process.*

One can hear in the wit of Conrad's descriptions the echo of Lady Bracknell, who famously proposes that to have a fashionable address one need only change the fashion.[33] Like Conrad, Wilde was an unnatural Englishmen: he had to learn how naturalness looks.[34] Invoking habitual phrases while also displaying them, Wilde's epigrams allowed readers to see their own expectations. Conrad extends Wilde's analysis of art to the analysis of everyday culture. As Wilde famously puts it, with only some irony,

> Where, if not from the Impressionists, do we get those wonderful brown fogs that come creeping down our streets, blurring the gas-lamps and changing the houses into monstrous shadows? . . . At present, people see fogs, not because there are fogs, but because poets and painters have taught them the mysterious loveliness of such effects.[35]

Wilde's blurred "gas-lamps" and "monstrous shadows" could have set the scene for Conrad's novel, which is full of similar, and similarly conventional, opacity. A few paragraphs after his discussion of the Impressionist fog, Wilde remarks that "nations and individuals" like to imagine that art refers to *them*, but rather it is art, Wilde contends, to which "human consciousness" refers ("Decay of Lying," 1087). Conrad takes this argument further: he presents adaptability, the projection of naturalness, as the source of English nature.

Conrad aims to make readers *see* the perceptual norms that keep people and cultures in place. If *Heart of Darkness* is Conrad's "most profound meditation on the difficult process of giving himself to England and to English," as James Clifford has argued, *The Secret Agent* asks what England and English are, displaying acts of "giving" as strategies of making (96). *The Secret Agent* suggests that fastidious editing and infamous lies originate, not over-there in the colonies, but over-here in Soho: the metropolitan culture that Marlow lies to protect, it turns out, has many origins and many lies within it. By imitating spectators, Conrad aims to change the way they see. By creating distrust for established reputations, Conrad creates a less natural conception of Englishness and a more cosmopolitan tradition of British writing.

2

A nation is the same people living in the same place. . . . Or also living in different places.

—JAMES JOYCE, *ULYSSES*

OVER THE PAST fifteen years, literary critics influenced by postcolonial theory, critical race theory, and the new cosmopolitan theory have sought to emphasize the political aspirations or "political content" of James Joyce's writing.[1] These critics have aimed to correct or at least to supplement previous studies that focused on Joyce's reputation as a European writer and aesthetic innovator. The new emphasis on what has been called the "subaltern" or the "semicolonial" Joyce is usually offered as a counterpoint to an old emphasis on Joyce's modernism, though many scholars now acknowledge that the renovation of Joyce studies has helped to produce in turn a renovation of modernist studies.[2] What it means to focus on and to analyze Joyce's modernism has changed: we no longer reduce literary modernism to a collection of literary techniques, nor do we assume that British literary modernism, with or without Joyce, constitutes a homogenous cultural movement or a retreat from political and social action. The emphasis on Joyce's anticolonialism has led to a new analysis of Joyce's cosmopolitanism, which includes his "dual identification," as Joseph Valente puts it, with "the conquerors and the conquered," with British culture and Irish counterculture, with "imperial agency and native resistance."[3] In order to emphasize these identifications, recent work on Joyce's cosmopolitanism has tended to privilege narrative themes of hybridity, border crossing, and cultural inauthenticity over narrative forms of perversity, decadence, and artifice.[4] This work has allowed us to see Joyce as a serious, significant writer of anticolonial, antiracist fiction. Yet Joyce's principal insight, that colonialism and racism rely for their political efficacy on norms of seriousness and significance, is sometimes lost in the bargain.[5] In this chapter, I argue that Joyce's cosmopolitanism, while committed to democratic collectivity and Irish liberation, eschews the heroic pieties both of local and of planetary belonging. He proposes instead that anticolonialism and antiracism require a model of cosmopolitanism that values triviality, promiscuous attention, and what I call "canceled decorum."

Joyce's focus on triviality—his emphasis on ordinary objects, everyday experiences, transient pleasures, and the tricks of language—leads him to generate two models of national culture: a fixed culture that can be described through the exhaustive collection of quotidian details and a transient culture for which quotidian details mark a principle of inexhaustible, proliferating characteristics. In the critical history of Joyce studies, the tension between these models is addressed sometimes as the tension between two literary modes, naturalism and symbolism, and sometimes as the tension between two political modes, the Irish Joyce and the international Joyce. In his recent book, Andrew Gibson aspires to "bridge the gap between Bloom-centered and Stephen-centered interpretations," between the emphasis on a "European and international Joyce" and an emphasis on an "Irish and/or colonial context."[6] While I share Gibson's aspiration, I argue in this chapter that the critical "gap" reflects the double imperative of Joyce's project: the affirmation of distinctive cultures in the service of Irish liberation and the rejection of cultural distinctiveness in the service of antiracism, democratic individualism, and transnational community.

It is a literary as well as a political truism that national movements need to bypass the disparate, quotidian experiences of living in the same place in order to produce collective, affirmative narratives of identification: common origins, common traditions, and common desires.[7] That this is a truism does not make it true, but the importance of national unity, especially during times of war or social embattlement, is a familiar claim. A great range of cultural critics, from Ernest Renan and M. M. Bakhtin to Etienne Balibar and Arjun Appadurai, have argued that the traditional premise of the nation requires the subordination, if not the suppression, of individual differences so that, as Balibar writes, "it is the symbolic difference between 'ourselves' and 'foreigners' which wins out and which is lived as irreducible."[8] Historically, this structure of subordination has been important for the political recognition that comes with coherent social visibility: if political recognition is based on cultural distinctiveness and value, then one may need to claim a distinct and valued culture even to speak at all.[9] However, bypassing disparate experiences can have aesthetic as well as political consequences: literature that repeats familiar generalizations, Theodor W. Adorno has argued in essays on the politics of literary style, helps to maintain fixed conceptions by living up to them, and it generates in its readers habits of inattention and intellectual automatism.[10] Literature that refuses to reproduce the social "façade," as Adorno puts it, shows readers that there might be something to change, that there is a difference between "living human beings and rigidified conditions."[11]

Adorno's account of novelists who refuse to accommodate rigidified conditions, who resist what this chapter calls "acquiescence" or "cheerful decorum," begins with James Joyce.[12] I will be using "decorum" to refer not only to conventions of social appropriateness but also and more particularly to conventions of literary judgment and political affect. Readers have long noticed that Joyce was indecorous in his refusal to abide by the moral norms of his day. I will be arguing, on the contrary, that Joyce's critique of decorum needs to be understood as an effort to revise literary conventions of national belonging and political assertion. From Aristotle and Horace onward, "decorum" has referred to the congruity between subject matter and style and between art and social experiences. The logic of decorum is conservative: it favors consistency rather than discrepancy, continuity rather than change. In this chapter, I aim to shift critical attention from the measure of Joyce's nationalism to the analysis of Joyce's "nation," his effort to revise what a "living" nation is. Joyce's project is cosmopolitan in two important ways: it is critical of authenticity as a measure of belonging, and it promotes intellectual vagrancy, what I call "triviality," as a condition of materialist critique and social transformation. Joyce develops a style of triviality to contest the political affects that he associates with British imperialism, Irish anti-Semitism, and Catholic evangelism; to induce comparison among examples of exploitation, such as colonialism in Ireland and religious conversion in Asia and Africa; and to reorient attention to an international politics of the everyday.

✳✳✳

While Joyce is considered perhaps the least "trivial," most influential twentieth-century writer in English, he is best known for the minutiae rather than for the majesty of his style. His work provides the most persuasive, most thorough example of epic triviality: through the obsessive, often repetitive thoughts of unremarkable or unrefined characters, Joyce adds fresh, often outrageous images to the repertoire of fiction in English. Using the materials of everyday life, Joyce forges new strategies of intellectual resistance and cultural improvisation. Joyce's triviality helps to inaugurate a practice of collage in the twentieth-century novel: the collage of foreign cultures, details from places such as England, Ireland, Palestine, and India, and also the collage of local cultures, high as well as low, details from places, in a different sense, such as street corners, music halls, houses, newspapers, and pubs. Moving from one place to another, Joyce's work gives texture to an insubordinate cosmopolitanism, embracing intellectual vagrancy as a practice of social critique. Unlike Raymond Williams, who rejects "vagrancy" as observation without judgment, Joyce values, in the process of judgment, more promiscuous styles of attention.[13]

I associate Joyce's triviality with several literary strategies from his early and later writing. Described generically, these strategies correspond to some of the principal characteristics of modernist narrative: the use of interior monologue and unfiltered observation; the unusual range and focus of narrative attention; and the rigorous inclusion of different social, cultural, and aesthetic registers, such as biblical verse and bawdy limerick, popular and philosophical theories of national allegiance, major life events and the color of a face. In this chapter, I will speak of "canceled decorum," "subtracted consensus," "unsubordinated attention," and "tactical discourtesy" to show how Joyce manipulates the conventions of literary description. In his early letters, Joyce argues that conditions of writing, created by publishers as well as by governments, serve to limit the visibility of Irish culture.[14] Extending this visibility, Joyce proposes to transform the consciousness of his readers.[15]

Subtracting consensus, Joyce knew that he was promoting discomfort, if not hostility. He suggests this knowledge in his refusal to alter or omit stories from his first book, *Dubliners*, about which he claimed, "I have come to the conclusion that I cannot write without offending people."[16] Joyce's comment may sound like a lament ("I wish I could write differently") or even an excuse ("I am unable to write differently"), but the stories imply something more aggressive: Joyce offended his readers on purpose. In some ways, Joyce's claim is specific to *Dubliners*, in that Joyce was aiming, at the turn of the twentieth century, to disrupt the social logic of Victorian reading. He knew that his audience, whether Irish or English, would find his topics and strategies either shocking or disconcerting or both. Joyce refuses to censor the less heroic, less salubrious aspects of Dublin life, and he refuses to present these experiences with requisite condemnation or carelessness. This refusal was widely received as Joyce intended it, as a rejection of "standards," by which one English reviewer, speaking later of *Ulysses*, meant both specific rules, those that would censor "our most secret and most unsavoury private thoughts," and historical continuity, the principle that keeps specific rules in place.[17] Joyce's work thus rejects not only literary custom but also literary tradition; it rejects the edifice of English literature and cultural pride, described by the reviewer as "the noble qualities of balance, rhythm, harmony, and reverence for simple majesty that have been for three centuries the glory of our written tongue." Making Irish life part of English tradition, Joyce's work reminds its readers that English "glory" is neither as noble nor as majestic as it once may have been possible to imagine.

That Joyce's refusal of representational norms functions as a revision of national belonging is first proposed explicitly in two important, early reviews of *Ulysses*. In these essays, the eminent French writer Valéry Larbaud and the influential English writer John Middleton Murry measure Joyce's "European" credentials by assessing the decorum of his work.[18] However much they disagree about Joyce's place in either national or cosmopolitan traditions, Larbaud and Murry concur that his work offends and that its offensiveness is directed at and against the traditions of national writing. In an article that was first presented as a public talk in 1921 and then widely circulated in English and in French, Larbaud praises Joyce by claiming that, with *Ulysses*, "Ireland is making a sensational re-entrance into high European literature" (253). *Ulysses* is European rather than merely Irish, Larbaud proposes, because it demonstrates a less celebratory, more descriptive shade of belonging: for Larbaud, the distinction between the national work and the national work that is also European is the author's refusal to "please" (his term) what Larbaud calls the "nationalistic" audience (253). To be European, one must be willing to offend. Larbaud suggests this most of all in his naming of the other European authors with whom Joyce should be compared: Ibsen, Strindberg, Nietzsche, Gabriel Miró, and Ramón Gomez, all of whom wrote against the social mores of their nation and time.[19]

Larbaud invokes the category of "European literature" only once in his essay, but his comment was enough to provoke several critical responses, both from those who sought to associate Joyce with a distinctive and valued Irishness apart from European connections and from those who found Joyce too nonconformist to have any "social" affinity whatsoever.[20] Writing in the *Nation and Anthanæum*, John Middleton Murry argued that *Ulysses* is part of no tradition, neither European nor Irish, because it demonstrates no respect for "Western" conventions of taste. Murry contends that a work of literature is European only if "the author, consciously or unconsciously, accepts the postulates of Western civilization. He accepts the principle of order, the social law (or convention) that certain things are good and certain other things are evil" (117). *Ulysses* is not European, Murry continues, because it does not display "obedience" and "submission," terms of social accommodation that Joyce specifically rejects in *A Portrait of the Artist as a Young Man*. Murry argues that writers cannot be European, or even Irish, if they do not reproduce traditional literary values. The author of European literature, Murry asserts,

> obeys the law [of convention] because he feels himself to be a member of society, and an instinct warns him that deliberate and continual disobedience leads to the disintegration of the society which is Europe. . . . A writer who is European not only makes this act of submission in himself, but regards his writing also as a social act. He respects the limitations which the essential social law of taste imposes; he acknowledges the social tradition of Europe.
>
> (117)

Murry is an important early reader of Joyce's work because he recognizes, if not Joyce's talent, at least Joyce's aim: he sees that his writing is meant to reject the established conditions of social collectivity. For this, Murry calls Joyce an anarchist: "He is the man with the bomb who would blow what remains of Europe into the sky" (118). Murry is speaking metaphorically, but he is plain in his concern that literary disorder can lead to political disintegration. Murry is unwilling to acknowledge social disobedience as an effective literary or political strategy, in good part because he wants to maintain "the conditions of civilization" more than he wants to change them (118).

While Murry can find no place for social commitment in Joyce's insubordinate, unsubordinated writing, Larbaud's account of Joyce oscillates between a familiar story of national affirmation and a less familiar narrative of international critique. Larbaud associates Joyce with two, not quite consistent projects: writing on behalf of the nation ("Ireland"), as it if were a valuable, coherent object; and writing for a community of artists that is broader than the nation and that serves to contest celebratory images of national tradition. For Murry, Joyce's refusal to adopt a conventional social posture means that he has no social position at all; for Larbaud, Joyce both represents Irish society and also resists the politics of coherent representation. Ultimately, Larbaud and Murry share the assumption that Joyce can meet his political and literary goals only by affirming a distinctive social or national tradition. They are unable to imagine that there is any other kind of tradition to affirm.

Many of Joyce's contemporaries, such as artists of the Irish Revival and the Harlem Renaissance, sought to promote political recognition for specific social groups by affirming the distinctiveness of their cultures. Joyce valued political recognition also, but he had a different image of culture in mind.[21] For Joyce, it is not because Ireland has a distinct culture that it deserves self-determination; rather, Joyce wants Ireland to have self-determination so that its culture may change and diversify, so that it may become less distinct. Joyce argues in an early essay that freedom of thought is stifled by social and political constraint, which is why the Irish artist has to leave Ireland:

> The economic and intellectual conditions that prevail in his own country do not permit the development of individuality. The soul of the country is weakened by centuries of useless struggle and broken treaties, and individual initiative is paralyzed by the influence and admonitions of the church, while its body is manacled by the police, the tax office, and the garrison.[22]

Joyce is committed to Irish independence from British rule and supports political efforts that would bring about this separation, but he does not seek to justify the political struggle by promoting a homogenous, wholly consistent image of Irish culture.[23] When Joyce speaks of politics, he promotes an Irish republic; when Joyce speaks of the Irish National Theatre, he promotes "European masterpieces," the plays of Yeats but also of Ibsen, Tolstoy, and Hauptmann.[24] These are not separate campaigns. Joyce contends that international art will bring fresh inspiration to Irish culture, which is paralyzed by economic and political domination; he looks to contemporary writers and dramatists such as Ibsen to bring freedom from "deliberate self-deception" (71). Joyce envisions a cosmopolitan Ireland, which values Irish traditions without seeking to codify or sentimentalize them, which rejects British occupation, and which welcomes the impropriety of art as a strategy of social transformation.[25]

***

Joyce's early works of narrative fiction may not emphasize cultural hybridity and other recognizable themes of cosmopolitanism,[26] but they develop models of insubordinate attention that are crucial to the cosmopolitan posture of Joyce's later writing. Wandering operates not only as an activity of Joyce's characters, as it is most famously in *Ulysses*, but also as an activity of Joyce's texts: the ceaseless movement of perspective allows Joyce to display and appropriate the paralyzing norms of colonial Dublin.[27] In "Two Gallants," the one story in *Dubliners* that Joyce's publisher initially rejected outright, the refusal to focus on appropriate and significant topics—a refusal in which both the characters and the narrative participate—is a principal theme, and a provocation.[28] The story relies on the effect of what I call "canceled decorum" to display and unsettle the façade of social consensus. In later texts, Joyce produces this effect by representing episodes of broken ritual, such as a ruined dinner or an insincere handshake; in "Two Gallants," he invokes and withdraws generic expectations of romance, chivalry, and moral concern. "Two Gallants" presents decorum as a scam of British imperialism. While it is sometimes read as an example of Joyce's naturalist style, as if it offered a "transparent representation of Irish culture," one should notice that the social and textual environment of the story is constituted by tricks, affectations, and echoes: styles of behavior that are, for the reader, neither transparent nor fixed.[29] Even the story's title is not exclusively Irish: it names two desperate, self-interested Dubliners by invoking the cosmopolitan tradition of courtly love.[30] In addition, one Dubliner's gratuitous and purposeful use of foreign words ("That takes the solitary, unique, and, if I may so call it, *recherché* biscuit!") suggests that ordinary Irishmen might be aspirant cosmopolitans, in the sense both of social cultivation and of cultural mixing (44). Joyce does not oppose the story's French affectations to some true Irishness located elsewhere; rather, he proposes that cosmopolitan posture is a social mannerism that is genuine to Dublin life.

"Two Gallants" is structured by two principal scams, each of which involves a strategy of diverted attention. The narrative seems to be about two unemployed, unappealing young men: Corley, who plans to extract money from a slavey (a domestic servant) by acting the part of a suitor, and his friend Lenehan, who admires Corley's ruse and hopes to benefit from the con. The first part of the narrative joins an ongoing conversation between Corley and Lenehan, as they discuss Corley's plan, and the rest follows Lenehan, who meanders through Dublin, buys himself a meager plate of peas for dinner, and waits for Corley, who meets up with the girl in a scene the reader is not shown. At the end of the story, Corley returns triumphant, with a gold sovereign—a British coin—in his hand. "Two Gallants" implies that romance is a scam, an unequal and untransparent exchange, in which the gestures of courtship point only to other, unromantic conquests. Corley's conquests are economic: he manipulates the slavey's trust (she gives him the equivalent of several months' wages), and he manipulates social expectations (he manages to subsist without a job). The story's most obvious scam is Corley's manipulation of the slavey through the promise of romance. The story's secondary scam is Joyce's manipulation of the reader, who is led to believe by Lenehan's coarse jokes and ringing insinuations ("Is she game for that?" [46]; "are you sure you can bring it off all right?" [47]; "Did you try her?" [54]) that Corley's goal is sex rather than money. The first scam, in which the slavey is diverted, in turn diverts the reader: one is surprised to find the banality of money posing as the titillation of sex; the surprise means that the reader, like Lenehan, ends up worrying more about his or her own deception than about the deception of the girl; however, the surprise also allows Joyce to suggest that moral judgments—our assumption, for example, that sex with the young woman, who looks at Corley with a "contented leer" (49), would have to involve a scam—tend to obscure the gravity of economic squalor. "Two Gallants" is a tale of impoverished romance that is also a tale of everyday fiscal poverty.

The primary and secondary scams are a set up for the story's most shocking acts of reoriented attention: not the replacement of romance with sex, or sex with money, but the replacement of moral judgment with economic conditions. The story makes its reader focus on a gamut of topics that seem trivial, even unethical by comparison to the topics on which the story might otherwise have focused: Lenehan's evening of meager fantasies instead of Corley's interaction with the girl; the feelings of Lenehan and Corley instead of the girl's feelings (she is never given a name); Lenehan's concern that Corley might trick *him*, but never his concern that someone else—the girl—is being tricked. Even Joyce's use of the word "trick" is confusing. Corley tells Lenehan, "I'm up to all their little tricks" (47), which seems to have two, opposite connotations: Corley is able to exploit women because he knows their vulnerabilities ("tricks"); or, Corley is able to imitate the tactics ("tricks") that women use to manipulate men. Either way, Corley's ambivalent phrasing diverts attention from his own dubious actions and towards the actions or vulnerabilities—it is he who calls them "tricks"—of the women he cons.

The specific trick that Corley describes to Lenehan is his habit of intentional tardiness—"I always make her wait a bit" (47)—which serves, presumably, to make women anxious about Corley's affections and thus more eager to please him. This trick is reproduced with a difference at the end of the story when Lenehan, left alone while Corley meets the girl, begins to worry that his friend might not be coming back. Lenehan imagines that Corley might have succeeded in his quest and then "given him [Lenehan] the slip" (53). Here, instead of facing the consciousness of the conman, the reader faces the consciousness of the dupe, except that the dupe is proposed not as the girl who is losing several months' wages but as the accomplice who wants to help spend those wages. Lenehan asks himself, in the story's single acknowledgment of ethical judgment, "Would Corley do a thing like that?" (53). Lenehan's question is striking because he has focused on himself rather than on the girl but also because he seems oblivious to his own engagement in tricks: his involvement in Corley's scam and his manipulation of Corley, whom he is pleased to handle with "a little tact" (47). Joyce invokes a collective spirit of ethical behavior—"Would Corley do a thing like that?"—but puts this sensibility in self-serving Lenehan's mouth: the story presents ethical norms, among the gallants and within colonial Ireland, as yet another scam.

The ethical decorum of Lenehan's question is canceled by the multiplication of referents, the things "like that," considered and unconsidered, which crowd the reader's mind: Would Corley pretend to like the girl in order to take money from her? Would Corley break up with her as soon as he gets want he wants? Would Corley take the girl's money and then keep it from Lenehan? The story is more interested in the comparison of scams than in the judgment of correct attention: there is no longer a necessary "that" in the local universe that Joyce describes. The final image of the gold coin suggests an ultimate scam and asks readers to question the politics of socialized attention: *one realizes that the figurative poverty of Irish morals has substituted for the literal impoverishment caused by British sovereignty.* Joyce implies that British rule in Ireland is one more example—though really the preeminent example—of economic exploitation posing as a gallant gesture. "Two Gallants" uses a style of insubordinate attention to offer a critical perspective on the scams of British imperialism. In the end, the conmen, who think they have managed their trick, remain dupes of foreign rule.[31] But this is not the final word: structuring his story as a scam, Joyce suggests that postures and affectations support cosmopolitan opportunities—his own—as well as imperialist manipulation.

In a letter to his publisher, Grant Richards, Joyce complained that the same printer who allows newspapers to report sordid divorce cases objects on moral grounds to the economy of scams that Joyce describes in his fictional stories.[32] For this, Joyce calls the printer "one-eyed" (82), which is a significant epithet, both because it casts hypocrisy as the failure to make comparisons between one stratum of culture and another and because it associates the conditions of literary production with the conditions of extreme nationalism and planetary cosmopolitanism, later personified in the "Cyclops" episode of *Ulysses*. In "Two Gallants," Joyce's style of promiscuous attention, most visible in the story's many diversions, serves to analyze rather than reproduce the scam of ethical consistency. Like the slavey and like the gallants, readers are duped. However, unlike the characters, readers learn the scam: the ruses of Irish gallantry and British imperialism are matched and best displayed by the ruse of Joyce's fiction.

✳✳✳

If "Two Gallants" trains readers to be promiscuously attentive, *The Portrait of the Artist as a Young Man* presents triviality as a tactic of heresy and insubordination. It is telling about Joyce's project that Stephen Dedalus, in an important scene from the novel, chooses intellectual freedom over social conformity by allowing his mind to wander. This freedom, while it ultimately leads to Stephen's embrace of exile rather than collectivity, prompts him to compare various examples of exploitation and to think historically and politically about the institutions in which he has been asked to participate. In this sense, wandering allows Stephen to generate a social context for creative innovation and a more complex account of the interrelationships among British imperialism, Irish poverty, Catholic duty, and familial obligation. Stephen's distraction takes place while he is shaking hands with the director of studies at Belvedere College; the director is a Jesuit, and he has been trying to recruit Stephen for the priesthood. For Joyce, the oscillation of Stephen's mind, as he focuses on the priest's conversation and on nearby sounds and images, both constitutes intellectual freedom and also produces it: once Stephen diversifies his attention, a life of unimaginative duty repels him. From this moment, Stephen embraces "wandering" rather than "acquiescence" (136–38). The scene of unsubordinated attention dramatizes the principles of Joyce's art.

As he shakes hands with the priest, Stephen hears a "trivial air," a passing melody played on a concertina; he prefers the quotidian pleasure of the song to the "mirthless reflection of the sunken day," which he sees before him in the priest's face (136). In this preference, Stephen realizes that he will not join the Jesuits. An entire paragraph narrates only this one, ephemeral moment:

He [the priest] held open the heavy hall door and gave his hand as if already to a companion in the spiritual life. Stephen passed out on to the wide platform above the steps and was conscious of the caress of mild evening air. Toward Findlater's church a quartet of young men were striding along with linked arms, swaying their heads and stepping to the agile melody of their leader's concertina. The music passed in an instant, as the first bars of sudden music always did, over the fantastic fabrics of his mind, dissolving them painlessly and noiselessly as a sudden wave dissolves the sandbuilt turrets of children. Smiling at the trivial air he raised his eyes to the priest's face and, seeing in it a mirthless reflection of the sunken day, detached his hand slowly which had acquiesced faintly in that companionship.

(136)

The reader knows that this is the moment of Stephen's decision, what will become his permanent disavowal of religion and social conformity, because the passing of the music takes "an instant," the same amount of time occupied by the "sinful thought" of disobedience that led to Lucifer's downfall (98). One should hear in Stephen's nonacquiescence the sound of Lucifer's declaration, *non serviam* ("I will not serve"), which Stephen repeats later in the novel to emphasize his separation from religious, political, and filial obligations (205). The repetition of instantaneous fall is partial rather than exact, however, because Joyce attributes to Stephen's consciousness nothing so willful and single-minded as disobedience: this moment exemplifies the difference between the style of attention that Joyce admires, which is flexible, in some ways even passive, and Stephen's embrace of "exile," which Joyce will present later in the novel as definitive and unyielding.

The freedom of Stephen's imagination depends on a "trivial" pun (air as breeze and air as music), whose combination of touch and sound creates a diversion: Stephen seems to be "smiling" at the breeze, at the melody, and also at the frivolity of the resonating experience. This style of attention allows Stephen to see the hypocrisy of single-mindedness. The pun is notable not only because it prefigures the importance of wordplay in Joyce's later writing but also because it aligns Stephen's choice of intellectual freedom with his refusal to distinguish between significant and insignificant interpretations. Jonathan Culler has observed that puns refuse to "reaffirm a distinction between essence and accident, between meaningful relations and coincidence."[33] Joyce's pun serves to create new meaningful relations by changing the way Stephen thinks: the open, resonating experience of evening and music makes the priest seem, by comparison, unseeing and insensitive. Thinking about the person he will not choose to become, "The Reverend Stephen Dedalus, S. J." (*Portrait*, 137), Stephen pictures "an undefined face or colour of a face . . . eyeless and sourfavoured and devout" (137). Joyce suggests in Stephen's image that the priest's static, devout attention is equivalent to blindness; it makes him incapable of paying attention at all, where paying attention requires distraction as well as sight.

Joyce's pun introduces play into a passage about duty. It introduces what Adorno calls "art's lightheartedness": a "change in the existing mode of consciousness" that acknowledges but does not reproduce "the brute seriousness that reality imposes on human beings."[34] Art is "lighthearted," not because it represents happy topics or because it shows indifference to reality but because it exceeds "the constraints of self-preservation" by representing more than is necessary or legitimate, or even politically expedient. Like Joyce, Adorno seeks to change social conditions by changing styles of thought. However, Adorno recognizes that writers who challenge standards of judgment or habitual thought will often seem "inconsiderate," "eccentric," or "foreign."[35] Joyce's writing seems cosmopolitan to his early readers because he expresses both erudition and vulgarity; indeed, Joseph Litvak has argued that sophistication, a characteristic often associated with cosmopolitanism, tends to imply not only snobbery but impropriety as well.[36] Joyce's writing seems foreign or cosmopolitan because, as Adorno's argument suggests, "the perpetuation of existing society is incompatible with consciousness of itself":[37] social immobility is maintained by the inability to sense it, or by the inability to imagine any other possibility. For Adorno, thinking transforms the social world because it is "not the intellectual reproduction of what exists anyway."[38] Culler argues, similarly, that the pun serves to encourage active thought because it involves a "conception of language which one must struggle to imagine" (14).

One should see two related kinds of active thought in the passage from *Portrait*: the diversion of Stephen's attention, from obligation to sensation, and the diversion of the reader's attention, from evening breeze to trivial melody. These diversions are part of single project in Joyce's novel. The seeds of this project, visible from the very beginning of *Portrait*, suggest how intellectual triviality comes to resist political acquiescence. By the time Stephen arrives at his meeting with the director of studies, during the fourth of the novel's five chapters, he has passed through an intellectual childhood punctuated by efforts to generalize and to parse. For example, in the first chapter of the novel, Stephen learns to give a single name to the same experience repeated several times, such as what happens "when you wet the bed" (*Portrait*, 1), and he also learns that single names can designate different experiences ("That was a belt round his pocket. And belt was also to give a fellow a belt" [3]). Joyce establishes in these early pages the gestures of trivial attention that will stimulate social critique later in the novel. One of Stephen's juvenile memories, from his childhood at school, intimates a more mature politics of imagination: Stephen's mind travels from the effort of solving a classroom equation to images of red and white roses that he and his rival wear on their lapels to the color of the cards ("pink and cream and lavender") that the most successful students receive to the thought of "lavender and cream and pink roses" to the thought of a "wild rose" to "the song about the wild rose blossoms on the little green place" to the impossibility of "a green rose" (6). While Stephen knows that "you could not have a green rose," the wandering of his mind allows him to imagine, for just a moment, that "perhaps somewhere in the world you could" (6). Stephen has replaced the cold utility of the schoolroom with the pleasures of artifice—a nonexistent rose—and momentary escape; however, it is the momentary escape from habitual knowledge ("what you can have") that allows Stephen to imagine the glimpse of possibility. Making the rose green, the color of Ireland, Joyce suggests that intellectual freedom, as exemplified by Stephen's trivial mind, establishes the conditions for political independence.

By the second chapter of the novel, Joyce is more explicit in his contention that political strategies of anticolonialism require thinking that is "heretic and immoral," thinking like Lord Bryon's and like Stephen's in his defense of Byron. The schoolboy Stephen defends Byron, whom he claims as his favorite poet, against his classmates' assertion that Lord Tennyson, the British poet laureate, is "the greatest poet" (67). The classmates base their claim about Tennyson on the fact that "we have all his poetry at home in a book," and they refuse to consider Byron because he "was a bad man" (67–68). The preference for Tennyson signals that the other students are unthinking in their intellectual conformity—they like what they already know and what has received the appreciation of others, in the form of awards and in the form of publication—and also that they are capitulating to British imperialism: Tennyson is the poet of Britannia. The students punish Stephen for his refusal of these values and for his refusal to observe the priority of religious judgment: when Stephen says he does not care that Bryon was a heretic, the students respond by beating Stephen with a cabbage stump, shouting "Admit that Bryon was no good" (68). Stephen reproduces heresy by refusing to condemn it; that heretics produce bad poetry, however "bad" is defined, is an article of faith that Stephen is unwilling to accept.[39] This is the first episode, chronologically, in which Stephen is asked to put religious judgment before all other perspectives, though it follows, in the novel, a second episode from several years later.

In the later episode, Stephen is asked, this time playfully, to "admit" his interest in an attractive girl (64). Instead of struggling, as he did when he was younger, Stephen pretends to acquiesce, "bowing submissively" and reciting the Confiteor, the prayer that is used in preparation for Confession (65). Stephen resists the teasing of his friends by adopting the rhetoric of religious submission; performing submission in this mocking context, Stephen trumps his friends by shocking them. When Stephen is older, his irreverence brings laughter rather than aggression. In the early scene of impiety, Stephen refuses to "admit" his sin (liking Bryon even though he is a heretic); in the later scene, he admits his sin (sexual interest) but only by sinning more egregiously (mocking the Confession). The two scenes of impious resistance are connected in the novel by the syntax of "while," which forces the reader to look across situations of time and circumstance, to rethink one circumstance in comparison with another, and to read without subordination of chronology or conventional significance:

> The confession came only from Stephen's lips and, while they spoke the words, a sudden memory had carried him to another scene called up, as if by magic, at the moment when he had noted the faint cruel dimples at the corners of Heron's smiling lips and had felt the familiar stroke of the cane against his calf and had heard the familiar word of admonition:
> —Admit.
>
> (65)

This syntax is repeated a few pages later, after Stephen has remembered the earlier episode, by the addition of another thought: "While he was still repeating the *Confiteor* amid the indulgent laughter of his hearers and while the scenes of that malignant episode were still passing sharply and swiftly before his mind he wondered why he bore no malice now to those who had tormented him" (68). Stephen bears no malice because he is not interested in questions of "honour" (69), particularly his own; he finds silence preferable to revenge because revenge repeats rather than changes the conditions of judgment. The word "while," which comes once again, points to the structure of thought that Stephen is resisting and introduces an alternative, insubordinate model:

> While his mind had been pursuing its intangible phantoms and turning in irresolution from such pursuit he had heard about him the constant voices of his father and of his masters, urging him to be a gentleman above all things and urging him to be a good catholic above all things. These voices had now come to be hollowsounding in his ears. When the gymnasium had been opened he had heard another voice urging him to be strong and manly and healthy and when the movement towards national revival had begun to be felt in the college yet another voice had bidden him to be true to his country and help raise up her fallen language and tradition. . . . And it was the din of all of these hollowsounding voices that made him halt irresolutely in the pursuit of phantoms.
>
> (69–70)

The syntax of "while" captures the wandering of Stephen's mind from his pursuit of thought, to his "irresolution" about that pursuit, and back to a state of unresolved consciousness. One might describe Joyce's style in these several pages as "stream of consciousness," but Stephen's associations are somewhat more purposeful and more critical than they are automatic or accidental. Responding to the noise of too many projects clamoring for exclusive attention, Stephen rejects any one, single voice. Joyce's sentences, like Stephen's thoughts, refuse to subordinate; they refuse to put any one perspective "above all things." This refusal to prioritize is insubordinate because it promotes conflict rather than acquiescence; it is trivial because it ignores "honour" and other standard priorities of social behavior.

Stephen chooses triviality—art rather than religion, critique rather than socialization—and a life "wandering among the snares of the world" (138). He chooses, instead of a "grave and ordered and passionless life" (136), a life "elusive of social and religious orders" (138). As Stephen walks away from the interview with the director of studies, his travels assume the metaphors of a disobedient consciousness: turning "for an instant towards the faded blue shrine of the Blessed Virgin," Stephen sees only the squalor of Dublin; he leaves the shrine by "bending to the left," toward "disorder, the misrule and confusion of his father's house" (138). It is important to notice that Stephen's wandering mind prepares the way for more literal, physical wandering; his distracted attention makes unconventional travel—through Dublin and from Dublin to Paris—something he is able to imagine. Once Stephen has "[bent] to the left," once he has embraced a sinister disorder, his social and physical self-restraint falls away: he smiles, "a short laugh broke from his lips," "a second laugh, taking rise from the first after a pause, broke from him involuntarily" (138). Stephen is pleased to think of the farmhand whom he and his siblings have "nicknamed the man with the hat": detaching himself from the social institutions of Ireland and from the social decorum of self-discipline and rigid custom, Stephen fashions an experimental, vernacular existence out of informality, made-up language, and the playful appropriation of everyday objects.

For Joyce, as for Salman Rushdie after him, nicknaming creates intimacy, a private world, and it serves in turn to disable official naming, which it reconstitutes as one more point of view. Nicknaming thus becomes the condition, and not the substitution, for proper names. By the end of *Portrait*, Joyce presents Stephen's turn away from proper naming as a critique of cultural distinctiveness and intellectual paralysis: Stephen, now at university, famously haggles with his dean, an Englishman, about whether "tundish" is an English or an Irish word (161). The debate between Stephen and the dean implies not only the word's etymology but also its usage: Is it a word proper to English speech? Is it (only) an Irish idiom? Is an Irish idiom less proper to English speech than an English idiom would be? Speaking pedantically, the dean tells Stephen that the best way to feed oil into a lamp is "not to pour in more than the funnel can hold" (161). Stephen is surprised by the use of the term "funnel" for an object that he calls a "tundish." The dean, who has never heard of a tundish, assumes that funnel is the correct word for the object and that tundish must be specific to Irish use: he asks, "Is that called a tundish in Ireland?" Because he is an Englishman, the dean believes that his use of English is natural, whereas Stephen's is secondary and perhaps incorrect. As Stephen exclaims in the final pages of the novel, "tundish" is "good old blunt English," derived from Anglo-Saxon (216). A further irony, not proposed by Stephen, is the derivation of "funnel" from Old French.[40] The point here for Joyce is not to replace one etymology with another but to display the characters' motivations—economic, political, and social—for establishing correctness.

Like the untrained readers of "Two Gallants," like the Jesuit priest, and like Stephen's colleagues at school, the dean takes intellectual norms for granted: Joyce suggests that attentiveness, literary evaluation, and even word choice are shaped by economic and political conditions. Representing these norms, making them the subject of his fiction, Joyce aims to subtract consensus from conceptions of national collectivity. The exchange between Stephen and the dean demonstrates the arrogance of British imperialism, the assumption that the Irish know less about British culture than the English do or that Irish usage, if "tundish" were used only in Ireland, is not part of British culture. The exchange also confirms, beyond the dean's arrogance, his intellectual limitations: he thinks only in generalizations, platitudes, and clichés.[41] To use a distinction that Stephen makes between literal and figurative language, the dean knows words only "according to the tradition of the marketplace," only in their most familiar usage, and not "according to the literary tradition" and enlivened by thought (161).[42] The dean uses the word "funnel" because it is the general term for almost any conical shaped object with a hole at the narrow end. Whereas the Englishman knows only one name and only the most banal designation, Stephen knows that objects have several names, that objects of a similar shape have different names and functions, that language, like culture, is diverse, changeable, and without definite origin. The dean is single-minded because he is insensitive to his own false courtesy, because he has no ear for metaphor or irony, and because he assumes that differences in language are a matter of national distinction rather than a matter of national or cultural or even semantic diversity.

✳✳✳

The false courtesy that Stephen rejects in *Portrait* is a principal topic in *Ulysses*, especially in "The Wandering Rocks," a chapter at the center of the novel. Joyce begins the chapter in a style of "cheerful decorum," the social attitude preferred by Father Conmee, whose consciousness Joyce has adopted for the initial narration.[43] For Joyce, even cheerfulness can be a kind of acquiescence when social and economic conditions inspire no cheer and when being cheerful takes the place of being mindful, or critical, of those who maintain those conditions. In *Portrait*, Stephen imagines his classmates "meekly bent as they wrote in their notebooks the points that they had been bidden to note," while he imagines himself "unbent" and aware, as his "thoughts wandered abroad," of "cheerless cellardamp and decay" (*Portrait*, 152). Joyce proposes that imperialist decorum involves accommodation, constant attentiveness, and unerring repetition, whereas cosmopolitan triviality involves distraction and new, sometimes vulgar sensibilities. In *Ulysses*, to perceive the cheerless world is to refuse optimism, blindness, and obedience. Joyce refuses these conditions in "Wandering Rocks," as he describes the cheerless families whose suffering he contrasts with the unsympathetic posturing of church and state. To understand the chapter's analysis of exploitation and hypocrisy, the reader has to focus on trivial details, reorder the presented world, and make insubordinate comparisons.[44]

Unlike Stephen, whose description of a person will move from standard vocational categories to habitual, disreputable characteristics, Father Conmee focuses strictly on official titles, social status, proper names, pompous clichés, and "practical" consequences (180). Stephen's description of his father's "attributes" at the end of *Portait* provides a ready example of indecorous triviality because it does not subordinate or censor different registers of behavior, whether respectable, professional, habitual, occasional, or embarrassing. "What was" Stephen's father? He was: "A medical student, an oarsman, a tenor, an amateur actor, a shouting politician, a small landlord, a small investor, a drinker, a good fellow, a storyteller, somebody's secretary, something in a distillery, a taxgatherer, a bankrupt, and at present a praiser of his own past" (207). Whereas Stephen cannot remember and does not care whose secretary his father was and what position in the distillery his father held, Father Conmee focuses his attention only on status, which is also all that he remembers. In "Wandering Rocks," Joyce introduces Conmee in Conmee's style, describing him, in the words that open the chapter, as "The superior, the very reverend John Conmee S. J." (180). Joyce's diction implies that the title describes as well as names: that anyone called "superior" and "very reverend" as a matter of custom will also turn out to inhabit these virtues as well. This, indeed, is the logic of aesthetic decorum: the assumption that people are what they are called, that every person has one proper name, that there is no difference between social façade and social conditions.

The opening of "Wandering Rocks" is worth close consideration because Joyce has embedded in Father Conmee's style an entire repertoire of subordinating thought. The priest's stingy attention, which poses as sympathy and good will, points to the model of national consciousness that Joyce has been resisting in his previous works and that he comes to criticize most explicitly here and two chapters later, in "Cyclops." Father Conmee reproduces social conditions by imposing ready aphorisms, which he justifies by their sound of familiarity and by their conservation of effort. Joyce uses literal stinginess (Conmee's decision that he will bless a wounded sailor rather than give him the single "silver crown" in his purse) to signal stinginess of mind and to suggest that the exchange of moral rhetoric for material goods is motivated by selfishness rather than piety. As he does in "Two Gallants," Joyce asks us to notice that decorum participates in a system of exploitation by substituting moral problems for economic ones. Decorum seems to offer what is fitting, when in fact it constitutes a ruse or a distraction that Joyce's more explicit strategies of distraction—his tricks—seek to criticize. As Father Conmee passes the one-legged sailor on the street, Joyce reports: "He thought, but not for long, of soldiers and sailors, whose legs had been shot off by cannonballs, ending their days in some pauper ward" (180). Conmee thinks of this image briefly because, as a rule, he protects his cheerfulness from the experience of distress and from unwelcome thoughts about social or institutional responsibility. Conmee is not sympathetic about what happens to soldiers and sailors, and he is not interested in the political decisions that cause cannonballs to fly. His observations are opportunistic: the encounter with the one-legged sailor burnishes the priest's self-regard by reminding him of a well-worn saying by Cardinal Wolsey (according to Conmee, "*If I had served my God as I have served my king He would not have abandoned me in my old days*"), which he repeats to himself pompously and which he uses to imply that the sailor alone is responsible for his impoverished, damaged condition (180; emphasis in original). Aphoristic decorum allows Father Conmee to substitute pious clichés for sympathy and social causality, and it allows him to mask complacency (thinking "not for long," displacing guilt from king to sailor) as intellectual grace.

Father Conmee expresses both appreciation and disdain only in formulaic terms: his attempts at *bons mots* always end in clichés; a woman who reminds him of Mary, queen of Scots, is said to have "such a queenly mien," and a Protestant minister is superficially pitied for his "invincible ignorance," the standard Roman Catholic evaluation of Protestantism (181). Joyce presents decorum as the perfect style for a man of limited imagination: he need only invoke the right statement for the right occasion. Of course, it is decorum's perfection that demonstrates its savage indifference. Decorous characters are so busy being just, in the most unimaginative fashion, that they have no time or no inclination to contemplate justice. Father Conmee uses gestures of worldly knowledge to reinforce what he already knows. His cosmopolitanism is provincial: when he thinks about "a dreadful catastrophe in New York," he thinks not of suffering or death or the grief of survivors but only of "unprepared" souls going to hell (182); when he thinks of "black and brown and yellow men" around the world, he worries not about colonialism or starvation or racism or genocide but only

about damnation, "a waste, if one might say" (183). Whereas sympathy initiates social encounters among the other characters in the chapter, it is for Conmee only a manner of speaking and a way to avoid encounters of any kind.[45]
Joyce proposes that Conmee's evangelism is congruous to the false courtesy of
British imperialism and the polite anti-Semitism of Anglo-Irish nationalism.
Conmee's concerns pose no risk to his cheerful demeanor because he is able
to reduce foreign circumstances to familiar, universalizing terms. This strategy
of generalization keeps him cheerful because it allows him to interpret all circumstances, no matter how disparate or unexplained, as comprehensible and
unavoidable conditions. Not "lighthearted" in Adorno's sense, Conmee's cheerfulness is committed only to practiced thought.

In the "Cyclops" episode, Joyce treats decorum by representing hostility. The
chapter is full of explicit references to anticolonialism, nationalism, imperialism, nativism, and anti-Semitism, and for this reason it has been a mainstay of
postcolonial, semicolonial, and cosmopolitan scholarship.[46] My own interest is
in the triviality of a single, well-known exchange between Leopold Bloom and
a group of Dubliners about the meaning of the word "nation." I say that this exchange is trivial not because it is unimportant or devoid of political significance
but rather because it emphasizes vernacular, personal, and economic details,
which Joyce uses to disrupt philosophical abstractions both of nationalism and
of cosmopolitanism. In this emphasis, the chapter resists not only the single-
minded nativism of the anti-Semitic narrator and the citizen but also the generalizing humanism of the antiracist Bloom. Andrew Gibson and Enda Duffy
have asked us to notice that the chapter does not restrict its satire of exaggerat-
ed, one-eyed perspectives only to the citizen, a Sinn Feiner, or to the Cyclopean
narrator.[47] I argue, in addition, that Joyce uses the vernacular anecdotes of the
other Dubliners—their ceaseless interruptions—to refine the politics of reason,
measure, and universal cosmopolitanism articulated by Bloom. In this refine-
ment, Joyce articulates a vernacular cosmopolitanism based on what Lauren
Berlant has termed "quotidian citizenship": the "banal and erratic logic . . . of
intimate relations, political personhood, and national life."[48]

Joyce's chapter chronicles an impromptu conversation among Bloom and several men whom Bloom knows from his life in Dublin. The men are drinking
friends, they are gathered in Barney Kiernan's pub, and their tolerance of Bloom's
company is fragile and ungenerous. The narrator, one of the drinkers, is recounting a scene that took place in the near past. There are several, recurring words
in "Cyclops": among the most important are "house" (265), "nation" (271–72),
"same" (271), "living" (272), and "place" (272). The repetition of these words
serves to emphasize the materiality of language (that language has a varied history and context of use) and to unmoor customary meanings from unthinking
social usage. Neil Levi has argued that the logic of *Ulysses*, which favors repeti-

tion and the instability of language, is directly opposed in "Cyclops" to the logic of the narrator, who complains of Bloom—as one might complain of Joyce—that he cannot simply recognize an object or a fact but must provide endless explanations that undermine the certainty of naming.[49] Levi argues that the narrator's critique of Bloom's rhetorical detachment is motivated by anti-Semitism: the narrator treats the desire to explain what others accept as fact as a symptom of Bloom's Jewish cosmopolitanism ("'See that Straw?'" 383–85). I see this also— that Bloom's dialogic pedantry functions for the narrator as one more example of perverse doubleness, along with Bloom's Irish Jewishness, his multiple religious conversions, his literariness, and the doubleness that anti-Semites associate with Jewish sexuality. Yet I do not see a perfect symmetry between Joyce's style and Bloom's, as Levi does: whereas Joyce values the materialist analysis and critical discrimination that characterize Bloom's consciousness in earlier chapters, he presents more ambivalently the detached idealism and universalist cosmopolitanism that characterize Bloom's speech in "Cyclops."

Bloom announces, speaking to one of his companions about "persecution":

—Persecution, says he, all the history of the world is full of it. Perpetuating national hatred among nations.
—But do you know what a nation means? says John Wyse.
—Yes, says Bloom.
—What is it? says John Wyse.
—A nation? says Bloom. A nation is the same people living in the same place.
—By God, then, says Ned, laughing, if that's so I'm a nation for I'm living in the same place for the past five years.

So of course everyone had the laugh at Bloom and says he, trying to muck out of it:
—Or also living in different places.
—That covers my case, says Joe.
—What is your nation if I may ask? says the citizen.
—Ireland, says Bloom. I was born here. Ireland.

The citizen said nothing only cleared the spit out of his gullet and, gob, he spat a Red bank oyster out of him right in the corner.

(271–72)

In Bloom's first two answers, he offers a general case that would apply to him but does not force him to speak directly about himself; in the last answer, because the citizen has personalized the matter, Bloom does not propose a general case (for example, "a nation is the same people born in the same place") but speaks only of himself ("I was born here. Ireland."). The citizen's racism is not to be admired, but his question has, for the reader, provocative effects: it negates the false courtesy by which racism had previously passed. Against the epic reconciliation of the chapter's genteel announcements, which project a continuous and heroic national past, against the narrator's preference for ideas that require no thought and no elaborate conversation, and against Bloom's utopian platitudes, the exchange about "nations" introduces a living, contested present.

Bloom invokes a view of national community that accommodates both philosophical and anthropological models of cosmopolitanism: he asks his companions to think of relationships among nations as well as those within them; he asks them to imagine a nation as a community of like values that need not be situated in the same geographic place. Bloom proposes that people living in the same community constitute a nation, whatever differences of culture, ancestry, and origin they may have; that a nation should be measured by its present ("people living") rather than by its past or by its future. Bloom is asserting that collective identity ("the same people") should depend on location ("the same place") or on self-determined association (despite "different places") rather than on ancestry or on genetic continuity (race). Ned, Joe, and the citizen offer two counterdefinitions, both of which contest the mutability, contingency, and unconstrained voluntarism that they associate with Bloom's account. The first counterdefinition is based on a philosophical difference about how communities are organized. Ned Lambert and Joe Hynes make fun of Bloom for speaking of place, as in mapped geography or legal territory, because they find it too vague, transient, and inclusive as a test of national belonging: people can change countries as easily as some people change houses, and, as patriots, they want national identity to be less easily acquired and less easily lost than, for example, property. The citizen's mute response at the end of the scene displays, through verbal silence and physical gesture, his conviction that living in a place, even from birth, is not sufficient proof of belonging: the citizen believes that the Irish nation includes only people of Celtic origin whose parents and parents' parents spoke Gaelic and who have participated in ancient Gaelic traditions for many centuries; for him, the nation is defined as people who participate, and whose ancestors participated, in an unchanging, homogeneous culture rooted in the ancient past.

The second counterdefinition is based on the quotidian experience of everyday life in Ireland: Ned and Joe, who offer details of this experience, do not mean to be defining all nations or even the Irish nation in their comments, but Joyce allows their jokes to introduce a trivial register of description. Critics have recognized Bloom's unwillingness to privilege a community based on race or immutable characteristics, but they have tended to ignore the Dubliners' retorts.[50] The retorts are significant because they allow a crude and promiscuous vocabulary of location to disrupt Bloom's decorous philosophy of national belonging. The punning responses focus on the difference between "place" as house and "place" as territory and on the serious fact that many impoverished Dubliners do not have a house to call their own: Ireland is a place made up of many people sharing small, rented houses ("the same people living in the same place," like Ned Lambert) and of many people whose poverty causes them to move houses frequently ("people living in different places," like Joe Hynes). However much the men are making fun in this passage, they are also telling the truth about what the Irish nation is like. Joyce's triviality—the punning definition of place and the assertion of vulgar definitions—introduces an indelicate, anticolonial, and unheroic image of Ireland in particular and of nations in general. Moreover, it is an image that emphasizes specific instances of living as well as international conditions of economic and colonial domination.

Bloom's comments replace one platitude with another, but the puns inserted by the others produce the effect of a changeable "nation." Joyce's nation now includes people who live sometimes within one territory and sometimes within another; people who were born within one territory but may or may not reside there; people who also define themselves by association with smaller groups within one territory or with other territories and cultural traditions. The "same" in Bloom's "the same people" is heterogeneous: a people may be similar by reasons of continual or occasional proximity, voluntary association, birth, or ancestry. Moreover, "living" has several different registers as well, as Ned Lambert and Joe Hynes suggest: it conveys a transnational community of people residing or traveling or both, and it also conveys a vernacular, localized experience of minimal self-maintenance—"living" in the slums of Dublin. While Ned and Joe emphasize the economic suffering of their national community, in a subsequent exchange Bloom will urge them to think ever more expansively, insisting that he, too, "[belongs] to a race . . . that is hated and persecuted," as the Irish are (273). Bloom's cosmopolitan comparison, between Irish and Jewish persecution, further annoys his interlocutors, who want to think of Ireland alone and before all other situations. They are aggravated by Bloom's use of abstract language: his talk of "injustice," "Force, hatred, history, all that." Bloom moves quickly from description to comparison and from comparison to generalization. He asserts that force and hatred are "the very opposite of that that is really life," which he calls "Love." The citizen makes fun of Bloom's rhetoric (he calls Bloom "a new apostle to the gentiles"), but so does Joyce, who inserts a childish parody—"Love loves to love love"—immediately after this conversation. The citizen's comment is motivated by racism and by the refusal to compare, but Bloom's generalizations seem obtuse and ossified in contrast with the specific and animate thought to which we have been introduced in previous chapters. Joyce wants to affirm the politics of transnational sympathy and yet to insist as well on the politics of vernacular difference. Joyce's triviality, his proliferation of many "nations," has the effect of provincializing Bloom's cosmopolitanism.

Within the "changing same" of the "Cyclops" episode, to invoke Paul Gilroy's image of cosmopolitan tradition, Joyce rejects the all-inclusive rhetoric of universal community while rejecting the too-exclusive rhetoric of anti-Semitic racism and Irish anti-imperialism.[51] More than any other episode, "Cyclops" suggests that styles of decorum not only support racism (by allowing it to function) but also inform it (by naturalizing what is fitting and right). The chapter resists decorum by making racism explicit and by refusing to install a traditional cosmopolitanism in its place. This is not the first time in the novel that Bloom has been mocked and insulted by his companions—it is a recurring, almost blanketing circumstance of the text—but this is the first encounter in which someone directly challenges Bloom instead of whispering in his absence or snubbing him indirectly. Joyce makes the reader notice that the novel's impersonal banter among Bloom and the other Dubliners has involved a muted, tactful racism, which this scene vocalizes by shifting from the general (what is a nation?) to the particular (what is your nation?) case. The citizen's question makes Bloom acknowledge that the indirect statements of anti-Semitism and xenophobia spoken casually and regularly in his presence have had a specific target: him. Joyce shows what is implied in the social exclusion and mocking treatment of Bloom in previous pages: to wit, a fixed conception of the Irish nation, which Bloom's social presence and style of wandering consciousness, though not always his speech, serve to challenge.

Joyce proposes that those who belong to the same community, or the same nation, do not necessarily share the same values, or even the same definition of community and nation and "same." By refusing to choose among these definitions and by valuing the triviality of minor diversions, Joyce transforms dead metaphors into living contestations. For Joyce, the tricks, the ruses, and the insistent pleasures of "living" are the necessary conditions of a truly critical cosmopolitanism.

3

WOOLF'S EVASION

Oh! thought Clarissa, in the middle of my party, here's death, she thought.
—VIRGINIA WOOLF, *MRS. DALLOWAY*

IN HIS RECENT work on international feelings, Bruce Robbins looks to contemporary novels about fascism, imperialism, and world war to investigate "the proper tone" of cosmopolitanism. The novel, Robbins proposes, is "a place where such matters of tone are most searchingly experimented and reflected on."[1] Robbins's gambit is telling in three important ways. First, it suggests that any philosophy or ethics of cosmopolitanism must have a "tone," a way of thinking about people whose lives are geographically or culturally unrelated to one's own and a way of acknowledging, though not only acknowledging, the ethical or affective compromises that go with that thinking. Second, it suggests that there are many possible "tones" (sympathetic, indifferent, arrogant, tolerant, outraged) that need to be examined and tested. Third, it directs the project of tone to the project of the novel and thus suggests that the tradition of narrative in the twentieth century has helped to develop existing strategies of cosmopolitanism. The echoes of this tradition have become increasingly audible in old and new essays about international conflict and wartime patriotism; while some of the authors of these essays are trained as literary critics, as Robbins is, others are importing the techniques and metaphors of narrative—and of modernist narrative, in particular—into disciplines such as philosophy and performance studies. Judith Butler, for example, has argued that U.S. patriotism, as it was formulated after the World Trade Center attacks ("9/11") demands a "first-person point of view" that precludes "accounts that might involve the decentering of the narrative 'I' within the international political domain."[2] To conceive a just role for U.S. foreign policy, one that acknowledges the global underpinnings of local conditions, Butler asserts, "we will need to emerge from the narrative perspective of

U.S. unilateralism and, as it were, its defensive structures, to consider the ways in which our lives are profoundly implicated in the lives of others" (181). Butler proposes that a more responsible view of global history requires less coherent, less exclusive perspectives.

Fred Moten has argued similarly that the rhetoric of terrorism promoted by the U.S. government has generated a new political "homogenization," which is based on the "equality" of suffering and fear, and not on the equality of persons.[3] This is manifest, Moten proposes, "not only as the liquidation of dissent or of whatever marks the possibility of another way of being political, but even as the suppression of alternative tones or modes of phrasing as well" (189). Moten takes the title of his essay, "The New International of Decent Feelings," from Louis Althusser, whose early treatise on "The International of Decent Feelings," first published in 1946, argues that the proper tone of internationalism after the catastrophe of the Second World War is not a "moralizing socialism" of equality in suffering but an analytic, antagonistic socialism of judgment and differentiation.[4] Wanting to preserve the class struggle against postwar existentialism, Althusser argues that the rhetoric of universal suffering by all tends to obscure the significance and reality of social and economic suffering by some. And these generalizations about class struggle allow him to see other generalizations about international violence and world politics. He shares with Butler and Moten a critique of self-absorbed "decency." Butler and Moten contest the assumptions of universal or "planetary" cosmopolitanism: that all people in the world have the same relationship to international events; that all people living in a single nation should have the same views about these events; that any one view is unambivalent and unchanging; that decent feelings are more important than dissenting thought.[5]

Decentering the first-person point of view, rejecting tones of comfort or confidence, and risking indecency: arguably, these are the principal hallmarks of modernist fiction. The tension between decent feelings and dissenting thought is especially visible in the writing of Virginia Woolf, but also in the work of many early-twentieth-century artists who, like Woolf, sought to imagine models of social critique that would resist social codification. Early-twenty-first-century theorists of humanism, such as Edward Said and Jacques Lezra, see in Woolf's fiction a model of what Lezra has called, after Said, "critical heroism": the attempt to "[operate] in the world with sympathy toward the richness of the past, [while] preserving a posture of resistance and critique towards that richness and towards the institutions in which its study is enabled and its value measured and propounded, and maintaining that sympathy, and that critical and resisting stance, without end."[6] Said proposes that "the practice of humanistic service" in which Woolf and other modernists engaged "always entails a heroic unwillingness to rest in the consolidation of previously existing attitudes."[7] Yet, as Said and Lezra acknowledge, it is not easy to be both critical and heroic.

How does one resist social postures of euphemism and blinding generalization—postures, Woolf felt, that lead to acts of imperialism and militarism, such as the First World War—without resorting to literalism or narrow description? How does one resist inattentiveness if one's attention can never rest, if one must always look away in order to keep looking? As these questions suggest, as the phrase "critical heroism" implies, one must risk being bad—uncertain, inconsistent, and unsuccessful—in order to keep being good.

Focusing on the past and on the margins of social activity, useless pleasures but also invisible labors, Woolf directs her readers to notice aspects of British society that have gone almost unseen: the mundane activities of upper-class women, but also the activities and existence of servants, immigrants, homosexuals, divorced women, educated working women, the insane, and the dissident or angry.[8] Offering only glimpses of servants, immigrants, and others on the margins of upper-class life, Woolf emphasizes the social conditions of blindness rather more than she rectifies invisibility. Indeed, Woolf will purposefully exclude significant episodes—a suicide, an engagement, the breakup of a relationship, the destruction of bodies during wartime, and the procedures of colonial efficiency—in order to highlight quotidian experiences of unsocialized pleasure, as well as echoes, tangential effects, and memories. In the past, critics have argued that Woolf's fiction is quietist and insufficiently patriotic because it speaks of fascism and war but fails to address those topics directly or appropriately: she mentions a newspaper but does not tell us what the headlines say; she describes someone thinking of war but does not describe a battle. For these reasons, M. C. Bradbrook called "the style of Mrs. Woolf" self-indulgent and "evasive," arguing that her books give primary attention to minor events, such as a party, and only indirect attention to major events, such as war and death.[9] Writing in the inaugural issue of *Scrutiny* in 1932, Bradbrook condemned Woolf's novels for failing to express unambiguous political values and then attributed this opacity to a "trick of style": namely, Woolf's tendency to disrupt or qualify narrated thoughts with dependent clauses and frequent asides. Woolf is evasive, Bradbrook explains, in refusing to devote her novels, or even her sentences, to any single topic and in refusing to limit her topics to those that seem pertinent or suitable to war.

As a woman, an artist, and a pacifist, Woolf saw herself as an "outsider," and in this way she was a traditional cosmopolitan, detached from her country but attached to artists and to other pacifists and to a community of "educated men's daughters," as she put it in *Three Guineas*.[10] Yet for Woolf, being an outsider also meant that she could be a different or limited kind of insider, and that she could challenge the values that the usual insiders upheld: she could consider comparatively and "in her own case" what words like "patriotism," "foreigner," and national "superiority" meant (*Three Guineas*, 233). In these ways, Woolf's

cosmopolitanism differs from the traditional gestures of supranational affiliation and demystifying reflection.[11] Not belonging to the university, the military,
or the government, Woolf lacked political efficacy, and she did not roman-
ticize this lack. But she did reject the protocols of unwavering attention that
she attributed to her country's most powerful social institutions. This led her
to develop in place of those protocols more agitated, more modest forms of
attention that were less effective, perhaps, but from her perspective also less
complacent. I argue that Woolf used the analytic resources of aestheticism—
thinking of perception as a social process; valuing transient communities and
experiences; cultivating a posture of distracted or limited participation—to
treat politically, historically, and internationally literary values such as euphemism and argument.

To be certain, the claim that Woolf was uninterested in the political urgencies and civic debates of her day no longer dominates modernist studies.[12]
Work on *A Room of One's Own* and *Three Guineas* has emphasized Woolf's
involvement with public issues of education, militarism, literary value, and
the role of women in political life.[13] Melba Cuddy-Keane has argued that even
Woolf's essays that do not address education or politics in explicit ways are
"pedagogical" and political in the "intellectual challenges" they pose to the ordinary reader, and new work on Woolf's most experimental novels has emphasized their social engagement.[14] I share Cuddy-Keane's belief that "Woolf's
commitment to independent, critical thinking ... was the foundation for the
model of social equality that she upheld" (9), but I propose in addition that
Woolf often expressed this commitment by developing narrative forms that
are *evasive* rather than *explicit* or even *utopian*. Woolf may have participated
in civic endeavors and written directly against war and gender inequality, but
her project remains challenging and often disturbing because she suggests that
international sympathy and national dissent are nourished in part by those
evasions of syntax, plot, and tone that qualify, unsettle, and redirect enduring
habits of attentiveness.

✷✷✷

In the 1930s, the critique of Woolf came from both sides of the political aisle:
the socialist writer R. D. Charques submitted that Woolf found "refuge or immunity from the worst in contemplation of—what shall we say?—a mark on the
wall," while the right-wing Wyndham Lewis argued that Woolf represents "mere
personality" instead of "ideas."[15] Q. D. Leavis, in a scornful review from 1938, as-
serted that Woolf's writing lacks the characteristics of true argument and thus
achieves only "'argument'" ("Caterpillars," 205; the word appears in quotation
marks in Leavis's text).[16] These writers contended that Woolf seemed too vari-

ous in her sympathies, too distracted in her commitments, and too cosmopolitan in her analogies between the psychology of marriages and the philosophy of treaties, between the world of parties at home and the wars of fascism abroad. The early critics of Woolf's style believed that art should be unwaveringly attentive, that any failure of attention led not only to bad writing but, worse, to "nasty," "preposterous," and "dangerous" writing (Leavis, "Caterpillars," 204). In Leavis's view, Woolf's work is dangerous because it refuses to generalize (about Germany) and because it generalizes too much (about misogyny and sexism). Decrying what she sees as Woolf's evasion of important matters (for example, her apparent failure to emphasize the risk of German militarism), Leavis is also critical of what she sees as Woolf's fixation on matters overly narrow, literal, or petty (for example, her observation that Hitler's efforts to limit women's roles in public life resonate with the sentiments of many English politicians).

The point here is that those who identify evasiveness in others assume some agreement within a community or among readers about the topics that deserve attention and the kinds of attentiveness that are attentive enough. For Woolf, there is no such agreement. She examines in her fiction the literary classifications that many of her critics take for granted, and she asks readers to see that interpretive judgments operate historically: that they help to shape the boundaries and meanings of British society and that they are, in turn, shaped by social contestations. Woolf's writing represents conflicts about international action and national culture as conflicts about literary forms of attentiveness. This is true not only of the work that seems to focus on domestic minutiae but also of the work that seems to focus on peripheral spaces (*To the Lighthouse*, *The Voyage Out*), education policies (*A Room of One's Own*), and the relationship between fascism and gender (*Three Guineas*). Her point is not simply to create a new ideal of attentiveness, more expansive and extensive, but to display the customs and conventions, social and psychological, that control what can be seen and what can be said.

Woolf's novels and essays return, over and over again, to problems of comparison and to conflicts about tone: How should artists present sociability or pleasure in the context of international catastrophe? How does one display systemic conditions without seeming to ignore the particularity of events or diminish their singular importance? How can one offer fresh comparisons among different experiences without seeming to treat the experiences as the same? For Woolf and her contemporaries, as Michèle Barrett has argued in an essay on modernism and memory, these questions were prompted not only by the task of looking backwards but also by the social and geographic conditions of the First World War: the spatial proximity of the trenches in France and gentleman's clubs in London, such that an officer might spend his morning in one place and his evening in the other; the horror of devastating losses at the front reported in newspapers side by side with racing results and other com-monplace records of everyday life.[17] Is it more appropriate for artists to rectify the confusion of tones by representing only the direct, violent experience of war in the trenches? Or should artists represent a more expansive, more entangled conception of war, one that includes the spaces of newspaper, gentleman's club, trench, and racetrack?

Woolf begins to engage these questions in her very first published story, "The Mark on the Wall." Given her subject matter—the value of questioning in a time of unsatisfactory answers—it is perhaps not surprising that this story has been central to Woolf's reputation as an evasive writer. "The Mark" oc-casioned this review from E. M. Forster: "Mrs Woolf's art is of a very unusual type, and one realizes that quite good critics, especially of the academic kind, may think it insignificant. It has no moral, no philosophy, nor has it what is usually understood by Form. It aims deliberately at aimlessness."[18] While For-ster may have recognized the purposeful "aimlessness" of Woolf's literary proj-ect, other critics have transformed "The Mark" into a metaphor of futility and lassitude: they invoke the story to assert the naïve myopia of Woolf's entire oeuvre. This is the implication of Charques's claim that Woolf finds "refuge or immunity from the worst in contemplation of . . . a mark on the wall," as if the story's title represents all that Woolf contemplates and as if it merely replaces the contemplation of other, more serious concerns. Charques proposes that looking at a mark on the wall allows one to avoid social and political circum-stances that are otherwise legible and definitive. In his quip, Charques pretends to speculate ("what shall we say?") about Woolf's interests in much the same way that Woolf is said to speculate about the mark: he imagines that Woolf's writing, once it ignores "the worst," might focus on anything at all, that its aim-lessness has no aim whatsoever.

Charques implies that those who write speculatively in a time of catastro-phe help to perpetuate catastrophe by refusing to address it directly. Theodor W. Adorno would later argue that this criticism, which targets a literary style, promotes a rigid politics of affiliation and exclusion. Adorno provides an im-portant context for Woolf's work because both writers share the conviction that social norms are embedded in traditions of literary style and that liter-ary style is embedded in the politics of national culture. Adorno makes these connections explicit. Like Woolf, Adorno asserts throughout his career that the homogenization of writing—at the level of narrative structure, diction, and syntax—helps to produce the homogenization of culture, which Adorno associates with fascism. Adorno addresses the dangers of a project such as Woolf's in an essay on literary form, in which he claims that the demand for literalism and directness in political writing is a demand for legible and con-sistent social classifications:

The person who interprets instead of accepting what is given and classifying it is marked with the yellow star of one who squanders his intelligence in impotent speculation, reading things in where there is nothing to interpret. A man with his feet on the ground or a man with his head in the clouds—those are the only alternatives. But letting oneself be terrorized by the prohibition against saying more than was meant right then and there means complying with the false conceptions that people and things harbor concerning themselves.[19]

Adorno proposes that those who suspend the work of classification become themselves classified; they are marked as traitors, outcasts, and degenerates. The "yellow star" is compensatory: it creates proof where self-evidence is no longer visible. Refusing to classify a mark on the wall, Woolf's narrator shows how intellectual speculation, because it thwarts compliance, resists the passivity of wartime.

"The Mark on the Wall" was published in July 1917, bound with Leonard Woolf's "Three Jews" in a pamphlet entitled *Two Stories*.[20] Circulated privately among friends and literary colleagues, *Two Stories* inaugurated the Woolfs' new Hogarth Press, which was later to publish all of Virginia Woolf's remaining novels, T. S. Eliot's *Waste Land*, the collected writings of Sigmund Freud, English translations of Dostoevsky and Gorky, and many other important works of British modernism.[21] Most readers know "The Mark on the Wall" from its third publication in *Monday or Tuesday* (1921), the only volume of short stories published during Woolf's lifetime, and from its later republication in posthumous volumes assembled by Leonard Woolf after the Second World War.[22] The 1917 publication is significant, however, because Leonard's "Three Jews" orients readers of Virginia's story to the production of national collectivity.[23] Both stories remind readers that there are diverse ways of being British, even or especially during wartime, and both stories imply that one must resist the pressure to assimilate. The 1917 publication presents Virginia Woolf, unmistakably, as the wife of a person both British and Jewish, a person of both national and international affiliations; and it presents Woolf's literary project within a social context of anti-Semitism and strong international feeling about the relative patriotism of British Jews.[24]

Leonard's story relates a conversation between two Jewish men, who wonder together whether they can be part of the "orderly English way," or whether they can have or should have only their own, separate order.[25] The story focuses on the difference between wishing that England "belongs to us" and wishing that we "belonged to *it*" (emphasis in original). These are two models of assimilation: in the first model, English Jews change what counts as "English," while in the second model, English Jews accommodate religious and social norms whose characteristics are static and definable (8). One of the two characters tells of an acquaintance, the story's third Jew, who decides that his son no longer belongs to his family because he has married a Christian servant. The son is disinherited not because he has married a Christian, however, but because he has married a servant, which is to say that the father makes himself more English, he imagines, by emphasizing class as a standard of exclusion. The story thus asserts that exclusion can be a characteristic of Jewish as well as English belonging, though it ends, inconclusively, with one character observing to the other that "times change" (18). This may mean that the standards of national belonging merely shift from one category to another over time, as in the anecdote, but it may also mean—and the story's ironic tone points to this unachieved but preferable outcome—that belonging could come to have fewer, or less rigid standards: England could belong to "us" because the meaning of England changes, from a homogeneous community defined by manners or race to a heterogeneous community defined by location or citizenship.

While Leonard Woolf's story reminds wartime readers that national collectivity tends to impose cultural norms, Virginia Woolf's story focuses on social rules of attentiveness, feeling, and thought to address, more specifically, cultural norms about war. The 1917 publication of "The Mark on the Wall" is significant not only because Virginia's story echoes Leonard's topic—England's diversity—but also because it examines an ongoing historical event: the story depends on the progress of war for the drama of its ending and for its effect of evasive thought and entangled spaces. "The Mark" is narrated in the first-person by a woman remembering a day in the recent past ("it was the middle of January in the present year" [83]) when she saw a mark on the wall above the fireplace. Sitting in her living room, she imagines what the mark might be, though she does not get up to see what it is for certain; neither the narrator's name nor the specific location of the house is ever given; the entire episode, we learn explicitly at the end, takes place during a war, whose damnation ("Curse this war; God damn this war!") by an unnamed person addressing the narrator is the most dramatic activity and only conversation that the story relates.[26] Contentiously and self-consciously, "The Mark" is a story about the refusal to act without thinking. It is about the refusal to *substitute* patriotic comfort or static outrage for critical anger and curiosity, and the refusal to *separate* the political "facts" of a European war (casualties and official reports) from the disarray of a living room in England. These are related gestures: redirecting outrage and yet refusing comfort, the story suggests, allows the narrator to consider how the social history of attentiveness creates the conditions for wartime complacency.

"The Mark" may serve as a metaphor for evasion (evading the "fact" of the mark on the wall; evading the "fact" of the war), but it is also a story that considers directly what evasion evades. First of all, "The Mark" is in a sense narrated backward: although one might paraphrase the story as a tale about a woman who is trying not to think about the war, the context of wartime is announced only at the end of the story, when a comment disrupts the narrator's thinking about the mark. This disruption makes the reader notice, really for the first time, that the story is trying to represent the experience of wartime thinking. Of course, anyone reading the story in 1917, as British casualties continued to mount, would have known this from the beginning. And there are clues at the beginning, even if one needs the ending to make them fully legible: in the first paragraph, seeing the mark interrupts the narrator's "fancy of the crimson flag flapping from the castle tower," which she imagines when she looks at the burning coals in the fire before her (83). The narrator is relieved to have this vision disrupted: this is the story's first image of militarism, and it gestures toward the fighting not many miles away. One imagines that the narrator is relieved because thoughts of war are distressing in themselves, but she attributes her relief to a more specific distaste: the narrator calls her vision of war "an old fancy, an automatic fancy"; it is a vision shaped by worn images of heroism and chivalry rather than by personal experiences or singular thought (83).[27]

Evading automatic fancies, Woolf's narrator is evading "generalisation," which she associates with the social rituals and fashions of the past. The narrator criticizes the generalizations of British culture and then attempts to avoid generalizing rhetoric: as she speculates about the future of the novel, how it will tend to omit the description of reality in favor of reality reflected in the minds of individuals, she breaks off, dismissing "these generalisations" as "very worthless" and then invoking "the military sound of the word" (85–86). Woolf criticizes "standard" interpretations and pious rules by first dismissing generalization and then engaging in it. She shows, by speaking abstractly and theoretically about genre, that all rhetorical terms have social contexts:

> The military sound of the word is enough. It recalls leading articles, cabinet ministers—a whole class of things indeed which as a child one thought the thing itself, the standard thing, the real thing, from which one could not depart save at the risk of nameless damnation. Generalisations bring back somehow Sunday in London, Sunday afternoon walks, Sunday luncheons, and also ways of speaking of the dead, clothes, and habits—like the habit of sitting all together in one room until a certain hour, although nobody liked it. There was a rule for everything.
>
> (86)

The military sound of the word is enough to remind the narrator that speculative thought can diversify a single perspective and also that a single perspective makes it difficult to think speculatively at all. Moreover, by noticing the *sound* of "generalisation," the narrator refuses to take the word literally; she refuses the efficiency of meaning in favor of sensation, poetry, and art. This strategy, insisting on sound rather than meaning, turning poetry against efficiency, will be important to Woolf's later work—not because she values the play of the signifier, although she does, but because she uses the provocation and vitality of figurative language to invigorate and replace what she sees as deadened thought.

Woolf demonstrates in "The Mark," as she will elsewhere, that to critique euphemism, which translates intense experiences into language that is habitual and therefore invisible, one must also critique literalism, which proposes that there is only one objective experience to present. She demonstrates also, however, that the critique of euphemism and literalism will have to involve gestures that are in some ways both euphemistic and literal because writing a novel or making an argument or maintaining a friendship requires moments of purposeful blindness as well as moments of direct attention. To put it another way, Woolf cannot reject generalization outright because she actually values some of the things that generalization facilitates: new analogies, strategic overlooking, parties, and even, I will suggest, national monuments. Nevertheless, we might distinguish Woolf's use of euphemism and literalism from the uses she criticizes by her effort to treat these styles politically, to show that civic language (the rhetoric of leading articles, ways of speaking of the dead) and literary classifications (generalization, evasion) help to shape the social meanings of war, colonialism, and education.

By the time of the story, as the narrator tells it, the "standard things" of childhood have been replaced by Whitaker's Table of Precedency and its list of the peerage, whose official order complements the informal rituals of upper-class life. If as a child the narrator mistook a "class of things" for the repertoire of all things and thus was unable to see that there was anything that she had neglected to notice, as an adult the narrator observes that Whitaker's tends to minimize thought by providing the "comfort" of precedency:

> The Archbishop of Canterbury is followed by the Lord High Chancellor; the Lord High Chancellor is followed by the Archbishop of York. Everybody follows somebody, such is the philosophy of Whitaker; the great thing is to know who follows whom. Whitaker knows, and let that, so Nature counsels, comfort you, instead of enraging you; and if you can't be comforted, if you must shatter this hour of peace, think of the mark on the wall.
>
> (88)

The surprising logic of this passage is that thinking of the mark on the wall provides not a refuge from discomfort but an alternative, implicitly superior way of shattering peace. The narrator has "contempt for men . . . [who] take action as a way of ending any thought that threatens to excite or pain," but she puts an end to those "disagreeable thoughts" by thinking of the mark on the wall (88): that is, for the narrator, the discomfort of thinking about the mark works to combat the discomfort of thinking about the blind comforts of others. It is action without thought that the narrator finds complacent. It is habitual patriotism that the narrator finds contemptible. Yet the story does not suggest that one should rest in this contempt: while acknowledging rage as the appropriate response to obsequious order and anesthetizing action, the narrator prefers the wandering unpeacefulness of agitated thinking (the form and content of the story) to the static unpeacefulness of sheer frustration (the desire to classify the mark).

The story ends with a disruption: the narrator's thoughts are broken when the voice of practicality arrives, like some person from Porlock, to announce, "'I'm going to buy a newspaper'" (89). The unnamed person introduces the story's conclusion, providing the cause of the mark, the political context of the narrator's thoughts, and the facts of a newspaper. Official reports thus replace speculation and the production of official knowledge:

> Someone is standing over me and saying—
> "I'm going out to buy a newspaper."
> "Yes?"
> "Though it's no good buying newspapers. . . . Nothing ever happens. Curse this war; God damn this war! . . . All the same, I don't see why we should have a snail on our wall."
> Ah, the mark on the wall! It was a snail.
>
> (89)

Woolf contrasts the contention that "nothing ever happens" with the happenings of the story: she resists the passive experience of war by making thought happen and by arguing that what "happens" in the world involves not only the events that newspapers report but also the daily sociability that shapes, interprets, opposes, and ignores those events. With "The Mark on the Wall," Woolf introduces a central trope of her career, speculating about what "happens" while war is happening or while war, in its violence and its precedency, keeps one from noticing that anything else does happen.

"The Mark" does not observe a sense of order: its narrative progresses by way of association rather than by way of cause or efficiency; it tends to stop, change direction, turn in on itself. While Leonard Woolf contests the orthodoxy of national culture, Virginia Woolf contests the habits of wartime attention. Speculating instead of accepting what is given, Woolf marks out the lines of entanglement between the public, official, and faraway spaces where men fight and the small, private, enclosed spaces where women think. Woolf's narrator uses private speculation and poetic language to introduce new topics and tones of cosmopolitanism.

In "The Mark," Woolf is critical of traditional narrative aims, those of realism and linear narrative progress, because she finds them all too comfortable, like euphemism, in a time of radical discomfort and international crisis. And yet a wide range of literary and cultural observers today—filmmakers such as Marleen Gorris as well as scholars such as Alex Zwerdling—have suggested that Woolf's hostility to social euphemism means that her approach to war, to patriotism, and to individual desire must repudiate indirection or artifice as symptoms of ethical complacency and political negligence.[28] Woolf addresses the tension between euphemism and literalism in her major novel, *Mrs. Dalloway* (1925). Extending the subject and style of "The Mark on the Wall," Woolf rejects the kinds of attentiveness that she associates with national triumphalism.

✳✳✳

In her 1997 film adaptation, *Virginia Woolf's Mrs. Dalloway*, Marleen Gorris adds transparency and explicitness to Woolf's project by rearranging the plot of her novel. While the book begins with Mrs. Dalloway's trip through London to buy flowers for a party in the evening, Gorris's film begins with Septimus Warren Smith's experience of trench warfare: the camera focuses on his terrified face as mortars and gunfire explode chaotically around him. Woolf's novel begins in London, in 1923. Gorris's film begins in Italy, in 1918. The time and place of the film's beginning are announced by a caption superimposed on a single shot of Septimus: we watch Septimus, who watches (the camera does not show what he sees) the death of his friend, Evans, who is killed by a mortar or a mine. The film seems to remedy what it establishes as a problem both of equation (death and a party) and of evasion (having a party instead of thinking wholly of death). The film tries to make good on Woolf's politics by clarifying the novel's concerns. Gorris's image of good modernism is a modernism matched to narrative clarity, direct representation, and achieved ethical priorities.

Of course, the first line of the novel is not a beginning but a middle: "Mrs. Dalloway said she would buy the flowers herself."[29] The first scene of the film has been added by Gorris—it exists nowhere in the novel—and it preempts the trip to the flower shop, which now follows in the echo of the war. It is worth noting these differences, not so much to complain that Gorris has deviated from a sacred original as to emphasize that the new scene seems to correct Woolf's omission. The invention of the scene in the trenches and its placement at the beginning of Gorris's film introduces the war as a preeminent topic: it comes first, and it is the only historical episode presented as an objective past rather than as a remembered one. Gorris's film reverses the structure of "A

Mark on the Wall": it shows a conventional scene of war, not an unconventional reflection; it starts with war, not with thinking; it gives priority to casualties, trenches, and men at the front, not to women in living rooms or in flower shops or at parties. By beginning her film with the war in Italy instead of a shopping trip in London, by beginning her film with a war that we see directly rather than through the memory or consciousness of one of the characters, Gorris's film gives Woolf's narrative a sharper, more definite face. Gorris contrasts a style of euphemism—common among most of the upper-class characters in the story, including Clarissa Dalloway—with a style of transparency, which is visible in the film's commitment to show what is made to seem like everything, even those scenes that Woolf chose never to describe.[30] Gorris's adaptation of Woolf seems to argue that social indifference and national triumphalism, which Woolf criticizes in her novel, are best defeated by a narrative style that is linear and unequivocal.

For Woolf, however, it is unequivocal style that generates upper-class euphemism. The face that Gorris gives to her film—a focused, objective image of war—is similar to the face that Clarissa Dalloway gives to herself, as Woolf describes it:

> How many million times she had seen her face, and always with that same imperceptible contraction! She pursed her lips when she looked in the glass. It was to give her face point. That was her self—pointed; dartlike; definite. That was her self when some effort, some call on her to be her self, drew the parts together, she alone knew how different, how incompatible and composed so for the world only into one centre, one diamond, one woman who sat in her drawing-room and made a meeting-point, a radiancy no doubt in some dull lives, a refuge for the lonely to come to, perhaps; she had helped young people, who were grateful to her; had tried to be the same always, never showing a sign of all of the other sides of her—faults, jealousies, vanities, suspicions, like this of Lady Bruton not asking her to lunch; which, she thought (combing her hair finally), is utterly base! Now, where was her dress?

(37)

Between looking into her mirror and looking for her dress is an account of single-mindedness that Clarissa's mind labors to assemble. The face is the result of compositional effort, the "contraction" of many parts and varieties of the self into one "pointed; dartlike; definite" image. Woolf presents this image as the face of social decorum: Clarissa displays only one self and also makes sure to conceal that there are any other selves to display. Woolf registers this sense of concealment in the doubling of selves: "that was her *self* when . . . some call on her to be her *self* drew the parts together." Clarissa's socialized face promises socialized thoughts and conceals the emotional intensity that Clarissa remembers from her youth. Later in the novel, Woolf will suggest that English patriotism, also, has a pointed, dartlike face, which in turn conceals the multiple attachments and unruly desires of cosmopolitan Britain. At the same time, Woolf will acknowledge that contraction makes possible those communities that serve as alternatives or supplements to patriotism: in the novel, communities of friendship; in Woolf's milieu, the subcultural community of pacifist artists and the imagined, transnational community of women. Indeed, Clarissa's euphemism of self, as grim as it may be, allows her to assemble the party that concludes the novel—a party that occasions the comparison of selves and the acknowledgment of unresolved differences.

To meet the demands of marriage and upper-class propriety, Clarissa generates a consistent, public self that does not reflect her many momentary, private desires. Her contracted face is marmoreal: not only definite but also unchanging, like the marble faces of the uniformed boys whom Peter Walsh, just returned from India, admires in the London street: "Boys in uniform, carrying guns, marched with their eyes ahead of them, marched, their arms stiff, and on their faces an expression like the letters of a legend written round the base of a statue praising duty, gratitude, fidelity, love of England" (51). Less purposeful than Clarissa, Peter allows his thoughts of a rebellious past to be "drummed" into step by the "regular thudding" of young men marching past him. Peter's thoughts are regularized in theme and in style: they become like the concrete letters written "round the base of a statue"—"like" these letters both because Peter has some sympathy for the specific praise of duty and because his sympathy is as automatic as the legend's cliché. Peter's agitated, recursive thoughts of the past are replaced by the deadened march of syntax, by the march of feet, and by the forward momentum of certainty and progress. Like Clarissa's social world, which requires contraction, the march of British triumphalism requires "renunciation," as Peter reports: "on they marched, past him, past every one, in their steady way, as if one will worked legs and arms uniformly, and life, with its varieties, its irreticences, had been laid under a pavement of monuments and wreaths and drugged into a stiff yet staring corpse by discipline" (51). It is through renunciation, Peter explains, that the marching boys come to resemble the military heroes whose statues they pass; having "trampled under" the temptations of life, the boys likewise achieve "a marble stare."

In this important passage, only a few pages after Clarisa's encounter with the mirror, Woolf indicates that public triumphalism requires an unagitated attentiveness: a face that is stiff and recognizable, that shows no "varieties" or "irreticences." Moreover, Woolf presents triumphalism as a style of history. Whereas the boys march steadily forward, never looking back, Clarissa and Peter remember moments from the past that change and develop and disorder the narrative progress of living. Clarissa's relationship with Sally Seton, for example, occasions "the most exquisite moment of her whole life" (35). Unlike the boys "drugged into a stiff yet staring corpse," Sally is remembered by Clarissa as a person of "abandonment, as if she could say anything, do anything; a quality much commoner in foreigners than in Englishwomen" (33). Woolf knows that a style of consciousness that abandons predictable conventions will tend to seem foreign, and she also knows that the decorum of gender—how women and men are expected to behave—is crucial to the definition of national culture. Sally is one of the many English characters in *Mrs. Dalloway* who are said to seem or act like foreigners: there is Miss Kilman, who loves Clarissa's daughter and whose friends and family are German; Peter Walsh, who has been living in India and who has fallen in love with a married woman; Septimus, whose thoughts are in Italy and not with his Italian émigré wife. Abandonment, like agitation, leads to improvisation and flexibility, but also to surprise and pain. The heroic past, captured in marble, is familiar and etched in stone; the momentary past, on the contrary, is "a present, wrapped up," which one uncovers slowly over time (35–36).

Resisting imperceptible contractions and the march of progress, Woolf extends the grammar of parataxis—in her novel, not only the lists of phrases and images that appear within a single sentence but also the many scenes that follow without immediate rationale—to the insubordinate arrangement of political imperatives and everyday pleasures. Adorno describes parataxis as "artificial disturbances that evade the logical hierarchy of a subordinating syntax."[31] In *Mrs. Dalloway*, parataxis serves to evade "a sense of proportion," which functions in the novel as a rule of thought, society, and speech (96). Proportion is the social theory promoted by Sir William Bradshaw, the specialist physician who treats Septimus for shell shock on his return from the European war. The symptoms of Septimus's condition, as Sir William identifies them, are disorders of thought and language: Septimus overinterprets and overelaborates; he distrusts the normative meanings of words and shows an unwillingness to follow conventional patterns of expression. Septimus's symptoms, like Woolf's strategies of evasion, serve to resist the "logical hierarchy" needed for patriotism and normative masculinity. One should see, also, that Woolf's critique of "logical hierarchy" extends to the foundations of British society, represented by imperial conquest and compulsory marriage: as agitation interferes with patriotism, so "susceptibility" makes Peter Walsh a mediocre colonial administrator and so remembering threatens to derail Clarissa's studied social poise (151).

During times of international crisis, Woolf proposes, boundaries of thought are patrolled even more rigorously than boundaries of land. Sir William exists to correct women like Miss Kilman, whom he never meets in the novel but whose forceful heterodoxy would conflict with his own, more socially accept-able kind of pushiness. Kilman tutors the Dalloways' daughter in history after being fired from the girls' school where she taught at the beginning of the war; her position lost because her family was of German origin and she had Ger-man friends, her career ruined as a result of patriotism, she feels "bitter and burning" much of the time (124). Though she tries to feel "calm" (124), having learned to think of God, she is "stricken once, twice, thrice by suffering" (133). Miss Kilman's bitterness seems too much for Woolf, who values pleasure as well as anger and has little sympathy, at least here, for the critique of economic privi-lege. Yet Woolf uses Miss Kilman's story to show that the control of indepen-dent women and shell-shocked men in England helps to prepare the control of independent cultures abroad.

Sir William's desire to discourage thinking is legible in his diagnosis of Sep-timus, whose illness he pronounces after "two or three" minutes of questioning (95). As Sir William interrogates Septimus, Woolf's narrative shifts from the doctor's point of view to the point of view of "the patient":

> "You served with great distinction in the War?"
>
> The patient repeated the word "war" interrogatively.
>
> He was attaching meanings to words of a symbolical kind. A serious symptom, to be noted on the card.
>
> "The War?" the patient asked. The European War—that little shindy of school-boys with gunpowder? Had he served with distinction? He really forgot. In the War itself he had failed.
>
> (96)

Septimus's wife, Lucrezia Warren Smith, answers Sir William's question on Septimus's behalf, as if the doctor had asked for a fact that Septimus could not remember. She assures Sir William that, "he served with the greatest distinc-tion" and "was promoted" as a result (96). But Septimus has forgotten what "distinction" means; he no longer values the rhetoric of valor and military heroism. He says "he had failed" not because he did not fight but because "he did not feel" (91). "War," "failure," and "distinction" are words whose meanings are no longer certain. By repeating the words, Septimus insists that he does not assume, as Sir William does, that he and the doctor are talking about the same idea of war or that there is only one idea of war to talk about. Sir William identifies the multiplication of perspectives, even the fact of perspective at all, as a sign of illness: "He was attaching meanings to words of a symbolical kind." In the shift of perspective from Sir William to Septimus, from "the patient" and "the War" to "the European War" and "that little shindy of schoolboys with gunpowder," Septimus recites the several names for which Sir William has only one name and, moreover, invents a new name along the way. Septimus insists that his war is not Sir William's war and also refuses to call his event a war at all; for Septimus, "war" celebrates without analyzing; it finalizes without modifying.

While Septimus suggests that words might have multiple, contested meanings, Sir William invokes euphemism, making words mean as little as possible. Euphemism is the opposite of symbolizing because it does not "attach" one meaning to another but replaces one meaning with a muted, more comfortable interpretation. The point of euphemism is to make what is replaced and the act of replacement invisible. Sir William explains to Rezia, who wants to know if Septimus is "mad," that "he never spoke of 'madness'; he called it not having a sense of proportion" (96). Septimus shows, through deflation, the fatuous spectacle that "war" covers up (a "little shindy of schoolboys with gunpowder"), while Sir William gives "madness" a new name so he does not have to speak of it at all. Giving uncomfortable experiences new names and embracing these names in lieu of discomfort, euphemism demonstrates a sense of proportion. Of course, it is perfectly true that Septimus's response is also in some ways euphemistic: he does not speak of bodily destruction, the death of friends, or the intensity of remorse. Yet unlike Sir William's euphemism, Septimus's deflation creates greater discomfort: speaking of the war sarcastically, he declines explicitness, to be certain, but he also declines mythification. That Septimus does not share Sir William's sense (meaning) of war is a sign that he lacks sense (sanity) altogether. Woolf explains that Sir William's method works by excluding any element that would challenge his views: "Worshipping proportion, Sir William not only prospered himself but made England prosper, secluded its lunatics, forbade childbirth, penalised despair, made it impossible for the unfit to propagate their views until they, too, shared his sense of proportion" (99). Proportion requires seclusion and prohibition: it makes things fit by calling them "unfit" until they do.

By fighting proportion as a system of representation, Woolf is fighting to reverse the contraction of individuality and antagonism within civic debates about national and international thinking. To do this, Woolf promotes several strategies of thought that correspond to strategies of writing: poetic language, nick-naming, excitement, stammering, revision, and parataxis. These strategies are crucial in *Mrs. Dalloway*, where Woolf develops an analogy between symptoms of shell shock and tactics of social critique, but they are also noticeable throughout Woolf's writing: Rachel Bowlby describes the feminist logic of "Woolf's equivocations" in *A Room of One's Own* and other essays (70), and Michèle Barrett proposes that Woolf's use of parentheses and square brackets "form part of a general writing strategy that represents the really important things for Woolf—the war, death, grief, the meaning of life, as well as love—

only obliquely.''[32] Barrett argues persuasively that the "strange withdrawal of obvious affect in the writing of Woolf" (195–96), part of what I have been calling "evasion," demonstrates Woolf's commitment to the multiple, transient self, as opposed to the contracted, marmoreal self required by proportion, conversion, and triumphalism.

In *Mrs. Dalloway*, Woolf promotes metaphor ("that little shindy of school-boys with gunpowder") against heroic clichés and against the presumption that any experience has one consistent and conclusive interpretation.[33] Similarly, "excitement" and "exquisite joy," which Septimus, Clarissa, and Peter experience in moments of intense, though not necessarily "comfortable" feeling, serve as alternatives to the march of ordered existence and the flood of "tolerable" circumstance (55).[34] Both of the physicians who treat Septimus, Dr Holmes and Sir William, tell Rezia that Septimus must avoid "excitement" (140). Septimus's observations, as Rezia describes them, are much like Woolf's prose, full of disparate ideas whose association depends more on inspiration than on logic: "Some things were very beautiful; others sheer nonsense. And he was always stopping in the middle, changing his mind; wanting to add something; hearing something new; listening with his hand up" (140). The parenthetical thought ("stopping in the middle"), the semicolon and its accretion of metaphors ("wanting to add something"), the visibility of thought in process ("hearing something new; listening with his hand up") are all strategies of thought that evade certainty and marmoreal knowledge.

Woolf evades marmoreal knowledge through poetic language and stammering; these, too, are "symptoms" of social dysfunction that Sir William aims to cure. When Sir William returns from telling Rezia that Septimus will need to be "secluded" in a "home," he finds his patient "muttering messages about beauty" (97). Informed of Sir William's intentions, Septimus asks, purposefully, "One of Holmes's homes?" Instead of keeping quiet or rejecting the doctor's advice, Septimus refuses to allow Sir William to dictate his behavior or to dictate the terms in which his distress should be articulated. Instead of taking Sir William seriously and respecting his authority, Septimus makes a little rhyme out of Sir William's cure ("Holmes's homes"), focusing on the sound rather than the meaning, allowing the sound to stand against Sir William's unspecified intentions. Sir William would replace the stark fact of enforced institutionalization with the euphemism "home," but Septimus draws attention to the term and to the fact of replacement, making Sir William's language sound ridiculous rather than sane. For Sir William, however, making art instead of "sense"—making art *against* sense—is a sure sign of proportion's absence.

Septimus finds it difficult to communicate in a language that his doctors are willing to hear: he speaks in metaphors and in rhymes, and he stammers:

"I—I —" Septimus stammered.

"Try to think as little about yourself as possible," said Sir William kindly.

(98)

Here, Woolf gives physical manifestation to social and psychological estrangement. The stammering is not purposeful, as were the rhyme and the metaphors; rather, it shows that Septimus is unable to speak as if he knows his desires and as if he has confidence that his listeners will understand him. Septimus stammers because he is uncertain about what he has to say and because his beliefs keep changing:

Love, trees, there is no crime—what was his message?

He could not remember it.

"I—I—" Septimus stammered.

(98)

Stammering is a well-known symptom of shell shock: on the one hand, it is the result of imposed censorship, a displacement of the protest or distress that is otherwise prohibited; on the other hand, it is the result of self-censorship, an unconscious refusal to say, or to say easily and with conviction, what is socially required. Soldiers lose the ability to speak because they are faced with situations that are unspeakable within the context of military discipline.[35]

Septimus performs the only literal stammer in *Mrs. Dalloway*, but Woolf's novel also stammers in its own way, by resisting the language of continuous, confident narration and by describing a national capital full of foreigners and foreign attachments. Gilles Deleuze presents stammering not as an unconscious failure of speech but as a willful and difficult achievement of writing.[36] "A style," Deleuze argues, "is managing to stammer in one's own language" (4). When Deleuze speaks of "a style," he means the specific projection of unorthodox, unsocialized thought. For this reason, he will say that "style" belongs to people "of whom you normally say 'They have no style'" (4); it belongs to people like Septimus, whose manners do not correspond to an appropriate, invisible fashion. Among his list of writers whose novels "stammer," Deleuze includes Kafka and Beckett because they are "bilingual even in a single language" (4). Deleuze proposes that "multilingualism is not merely the property of several systems each of which would be homogeneous in itself: it is primarily the line of flight or of variation which affects each system by stopping it from being homogeneous" (4). Any intellectual committed to social critique, Deleuze argues, should write "like a foreigner" and thus make the process of communication both more vexed and more visible (5).

Woolf produces the effect of stammering by describing the process of thought, and this is a strategy that Adorno would later echo in "The Essay as Form." Compare, for example, Woolf's call for stream of consciousness in "Modern Fiction" (1925) with Adorno's assertion that the essay as a genre should describe "intellectual experience."[37] Promoting a novelistic prose that aspires to critical reflection, Woolf asserts: "Let us record the atoms as they fall upon the mind in the order in which they fall, let us trace the pattern however disconnected and incoherent in appearance, which each sight or incident scores upon the consciousness" (150). In turn, defending a critical style that aspires to the novelistic, Adorno defines "the essay" as the record of thought in process:

> The word *Versuch*, attempt or essay, in which thought's utopian vision of hitting the bullseye is united with the consciousness of its own fallibility and provisional character, indicates, as do most historically surviving terminologies, something about the form, something to be taken all the more seriously in that it takes place not systematically but rather as a characteristic of an intention groping its way.
>
> ("THE ESSAY AS FORM," 16)

Adorno's definition of the essay is useful for a reading of Woolf's fiction not because his definition is new—essayists since Montaigne have described the effort to record thinking—but because it helps to show that the genre of the essay, in its strategies of self-reflection, informs Woolf's new project for the genre of the novel.[38] For Adorno as for Woolf, modernist writing should generate a new condition of thinking, a "pattern however disconnected and incoherent." Uniting an aim with the risk of aimlessness, Adorno proposes that risk is constitutive of the essay's achievement: only by avoiding systematic thought can the essay avoid the inevitable result of preconditioned thinking. Through techniques of coordination rather than subordination, "cross-connections" among elements rather than "conclusive deductions," Adorno seeks to "violate the orthodoxy of thought," to risk the accusation of evasiveness, so that something "becomes visible which it is orthodoxy's secret and objective aim to keep invisible" (22–23).

Like Adorno's "orthodoxy," the "sense of proportion" that Woolf attributes to Sir William is characterized above all by disguise and invisibility: disguise, because individual experiences are replaced and covered up by a single, standardized account; and invisibility, because the mechanism of disguise is kept out of sight. Sir William's renaming of "madness" and his presumption of shared, transparent language ("war," "distinction") serve to make opinions that are merely conventional into thoughts that are necessary and unequivocal. This is proportion's "secret": it makes contraction natural. In two of the essays she wrote in the final years of her life, "The Artist and Politics" (1936) and "Thoughts on Peace in an Air Raid" (1940), Woolf transforms the too-easy rhetoric of distinction (the distinction between Britain and Germany) into a stammering, agitated language.[39] The key element in Woolf's strategy is "camouflage," which Woolf appropriates as a metaphor.[40] Woolf aims not to eradicate camouflage—she does not think this is possible, or even desirable—but to make it less hidden.

In "Thoughts on Peace in an Air Raid," Woolf proposes that it is necessary during wartime both to fight and to think (243–44). "To make ideas effective," Woolf argues, one must "put them into action"; one must engage in what Woolf calls, after Blake, "mental fight," which means "thinking against the current, not with it" (244). Woolf addresses the relationship between fighting and thinking by describing her experience of trying to think while planes fly overhead and guns explode nearby. Thinking about the opposition between "peace" and "war" that the essay's title seems to promise, Woolf comes to consider the similarities between "tyranny" at home and "tyranny" abroad (245). Woolf refuses in this essay to separate a discussion of Hitler's dramatic, genocidal tyranny from a discussion of militarism and imperialism in Britain; risking a naïve pacifism in the context of Hitler's threat, Woolf proposes that there is complicity between Germany and Britain, that what looks like liberalism can contain elements of fascism, that "guns" are sometimes concealed beneath "the hues of autumn leaves" (245–46).[41]

One might find Woolf's argument uncomfortable, if not impractical, in the face of Hitler's aggression, but Woolf's intention is neither comfort nor practicality. Woolf's project is this: to show and resist the kind of "thinking" that is encouraged by "fighting" by appropriating the strategies of war. Woolf transforms the physical impotence of wartime, being on the ground during an air raid, into "mental fight" and into "Thoughts on Peace in an Air Raid," the title and subject of an essay. One should notice the implicit analogy between the passivity and helplessness that soldiers in the trenches experienced during the First World War and the experience of women beneath an air raid during the Second World War. While Septimus returns from the war unable to think or feel, Woolf seeks to retain her sanity by refusing peaceful thoughts. Woolf transforms the everyday objects of passive resistance—"a gas mask," for example—into metaphors of rhetorical aggression: "Down here, with a roof to cover us and a gas mask handy, it is our business to puncture gas bags and discover seeds of truth" (244–45). Insisting that "thoughts," if they lead to peace, constitute "the only efficient air-raid shelter," Woolf uses metaphor to supplement military efforts ("fighting with the mind," while servicemen fight with guns) and also to examine the "freedom" that these efforts claim to protect (243). Given the conditions of international crisis and the real danger of Hitler's triumph, Woolf's argument may seem trivial in its concern with domestic issues and in its contention that domestic issues are also international ones. However, as Jessica Berman has argued in her study of Woolf's *Three Guineas* (1938), one kind of inaction may make other kinds of actions possible (*Modernist Fiction*, 115). If Woolf focuses in her late essays on "the question of how people like her—artists—should act politically," as Michèle Barrett has proposed, she also questions how acting "politically" should be defined.[42]

***

Appropriating camouflage to write against war and against patriotism, Woolf's work specifies the different objects whose comparison camouflage regularly conceals. Woolf assembles objects and ideas that are neither homogenous nor entirely distinct, refusing both the logic of replacement and the logic of equivalence.[43] Woolf's aim is entanglement, which means displaying self-consciously, perhaps aggressively, topics that will seem inconsequent alongside those that, traditionally, are thought more significant. The contrast between the inconsequent and the significant is pivotal to Erich Auerbach's canonical account of the "minor, unimpressive, random events" that Woolf emphasizes in her novels.[44] For Auerbach, whose essay on "the brown stocking" in *Mimesis* hails Woolf as the exemplary figure of modernist fiction, the "random moment" is a defining characteristic of Woolf's work and of the commitment to subjective impression that Woolf shares with Marcel Proust and James Joyce (541–44). Writing during the Second World War, Auerbach embraced randomness as a promise of intellectual refuge and transcendent humanity that is "comparatively independent of the controversial and unstable orders over which men fight and despair" (552). For Woolf, however, the "random moment" is made up of thoughts and experiences whose perceived inconsequence is inseparable from war and from the social institutions that legislate priority. While "randomness" may describe Woolf's refusal to embrace what is necessary or conventional, it withholds in the language of chance the evaluation and comparison that Woolf is eager to provoke.

Perhaps the best account of this provocation and of its social implications comes in Georg Lukács's important essay "Narrate or Describe?" which was published in 1936, the same year that Woolf published "The Artist and Politics." Lukács argues that the narrative technique of "description," which he traces from naturalist writing in the late nineteenth century to contemporary "subjectivist" (stream of consciousness) writing in the beginning of the twentieth century, demonstrates a failure to prioritize.[45] Because it is focused on observation, Lukács argues, description values the refusal to evaluate. Lukács criticizes texts that fail to make significance and causality explicit; in this failure, these texts obscure the evidence of class struggle and capitalist exploitation. Whereas narration provides "a proper distribution of emphasis and a just accentuation of what is essential" within a novel's social world (126), Lukács contends, description will not affirm that things have an order: "Narration establishes proportions, description merely levels" (127). By leveling, Lukács continues, description does not establish boundaries and may in fact lead to "something much worse": "a reversed order of significance, a consequence implicit in the descriptive method since both the important and the unimportant are described with equal attention" (131). Lukács is right to see that writing such as Woolf's obscures causality and actively refuses to emphasize only "what is essential," but he is unable to see that Woolf's work serves to challenge the rules both of relevance and of essence.

Lukács opposes "description" to "epic" and argues that the leveling of attention and objects suspends the mechanism of priority—what Mikhail Bakhtin in his study of epic calls the "world of 'firsts' and 'bests'"—and the possibility of consensus.[46] The most important aspect of epic, Bakhtin explained in 1941, is not the rendering of "actual facts" but the expectation of their "absolute" acceptance; the epic is distinguished by "its reliance on impersonal and sacrosanct tradition, on a commonly held evaluation and point of view—which excludes the possibility of another approach—and which therefore displays a profound piety toward the subject described and toward the language used to describe it, the language of tradition" (16–17). Lukács argues that the world represented in fiction should seem like "something not invented, but simply discovered" (126): not intention groping its way but experience realized.

For her part, Woolf tries to resist the hierarchy of objects she associates with patriotic thought. She contests the war by rejecting its models of attention. Woolf approaches the war parenthetically, never erasing its violence but not allowing violence to absorb, in the total attention violence demands, the partial attention that resists it. *Mrs. Dalloway*, in particular, reproduces a conflict about attention at several levels (syntax, theme, and plot). The novel shuttles between remembering and forgetting, between the rejection of complacency and the suspicion of prescribed action, whether this action involves forgetting or remembering to the exclusion of everything else. With the arrival of Sir William at her home, Clarissa hears that Septimus has killed himself: "Oh! thought Clarissa, in the middle of my party, here's death, she thought" (183). If one thinks that the gravity of death means considering death first and by itself, and not in the middle of a party, and not in the middle of a sentence about a party, then Clarissa's thought may seem insensitive and unsympathetic. But there may be something valuable in a reiterated "thought" that equates the significance of a party with the significance of death—that places these topics, syntactically and ethically, on the same plane. Clarissa recognizes in Septimus "an attempt to communicate" (184). She admires his death because he has done something unreasonable. He has rejected the "corruption" of life: "A thing there was that mattered; a thing, wreathed about with chatter, defaced, obscured in her own life, let drop every day in corruption, lies, chatter. This he had preserved" (184). As for herself, Clarissa reports: "She had schemed; she had pilfered. She was never wholly admirable" (185). Clarissa's party may facilitate chatter and perpetuate exclusion (Miss Kilman and Septimus were not invited), but it creates opportunities also—for measuring the past, recognizing friends, and saying "things you couldn't say anyhow else, things that needed an effort" (171). Presenting death in the middle of a party, Woolf refuses to accept the structure of choice—war or peace; party or death; reasonableness or insanity—that Clarissa's milieu takes for granted. The refusal of linearity and choice is a signal characteristic of Woolf's modernism, and it is one of the reasons why aesthetic success in her terms often seems like political failure.

Arguably, *Mrs. Dalloway* achieves its climax not at the party, where Septimus's suicide is announced and considered, but at the start of the novel's penultimate section, in which Peter Walsh calls a passing ambulance "one of the triumphs of civilisation" (151). Woolf places this sentence in Peter's thoughts only sentences after Septimus has killed himself and Dr. Holmes has disclaimed all responsibility. While Peter's comment does refer to the ambulance, it seems also, by proximity, to describe the scene of suicide that comes—in the novel—immediately before (though it is not known to Peter). Woolf uses Peter's interior monologue to register both the cruelty and the kindness of civilization's triumph and to suggest that technologies of kindness, which arrive in the novel as a doctor or as an ambulance, may generate cruelty in their wake. Throughout *Mrs. Dalloway*, Woolf makes the monuments of English civilization into symbols in the very sense Sir William uses: progress, an ambulance, war, and a wedding ring, all of which at first seem to have definitive meanings, no longer convey an unequivocal achievement.

In the novel's sudden shift from death to "triumph," we see right away that even in an ambulance there is nothing "wholly admirable." Peter sees the ambulance as a triumph because it functions as an agent of rescue and as an example of imperial "efficiency" and "communal spirit" (151). It symbolizes both English society at its most humane and the beneficence of this superior nation's rule elsewhere (as in India, from whose colonial service Peter has just returned). While the first may seem to us far more appealing than the second, Woolf would have us notice, by the nearness of the ambulance and the suicide and by Peter's clanging words (he repeats the word "civilisation" several times), that the very doctors who tend to the injured may be those who have driven Septimus to his death. Peter's triumphalism is made possible by three kinds of blindness: he does not know about the suicide of Septimus, or even that the treatment of shell shock is causing rather than correcting injury; he cannot recognize that the "communal spirit" at home, which he unreservedly admires, has been financed by the exploitation of communities abroad; and he cannot see that the social values he admires (progress, efficiency, usefulness) are continuous with those that led Clarissa to marry Richard, making Peter "more unhappy than I've ever been since" (42). In this scene, Woolf proposes forcefully what she has suggested elsewhere: that English manners have a "cosmopolitan geography"; efficiency and "communal spirit" are made possible—and belied—by colonialism on the one hand and by European war on the other.

Peter's thoughts of efficiency may distract readers from the contemplation of Septimus's mangled body and his wife's misery, and from wondering whether it is, indeed, Septimus whom the ambulance carries. Yet turning away from death, the novel brings to light the uncivil, unwavering attention of triumphalist thought, represented in the novel by the affective priorities of upper-class marriage, colonialism, and patriotism. By creating this diversion, Woolf's style of composition rejects what Adorno has called "the dream of an existence without shame."[47] For Adorno—who is perhaps most known for insisting that poetry after Auschwitz is barbaric and who is perhaps least known for retracting or at least revising this declaration[48]—writers seeking to resist social conformity must develop strategies of critique that exceed homogeneous or merely pious styles of expression; they must accept, if not embrace, the profanity of conflicting sensibilities—beautiful metaphors and ugly events, acts of kindness and scenes of cruelty, suicide in the afternoon and a party in the evening—and they must accept the ethical discomfort that this profanity may evoke. Adorno argues that the writer must acknowledge "the complicity that enfolds all those who, in the face of unspeakable collective events, speak of individual matters at all."[49] While "collaboration" should be resisted, Adorno asserts, "there is no way out of entanglement" (26–27). In *Mrs. Dalloway*, Woolf's shame is marked by her willingness to contemplate both the opportunities and the dangers of evasion.

By cultivating moments of diversion and by rejecting wartime priorities of attention, Woolf makes her readers more aware of social networks and helps them to distinguish between specific perspectives and universal ones. For example, Peter transforms a modest triumph into triumphalism by assuming that the limited success of the ambulance in recovering injured bodies can be simply extended to the entire success of London; that London's success can be extended to the success of the British Empire; that the success of the British Empire is equivalent to the success of civilization. Whereas the generalizing perspective assumes that triumph extends to every action and every actor, the agitated or distracted perspective acknowledges that one person's triumph is often the cause of someone else's loss. This is the point that Walter Benjamin makes in his claim, "there is no document of civilization which is not at the same time a document of barbarism."[50] Benjamin observes that "cultural treasures," now collected in museums, are the spoils of forgotten wars; that those discoveries that mark the advance of science and technology, however much they owe to individual inspiration, have been produced in part by anonymous laborers who received no benefit from their efforts. Benjamin's observation emphasizes causality and history, but it also speaks of the present and the future—the "triumphal procession," as he puts it, "that steps over those who are lying prostrate" (256). For Benjamin, forgetting and ignoring are not the unintended or necessary consequences of civilization's triumph, but rather they are the inaugural moments in which destructive self-righteousness are achieved. Writing in a time of too many processions, Benjamin proposes, as Woolf does, that looking backward and looking below are principal tactics of antitriumphalism.

And thus for Woolf even monuments are usable and potentially critical when their marmoreal substance is modified by the incitement to speculation. In *The Years* (1938), one of Woolf's characters refers to the statue of Edith Cavell, a British nurse who was executed by the Germans in 1915 and whose monument was erected near Trafalgar Square in 1920.[51] Initially, the statue was inscribed with the usual patriotic phrases: "fortitude," "devotion," "for King and country." Four years later, however, the Labour government added a statement that Cavell made before her death: "Patriotism is not enough, I must have no hatred or bitterness for anyone."[52] In Woolf's novel, Eleanor calls these words the "only fine thing that was said in the war" (319). Neither embracing patriotism nor rejecting it outright, Cavell's tentative universalism forces readers to speculate about the statue's message and about its function as a national monument. Woolf seems to appreciate the statue for its articulate evasiveness: the way it acknowledges (and even records) a history of conflict about the appropriate meanings and necessary objects of British devotion.

Woolf suggests that political engagement in an international context requires the willingness to march but also to think; the willingness to have a mind but also to change it; and the willingness to embrace uncommitted styles of attention. Woolf's analytic strategies depend on the persistence of effort rather than the production of efficiency. She uses evasion to reject the consistency and intensity of affect that she identifies with imperial progress and civic hypocrisy. Woolf's project brings together two strains of cosmopolitanism: a decadent, urbane tradition of dissenting individualism and a philosophical tradition of transnational sympathy based on similarities greater or less than the nation. Seeing the mixture of these traditions in Woolf's work has two principal consequences: first, it suggests that Anglo-American modernism includes antiheroic impulses that help to shape alternative modes of political consciousness; second, it suggests that critiques of modernity that focus on Europe, such as Woolf's, share analytic insights with critiques that emphasize the experiences of colonialism. Among these insights is the idea that resisting the politics of imperialism may involve refining or even rejecting some kinds of attentiveness.

When we read Woolf's fiction in the context of theories of cosmopolitanism and social theories of dissent, we can see and question what is valued as literary innovation, political action, and international sympathy in the twentieth century. Her critique of heroism and her emphasis on the political nature of intimacy will be crucial to the work of later cosmopolitan novelists.

MODERNIST COSMOPOLITANISM

PART 2

*Today, when I try to recall that evening I find my memory of it merging with the
sounds and images from all those other evenings.*

—KAZUO ISHIGURO, *AN ARTIST OF THE FLOATING WORLD*

IN KAZUO ISHIGURO'S second and third novels, *An Artist of the Floating
World* (1986) and *The Remains of the Day* (1989), the narrators look back from
the middle of the twentieth century on events that took place in the years before
the Second World War.[1] While the novels never mention their own time period,
the 1980s, their sly humor and dramatic irony depend on the reader's sense of
distance both from the interwar confidence of the early 1930s and from the
Cold War hypocrisy of the 1950s. In these works, interwar confidence comes
in the form of English racism, German militarism, and Japanese expansion-
ism, while Cold War hypocrisy is represented, often more subtly, by Englishmen who praise democracy but oppose the decolonization of "all kinds of little
countries" that once belonged to Britain (*R* 192) and by U.S.-influenced Japanese who think that establishing positive, anti-imperialist role models means
encouraging children to imitate cowboys instead of samurais (*A* 30). Comparing the fascisms of the 1930s, the imperialisms of the 1950s, and the nativisms
of the 1980s, Ishiguro develops a critical cosmopolitanism that allows us to see
how aspects of fascism and triumphalism function not only in Japan and Germany but also in the United States and England, and not only in the 1930s and
1950s but also in the 1980s; in Ishiguro's narratives, no country looks like a perpetrator or a victim only, or like a major power or a minor supplicant all of the
time. Ishiguro generates comparisons not to create equivalences but to notice
continuities and mergings among different political circumstances (of the early,
middle, and late twentieth century) and among various, conflicting allegiances
(to children, parents, teachers, students, art, country, friends, and so on). Ishiguro's novels are treasonous because they suggest that steadfast and unconflicted

allegiances are neither possible nor desirable, because they propose that critical artworks will need to project a limited or only partial faithfulness, and because they use unreliable narratives to generate in their readers self-reflective and contingent kinds of loyalty.

If Ishiguro is eager to compare scenes and kinds of coercion, he is reluctant to treat every instance of coercion as the same. He is also suspicious of social or political movements that aim to make all aspects of individual life accountable to a collective program. *An Artist of the Floating World* suggests that the production of decadent art—here, the representation and valorization of fleeting, intense moments of consciousness, usually involving pleasure or sexuality—constitutes treason in Japan of the 1930s because it does not express, encourage, or generate "the new spirit" of military conquest (64). Ishiguro's own emphasis on past moments, on partial or "pale" views, and on intimacy, within a group of novels that focus on the physical and psychic damage of militarism, racism, and neo-imperialism, allows us to see decadence not only as a refusal to participate in the expansionist project but also as a critique of the consolidating "spirit" or aesthetic protocols of that project. In *Artist*, the narrator recalls a banner that used an image of marching army boots displayed against the name of a popular bar to associate drinking and carousing there with Japanese patriotism (64). To be certain, the banner conformed to the new spirit because it celebrated military activities such as soldiers going to war. But it performed that spirit, too, by reducing acts of pleasure and sociability to an ethic of ineluctable progress: the marching boots represent the forward momentum of war as well as the instrumental and conformist way of thinking that would make all activities subservient to that momentum.

Ishiguro's treason differs from the idea of treason invoked by most of his characters: he sees it as a principle of imperfect unanimity that informs antifascist and antinativist ideas of community, whereas they see it as a failure of the "fierce and total" devotion that participating in a community requires (*A* 144). Perhaps the most visible footprint of the 1980s in Ishiguro's early novels is their frequent use of the word "misunderstanding," which characters invoke whenever they want to claim that there is confusion rather than conflict. Misunderstanding invokes the ideals of tolerance and mutual inaccessibility that readers trained in multiculturalism, at its height in the 1980s, often bring to Ishiguro's texts. And it facilitates the assumption of natural inaccessibility that the West has often attributed to the East. To this kind of tolerance, Ishiguro prefers the agency and open antagonism of treason.

However, by placing his characters between one imperial power and another, between social confidence and social questioning, between past and present, and between several national cultures, Ishiguro in some ways cultivates misunderstanding in his readers. His strategies of description and narration can seem to imitate the characteristics of the place and people he is representing. Readers often assume that his novels are expressing specific national traditions or attributes: this is true for the apparent Englishness of *When We Were Orphans* (2000) and *The Remains of the Day*, and for the apparent Japaneseness of *An Artist of the Floating World* and *A Pale View of Hills* (1982). If Ishiguro's oeuvre is cosmopolitan in a critical sense because it involves comparison and distinction, it is also cosmopolitan in the most traditional sense: the novels present characters who move from East to West and from West to East; they refer to works of literature, painting, and popular culture from Great Britain, France, Japan, the United States, and elsewhere; they are published originally in English, though some of the narrators do not speak or think in English at all. In another respect, also, the novels are cosmopolitan: they emphasize sensory experiences, such as familiar spaces, evocative smells, and the sound of habitual phrases. Ishiguro uses these spaces, smells, and phrases to associate major events with those that seem to be minor and to ask us to notice that the international politics of immigration and imperialism is shaped by intimate disputes about social achievement, education, and childrearing.

Marcel Proust's work provides an important comparison for Ishiguro's because he theorizes the relationship between narratives and selves and also allows that his texts might produce a self, defining in their style a particular persona or experience. By his own account, Proust imagines the "function and task of a writer as those of a translator," one who mediates (and knows the difference) between an "impression" in life and its "expression" in literature. He will name this difference and yet propose, at times, that expression may suggest what impression was: one may "recognize" in retrospect the telling "evidence" for a self invented in the act of retrospection; a narrative may articulate for the first time the identity whose characteristics it claims merely to recall.[2] Ishiguro's early works register this dialectic, between the narratives that generate identities and the narratives that describe them, as the origin of national fictions. Ishiguro's characters maintain these fictions by invoking what Maud Ellmann, writing about Henry James, calls "vulgar truth."[3] Refusing to endorse a static view of the past, Ishiguro abjures "vulgar truth" in order to abjure "vulgar falsehood" as well. This is to say, as Ellmann explains of James, Ishiguro is unwilling to reduce his narratives to a single, transparent event because in a world of political interpretations such truth is a kind of deception. "As soon as there is representation," Ellmann proposes, speaking both of narrative and of politics, "there is treason" (509). To represent this treason, Henry James built his late work on the foundation of absent narrative and envisioned his task as the evocation of insufficient representation: he hoped to convey to his readers the sense of "ever so many more of the shining silver fish afloat in the deep sea of one's endeavour than the net of widest casting could pretend to gather in."[4] For James, the floating world was the condition to which fiction aspired. Likewise, Ishiguro proposes that treason in people, nations, and art is more reliable and sometimes more responsible than absolute or merely dutiful allegiance.

Ishiguro's novels plainly reiterate the many generalizing utterances that characters use to obscure differences over time and within a community. These generalizations are audible in Ishiguro's novels as the echoes of nationalism and cultural stereotype. Ishiguro shows how cultural stereotypes work by presenting his novels as national allegories,[5] allowing the characteristics of his texts to stand for the characteristics of the cultures they seem to describe. Ishiguro reproduces these allegories and then displays them, embedding their cultural truths in narratives about the fictionalization of cultural truths. The novels thus demonstrate an "aberrant grammar," to use Roland Barthes's term, which disorients systems of meaning and patterns of reference.[6] Ishiguro's aberrant grammar is, like the Deleuzian stammer,[7] an effort to make the process of representation both more vexed and more visible; it is an effort to write "like a foreigner," if only to assert the necessity of translation even—or especially—within a novel that seems to be about a single national culture.[8]

Theodor W. Adorno has proposed that readers perceive foreignness in language whenever there is a disruption in the conventions of syntax: texts will seem "foreign" when they perform and require interpretation because readers attribute such efforts to a difference between cultures rather than to a difference within them.[9] Adorno explains, performing the contrast and the subordination that he is describing,

> With great narrative prose, interpretation easily takes on the coloration of the foreign word. The syntax may sound more foreign than the vocabulary. Attempts at formulation that swim against the usual linguistic splashing in order to capture the intended matter precisely, and that take pains to fit complex conceptual relationships into the framework of syntax, arouse rage because they require effort.
>
> (185)

Readers are enraged, Adorno argues, because they are encountering an unfamiliar idea, and they attribute their lack of familiarity to the author's use of foreign words rather than to the author's effort to generate unfamiliar meanings. This may explain why the persistent approximation of cultures in Ishiguro's novels is for many readers mimetic of places rather than displacement:[10] readers attribute the effect of translation to an objective, definable "foreignness," making a scene of distance out of a story of proximity, immigration, and comparison. This chapter will consider how Ishiguro anticipates, even entices these transformations and how he uses misunderstandings to resist exclusive allegiances and to affirm more critical, more cosmopolitan loyalties.

* * *

The "floating world" of Ishiguro's second novel names a subject for art—"those pleasurable things that disappear with the morning light"—as well as a country, a social milieu, and a past (180). The "artist" of the title is Masuji Ono: in the 1930s, he was a respected painter and imperial propagandist; in the 1950s, after the Second World War, he is a collaborator in disgrace. Ono's story is elusive, gestural, and translated in every sense, for Ono is a Japanese man speaking his native language, ostensibly Japanese, in formal English. For many readers, the difference between English discourse and Japanese setting does not call attention to the artifice of the novel so much as it articulates a cultural estrangement or simply a culture: Japan itself. These readers thus reproduce a metonymic logic that Ishiguro attributes ironically to many of his characters. It is worth remembering that narratives may project national fictions, even if the assembly of those fictions is part of the stories they tell. By embedding Japanese stereotypes within his work, Ishiguro prefigures and theorizes the interpretations that have come to pursue him.

In several reviews of Ishiguro's novels, the artist Ono and the artist Ishiguro are metaphorically interchangeable. Critics associate the novelist's technique with an authentic Japaneseness, and they propose this affiliation as a natural rather than a cultivated element of Ishiguro's craft. The author's "instincts," we are told, "are for the nuanced, the understated, elegant but significant gesture, similar to the deft brushwork of Japanese paintings."[11] It is more common for readers to attribute Ishiguro's non-English qualities to his style of writing than to his subject or biography, but some have attached a specific cultural particularity to the latter elements as well. For one reader, Ishiguro "remains inalienably Japanese" *despite* "Western literary techniques," in good part, it would seem, because the contrast between "the West" and Japan is itself "a favourite subject for Japanese writers."[12] Ishiguro has lived in England since the age of six, was educated in England, writes in English, but he is regularly compared with "modern Japanese novelists" all the same.[13]

Homi K. Bhabha has suggested that this kind of critical transformation, from difference into identity, attempts to convert what escapes the reading, authoritative gaze—those floating fish, the floating world, those "things that disappear"—into a containable metonymy. For Bhabha, the reader's failure becomes the object's abstract noun: "the *inscrutability* of the Chinese, the *unspeakable* rites of the Indians, the *indescribable* habits of the Hottentots."[14] The floating world of the Japanese. While these metonymies generate the racism of fixed characteristics, Bhabha argues, their opacity also reflects an impotent gaze and the potential failure of definitive sight. Whereas in Bhabha's account inaccessibility becomes an accessible, if somewhat menacing content, Rey Chow argues that obstinate strangeness justifies for many a distance that need not be measured. "When that other is Asia or the 'Far East,'" Chow has proposed, it is typically represented in "absolute terms, making this other an utterly incomprehensible, terrifying, and fascinating spectacle."[15] The problem, Chow explains, is not the incomprehension of difference but the embodiment it provokes: readers transform a subjective, idealized fantasy into an objective place or person; they "(mis)apply [this otherness] to *specific other cultures*."[16]

Ishiguro's approach to these transformations is unusual because he suggests that national identities are generated not only to maintain a boundary from the outside but also to erect a boundary in the face of new, perhaps internal estrangement. Ishiguro describes a world of metonymic reading, but he is careful not to suggest either that one might replace it with a more authentic, less figurative form of description or that its consolidating tactics are solely the strategy of an Orientalist perspective. Both Bhabha and Chow have criticized those models of anti-ethnocentrism that, in seeking to replace bad images with good ones, reproduce racist stereotypes by making foreign persons into objects of persistent nobility.[17] Chow is suspicious of any discourse that would transform other cultures into sites of "authenticity and true knowledge" not only because this authenticity forecloses the agency of self-definition and self-fashioning but also because it suggests that observers of these cultures might gain from them a "true knowledge" uninflected by translation and self-interest (52–53). Chow takes up Slavoj Žižek's observation that those who think themselves "non-duped," or "undeceived," are in fact the most deceived of all.[18] She extends Žižek's argument to assert that "our fascination with the native, the oppressed, the savage, and all such figures is therefore a desire to hold on to an unchanging certainty somewhere outside our own 'fake' experience. It is a desire for being 'non-duped,' which is a not-so-innocent desire to seize control" (53). The desire to be undeceived, like the desire for a "vulgar truth," leads to falsehood and coercion.

In Ishiguro's novels, the fictions of national definition are as often a product of local imagination as they are an imposition of foreign scrutiny. Moreover, Ishiguro proposes, the fixing of national identities depends on a style of representation whose claims to mimetic transparency assume norms of unwavering allegiance and historical continuity. Refusing this transparency at the level of narration, Ishiguro's novels generate a kind of "hesitant" knowledge that is neither homogenous nor absolute: Ishiguro's aberrant grammar resists political and cultural norms by reproducing a normalizing rhetoric (for example: "I always think it's so truly like England out here" [P 182]) excessively and inappropriately. It is important for Ishiguro's project that his novels are *not* incomprehensible, for any absolute ignorance would preserve, in its opposite, the fiction of unanimity. Against the ideal of understanding, Ishiguro commits his writing to meanings that change and to people who change their minds. Ishiguro's characters, for whom lapses in unanimity constitute a disquieting lapse in self-confidence, frequently claim incomprehensibility in order to disclaim conflict and bad feeling. The words "misunderstanding" and "mistake" thus repeat throughout Ishiguro's texts in the voice of characters and narrators whose response to conflicting interpretations is not acknowledgment but correction. So the English butler of *The Remains of the Day* calls his employer's decision to dismiss two maids because they are Jewish a "misunderstanding" (153). And Ogata-San, a former teacher and a supporter of Japanese imperialism before the Second World War, imagines in *A Pale View of Hills* that his son's criticism of imperialist education shows that he "clearly [doesn't] understand" (66). "Misunderstanding" and "mistake" are most prevalent and most significant, however, in *An Artist of the Floating World*, where they identify all those disagreements and disloyalties that the characters find too difficult to acknowledge (44, 49, 123, 155, and passim). Readers can only make sense of these novels once they, like Ishiguro's characters, exchange the rhetoric of correction for the condition of ongoing conflict.

Many of Ishiguro's reviewers have wanted to separate the practical difficulty of reading the novels from the cultural complexities that the narratives present. The reviewers attribute a Japanese style or repertoire to Ishiguro, while they remain otherwise self-conscious about the use of ethnographic language. This ambivalence tends to produce a reflexive denial of cultural or national metonymy, which often constitutes the reviewer's only articulation—and explicit circulation—of the classification he or she is trying to avoid. Consider, for example, this statement, which introduces a discussion of Ishiguro's fourth novel, *The Unconsoled*: "First, Ishiguro himself is a puzzle (I am not referring to his name or country of origin)."[19] The effect of the sentence depends on what is withheld: the reviewer's meaning, though not Ishiguro's, is so self-evident that it need not be specified; there is nothing in the review, at least before this statement, that either identifies Ishiguro's name as Japanese or justifies a connection between "name" and "country of origin." Moreover, there is nothing to tell us why or how a man or a place, if he or it were Japanese, would be "a puzzle." The reviewer imagines that this information is obvious, or at least understood; he presumes that his readers might read the name Ishiguro in the same way he says he does not. The reviewer denies a cultural specificity in the grammar of negation, but he reproduces its effect in the rhetoric of presumption: leaving his comment to speak for itself, he affiliates his readers with the clarity of his referent (what he and "we" understand) and thus contrasts them against the "puzzle" of Ishiguro's prose. The denial of reference ("I am not referring . . .") initiates the reviewer's incomprehension (puzzlement) as that which results from and distinguishes Japanese incomprehensibility.

Readers find it difficult to discuss what signifies Japan without repeating the signifiers as natural or necessary. Gabriele Annan proposes in *The New York Review of Books* that "the elegant bareness [of Ishiguro's style] inevitably reminds one of Japanese painting."[20] While Annan comes to dispute the simplicity of this association, she assumes that her readers will share her initial, "inevitable" thought. Annan describes Ishiguro's indictment of "cliché," but she produces clichés of her own:

> He writes about guilt and shame incurred in the service of duty, loyalty, and tradition. Characters who place too high—too Japanese—a price on these values are punished for it. . . . Compared to his astounding narrative sophistication, Ishiguro's message seems quite banal: Be less Japanese, less bent on dignity, less false to yourself and others, less restrained and controlled.[21]

There are three main assumptions posed as "inevitable" here: first, that "elegant bareness" points a straight line to Japanese painting; second, that a "Japanese style" would suggest a celebration of Japanese culture; and third, that Ishiguro's critique of "cliché" is a critique of "being Japanese" rather than a critique of cultural stereotypes. In the reviews of Ishiguro's work, Japanese painting *has become* the "inevitable" comparison for the novelist's style, if only because so many reviewers make the association. It might be "inevitable," then, because Ishiguro identifies and evokes the signifiers that produce the collateral effect. In any case, Annan makes no distinction between the claim that emotional restraint *is* Japanese and the possibility that such restraint reflects disagreement and uncertainty over what being Japanese involves.

As a style of art and self-presentation, restraint—like evasion—is for good reason often associated with ethical failure and political quietude. To be sure, the narrator of *The Remains of the Day*, the novel that brought Ishiguro the Booker Prize, cultivates restraint to excuse his complicity in decisions that he allowed others to make for him. However, one sees that another character in the novel, while full of "good strong opinion" (184), is not wholly admirable: he may speak for democracy among Englishmen, but he laments the decline of empire and "all kinds of little countries going independent" (192). Ishiguro suggests that literary and artistic styles that seem opinionated do not necessarily express sentiments that are honest, or even ideal. In *An Artist of the Floating World*, Ono seems to exchange cartoon stereotype and impressionist shadow for realist transparency: the narrator recalls moving in his apprenticeship from the commercial studio of Master Takeda, where the presence of "geishas, cherry trees, swimming carps, temples" (69) defined Japan in paintings sold abroad; to the workshop of Mr. Moriyama, or Mori-san, artist of pleasure houses and social decadence; and finally to the tutelage of Chishu Matsuda, an advocate of

Japanese militarism, for whom Ono turns out imperialist propaganda. There are two versions of this trajectory, which the reader is left to assemble. In the first version, which Ono describes, the career moves from one extreme to another: Ono reports that his later art had a political message but no artifice, while his earlier art was commercial or aesthetic but not political. In the second version, which Ishiguro only implies, one sees that Mori-san advocates impressionism with the enthusiasm of a dictator—those who paint in a style that differs from his example are considered "traitors" to his cause (165)—and that Ono's art is most cunning when he adopts a style of painting that seems direct and explicit.

In a work called *Complacency*, which Ono painted in support of Japanese militarism in the 1930s, the artist fuses an image of three impoverished boys with an image of three samurai warriors. The fusing is meant to suggest that the fact of poverty can only be redressed by the activities and spirit of imperialist expansion (167–68). Ono's art as a propagandist is not truer than the illusoriness of the style he adopted under a former teacher: rather, in *Complacency*, the fact of illusion is no longer represented. The propagandist style acts as if it is true, whereas the impressionist style never makes this claim: in this sense, Ishiguro suggests, the style that claims openness and truth is most deceptive. Restraint, which corresponds both to the impressionist style of painting and to the style of Ishiguro's novel, seems more honest than the apparent sincerity of wartime propaganda, though it seems only more Japanese to the extent that it is part of a long tradition of Japanese art.

In Ishiguro's novels about Japan, what counts as Japanese is what James Clifford would call, ethnographically speaking, "an achieved fiction."[22] The point of Clifford's metaphor is that cultural narratives are by definition "novelistic," which makes them no more and no less "fictional" for all that. One of Ishiguro's short stories provides a good example of the relation between what we might call insider and outsider ethnographies, Japan's stories about itself as opposed to the stories told about Japan. Japan can be fictionalized, Ishiguro suggests, but the "true" Japan is already a fiction, and not just someone else's. In "A Family Supper" (1990), suicide is offered up both as a fact of Japanese nostalgia and as a myth of Orientalism.[23] Ishiguro's story begins with a parodic account of *seppuku* in which the narrator's mother dies not through her own purposeful and ritualized disembowelment but by the accidental ingestion (at a dinner party) of a fish whose poisonous glands had been imperfectly removed. In case the reader has missed the replacement of one gutting for another, the narrator reports that in Japan "after the war," it was "all the rage" to serve *fugu* to neighbors and friends, as if to replace the traditional *seppuku* with a more sociable form of collective remorse (207).

Ishiguro's parody is recounted in the first-person voice by a young man who was born in Tokyo but has been living in California in the years just before the beginning of the story. The narrator is returning to Japan some two years after the death of his mother, which is described in the opening paragraphs. Since Ishiguro's name sounds Japanese, since he is writing in English and publishing his story in *Esquire* magazine, since he seems to know about Japanese rituals and describe them much as one who has been living far from home, perhaps in California, readers might imagine that the story of poisonous fish and hazardous dinner parties is true. Or maybe that some of it is true. But which part? Even before one gets past the framing narrative of return to the supper that is the story's putative topic, there are details—both personal and historical—that the narrative encourages its readers to accept. The parody inheres in its assumed referent, in the expectation that readers will find the fish story grotesque, bizarre, unlikely, at best, though they will recognize in it, perhaps, that common and persistent trope of "Japanese" melodrama: suicide.[24]

Left with this "reminder" of Japan's predisposition, one enters the body of the tale and the narrator's supper with his father and sister. Readers learn through dialogue, though not through narration, that the father is melancholy because his business has recently collapsed. Moreover, there are some family conflicts that Ishiguro presents only indirectly: the father is "prepared to forget" his son's unspecified "behavior" (208) in the past and longs for that time when his business did not involve "foreigners"; the son (the narrator) recalls his father striking him when he was a boy; the sister contemplates immigration to the United States with her boyfriend. These conflicts are what the characters do not talk about: the father does not want to consider the future; the narrator is reluctant to reopen prior disagreements; the sister has not told her father about her thoughts of leaving Japan. What the family does talk about, in implicit and explicit terms, is suicide: for while the mother may have died by accident, the father's business partner, we learn from the narrator's sister, has "cut his stomach with a meat knife," after killing his wife and children (210). The narrator and his father, as well as the narrator and his sister, separately discuss versions of this story twice before the meal is served. The father seems to approve his partner's action for its particular ethic and its general bravery: he calls his partner "a man of principle and honor" (208); later, the father says he wishes that he had been a pilot during the war, because "in an airplane . . . there was always the final weapon" (210). With the mother's death as background and the partner's suicide as foreground, one learns that the family is having fish for dinner, which the father has prepared by himself in the kitchen.

Ishiguro's story is about Japanese suicide, though not because the story is solely about Japan and not because Ishiguro thinks that suicide is a natural inclination of the Japanese. Rather, Ishiguro's tale is about the expectation that suicide is likely to figure in any narrative of Japanese life and about how this expectation, in its generalization about Japanese people, obscures conflicts within

Japan and within a Japanese family. "A Family Supper" is a cosmopolitan story not only because the characters think and live between nations but also because the most intimate topics within Japan, such as suicide, parenting, and shame, are generated by international concerns. As Woolf did before him, Ishiguro is marking out lines of entanglement between kitchen and battlefield, between Japanese travel and American occupation. Like many readers, the characters in the story do not see these lines because they tend to assume that collective rituals will resolve local conflicts, including local conflicts about national identity and international identification. Suicide functions as a form of nostalgic citation: it points to a past whose continuity and authenticity can be affirmed, through iteration, in the present. Ritual suicide, for the business partner and even for the air force pilots extolled by the father, is a Japanese anachronism: it seems to reproduce, but in fact merely invents a purely Japanese Japan.[25]

Ishiguro thus promotes the double consciousness that I have associated with critical cosmopolitanism: if readers see suicide as an essential, defining characteristic of Japaneseness, they may miss its fictionalization, but if they see it *only* as a Western fiction, they risk underestimating its position within Japanese culture.[26] "A Family Supper" leads its readers to believe that the father might intentionally repeat the scene of his wife's accident, but it is clear by the end, after the fish has been entirely consumed, that the remaining family disapproves of the partner's actions. The ending of "A Family Supper" seems to surprise the narrator as much as it may surprise the reader. The son, who had been living in America, does not approve of his father's values, but it is clear that he has assumed he knew what his father's values are:

> "Father," I said, finally.
>
> "Yes?"
>
> "Kikuko tells me Watanabe-san took his whole family with him."
>
> My father lowered his eyes and nodded. For some moments he seemed deep in thought. "Watanabe was very devoted to his work," he said at last. "The collapse of the firm was a very great blow to him. I fear it must have weakened his judgment."
>
> "You think what he did . . . it was a mistake?"
>
> "Why, of course. Do you see it otherwise?"
>
> (211)

Ishiguro's story closes a few paragraphs later without resolution or consolation; it ends, moreover, without the sense that suicide *is* consolation for what cannot be found or retrieved, either as national past or even as national difference. Although they do not affirm suicide as a positive act, the son and father are reluctant—the word "mistake" suggests this—to acknowledge that the business partner's values differ from their own, or that their own values in the present are different and opposed to the values of the past. "Mistake," like "misunderstanding," transforms political choice and individual action into accident and misapprehension; it implies a continuous self who has merely strayed involuntarily from a course now correctly identified.

It is significant in Ishiguro's story that there are two suicide effects in play. The business partner seems to think that suicide can compensate for the assault of foreigners and economic decline. The narrator attributes less decisiveness to the business partner's action: he seems to think that Japanese "restraint" or "despair" naturally leads to suicide. There are multiple agents in the making of the suicide fiction, and their differences can be seen most clearly in two scenes from Ishiguro's early novels. As in "A Family Supper," these scenes involve suicides described but not performed in the text. In *A Pale View of Hills*, suicide haunts the narrative: a young woman has hanged herself in the immediate past of the novel's present, but there may have been an earlier suicide—the memories are not clear—in the distant past that the narrator recalls in the middle and in the margins of her framing story. The novel opens with a stereotype of Japanese suicide, rendered clearly in the contrast between the narrator's report of her daughter's death and her description of an account written in an English newspaper.

The reader learns that the narrator's daughter, Keiko, has hanged herself just before the story begins. Keiko was born in Japan, but she and her mother later moved to England, where the mother, Etsuko, remarried in the years after the Second World War. Etsuko's second daughter, Niki, has come home after hearing about her half-sister's death. The narrator tells us:

> Keiko, unlike Niki, was pure Japanese, and more than one newspaper was quick to pick up on this fact. The English are fond of their idea that our race has an instinct for suicide, as if further explanations are unnecessary; for that was all they reported, that she was Japanese and that she had hung herself in her room.
>
> (182)

Etsuko presents Japanese suicide as "an instinct" of English invention, and this "instinct" is made newsworthy by the juxtaposition of a "pure Japanese" woman and the English room in which she died. The newspaper offers this contrast as the *effect* of death, but the novel suggests instead that it may be a *cause*: in her suicide, Keiko seems to be asserting a particular identity and a ritualized history against the demand for assimilation, perhaps also against the racism, of her English home. One might say that she is acting Japanese in order to adopt and stabilize a cultural difference that is otherwise unnoticed or superficially described. Ishiguro presents suicide as the preeminent signifier of Japanese culture, a story so common that "further explanations are unnecessary," and, at the same time and for this reason, it is a story to which he returns over and over again. Ishiguro uses suicide as a model for national fictions in other contexts: the Japanese "instinct" for suicide, which Etsuko critiques, resonates ironically with the "truly" English landscape that Etsuko celebrates at the end of the novel (182).

In *An Artist of the Floating World*, the assertive Japaneseness of suicide complicates its status as a form of antinationalist apology. Ono argues, for example, that the suicide of a former patriot, in disgrace after the war, is "honorable" because it acknowledges "mistakes," even though it maintains the codes and rituals of the past it claims to regret. Ono explains at length to his young grandson, Ichiro:

> "No. He wasn't a bad man. He was just someone who worked very hard doing what he thought was for the best. But you see, Ichiro, when the war ended, things were very different. The songs Mr Naguchi composed had become very famous, not just in this city, but all over Japan. They were sung on the radio and in bars. And the likes of your Uncle Kenji sang them when they were marching or before a battle. And after the war, Mr Naguchi thought his songs had been—well—a sort of mistake. He thought of all the people who had been killed, all the little boys your age, Ichiro, who no longer had parents, he thought of all these things and he thought perhaps his songs were a mistake. And he felt he should apologize. To everyone who was left. To little boys who no longer had parents. And to parents who had lost little boys like you. To all these people, he wanted to say sorry. I think that's why he killed himself. Mr Naguchi wasn't a bad man at all, Ichiro. He was brave to admit the mistakes he'd made. He was very brave and honourable."
>
> (155)

Suicide functions here as a disavowed apology: it offers to negate a nationalist fervor that its performance reiterates. The suicide of Mr Naguchi shows its support for political change through a public act of cultural conservatism; by choosing death, the composer recasts his "mistake" as a "brave and honourable" life. In this context, suicide is not what the West sees when confronted with Japan, but instead it is what Japan invokes and reinvents in its confrontation with the West.

Ishiguro thus represents the national allegory of Japanese suicide as an achieved fiction of English convention, as in *Pale View*'s newspaper report, but he also suggests that Japanese nationalists, Japanese migrants, and even novelists like himself have used this trope to revive and reappropriate the dead metaphors of national identity. Ishiguro's "suicide" serves to distinguish East and West: in *Pale View*, it confirms for English newspapers the Japaneseness of a Japanese-born girl living in England, and it also performs the foreignness that, for the girl, cannot be assimilated or described. In *Artist*, suicide summons Japanese tradition in the face of military defeat and "foreign" intervention. For Ishiguro, Japanese fictions do not originate, or do not only originate, from a distinctly measured outside to be found in a Western, colonialist, or Orientalist gaze. To the extent that Ishiguro's Japanese characters attribute innate values to common rituals—they attribute "honor" to suicide, for example—these Japanese fictions are what Roland Barthes calls "myths": "less reality than a certain knowledge of reality."[27] Nature is defined by use, as Barthes writes: "A tree is a tree. Yes, of course. But a tree as expressed by Minou Drouet is no longer quite a tree, it is a tree which is decorated, adapted to a certain type of consumption, laden with literary self-indulgence, revolt, images, in short with a type of social *usage* which is added to pure matter."[28] In Ishiguro's novels, characters *use* suicide to confirm a past and to define it. Making history, the myth of Japanese suicide establishes roots in world that otherwise seems to float.

Ishiguro undoes national allegory by allegorizing the invention of national identities. Seen this way, Ishiguro's novels are both more and less mimetic than most of his readers would have it. Ishiguro resists not simply the readers who find Japan or England embodied in his texts but also those who acknowledge his fictionalizing only to argue that a true Japaneseness exists somewhere else. Reviewers who notice that the stories produce "the sound of authenticity," "what looks to a Western reader like a Japanese text," or "the illusion of depth and feeling where there is only cartoon drawing and cliché" still oppose these reality effects to the reality of Japanese characteristics that have not been represented.[29] It is Ishiguro's analogy between reality effects in novels and social realities in life that bring his texts closest to the truth of national fictions.

✳ ✳ ✳

Even as Ishiguro's texts suggest that "restraint" is not simply, or not necessarily metonymic of Japanese culture, they regularly propose that styles of presentation are characteristic of particular identities. The works least identified with a Japanese setting or experience, which offer no explicit references to Japan whatsoever, provide a helpful template for Ishiguro's project, since they allow us to disaggregate narrative estrangement from the representation of worlds that are, for most English readers, already strange. Stevens, the narrator of *The Remains of the Day*, proudly attributes his own purposeful discretion to the essential reticence—"dignity"—of a genuine Englishness. For Stevens, discretion is neither an intention nor a failing; it is an indispensable characteristic. The countryside of England, where Stevens manages Darlington Hall, may be distinguished from the "sights offered in such places as Africa and America" by its lack of "unseemly demonstrativeness." Lest one fail to connect such scenic moderation with the narrator's own taciturn performance, Stevens offers a closer metaphor: it is, he explains, "the very *lack* of drama or spectacle that sets the beauty of our land apart" (28). If a distinctive artlessness is the hallmark of English manner, it is the accomplishment of this effect, everywhere boasted by Stevens, that nevertheless gives its claims away. "Dignity" turns out to be a cover story, not a disinterested attribute of English identity but a purposeful stylization of it; it is, in this case, merely the strategic defense of a guilty butler. The emotional restraint necessitated by "dignity" leads Stevens to facilitate the Nazi sympathies of his employer, Lord Darlington, by refusing to consider them. Playing valet to the German officers who frequented Darlington Hall before the war, Stevens fancies his circumspection as a kind of British patriotism. In *The Remains of the Day*, therefore, Ishiguro allows us to imagine that the text is not simply a description of England but an expression of it.[30]

For Ono in *Artist*, as for Stevens in *Remains*, the perceived authenticity of local characteristics depends on an exoticism displaced elsewhere. Ishiguro wants us to see that national traditions are forged by international encounters. Ishiguro's narrative thus conveys the nearness of Japan in the distance of other cultures. Salman Rushdie has proposed "authenticity" as "the respectable child of old-fashioned exoticism,"[31] and Ishiguro exploits this family relation: what seems most Japanese in *Artist* is the fascination with and seeming mistranslation of American culture. Chantal Zabus has included Ishiguro among other contemporary writers who write in English but were born outside of Great Britain. These writers, Zabus posits, are "exiled in English" and often "write with an accent" to express their alienation within the Anglophone literary and cultural tradition.[32] On his own, Ishiguro has indeed called himself "a kind of a homeless writer," neither "a very English Englishman" nor "a very Japanese Japanese either."[33] His sense that national identities require emphatic participation—if one is not "very," one is not quite "at home"—leads him not to reject or hybridize standard English (as Rushdie does) but to reproduce it aberrantly.

In *Artist*, there is rarely a break in the frame of English narration. Typically, Ono's voice comes with all the elements of polite and educated British speech, and little sounds "Japanese" about it. A meal one enjoys is "very nice" (136); a routine matter is "some such thing" (20). However, what seems "standard" or beneath notice does become conspicuous at times. The naturalized vernacular of the novel's English is strikingly ruptured in those moments when Ichiro, Ono's grandson, imitates characters from American popular culture:

"Very impressive, Ichiro. But tell me, who were you pretending to be?"

"You guess, Oji."

"Hmm. Lord Yoshitsune perhaps? No? A samurai warrior, then? Hmm. Or a ninja perhaps? The Ninja of the Wind."

"Oji's completely on the wrong scent."

"Then tell me. Who were you?"

"Lone Ranger!"

"What?"

"Lone Ranger! Hi yo Silver!"

"Lone Ranger? Is that a cowboy?"

"Hi yo Silver!" Ichiro began to gallop again, and this time made a neighing noise.

(30)

Ichiro's "Hi yo Silver!" and, later, "Popeye Sailorman" (152) are not quite right. They are a long way from his other Anglophone pronouncements, which are usually rather precise, if somewhat imperative. Ono cannot identify his grandson's appropriations of either the Lone Ranger or Popeye; he does not know who these characters are or even that they are American. It is the reader's ability to recognize America, and Ono's failure to do so, that registers Japan as a place, if not itself foreign, then surely foreign to us.

Ichiro's mispronunciation of American popular culture early in the novel serves to demonstrate both an international and a generational drama, in which Ono's daughter and son do not speak English but are willing to learn, while Ono finds the idea of English speech from his Japanese grandson "extraordinary" (35). Ono is shocked by two developments: his grandson is trying to speak a language other than Japanese, and his grandson is imitating not Japanese heroes but American ones. The generational conflict registers a change in the private choices made by Ono's family and also within the public choices made by the Japanese government, which before the war had tried to exclude European and American influences from Japanese art and culture. In the substitution of American cowboys for Japanese warriors, Ishiguro does not propose that images of militarism and imperialism have been removed from family life—the cowboys-and-Indians motif suggests otherwise—but only that everyday family decisions, such as whether to go to a movie, have national as well as international consequences.

Of course, even if Ichiro had gotten his imitations right, an America defined by Popeye and the Lone Ranger is not so very different from a Japan identified by geishas and cherry trees. America as foreign trope—"Hi yo Silver!"—partakes of the metonymic exoticism that is everywhere criticized in Ishiguro's work.[34] In *Pale View*, Etsuko's fantasy of English pastoral prompts, like Ichiro's fantasy in *Artist*, a lexical awkwardness: "I always think it's so truly like England out here," the Japanese-born narrator tells her daughter, Niki. *Pale View* is narrated from an unspecified English village where Etsuko now lives. Reflecting on her arrival from Nagasaki after the Second World War, Etsuko continues and reiterates: "When your father first brought me down here, Niki, I remember thinking how so truly like England everything looked. All these fields, and the house too. It was just the way I always imagined England would be and I was so pleased" (182). Etsuko refuses to recognize the difference between the imperfect England she experiences (recall that her eldest daughter, born in Japan, hanged herself) and the idealized England she conjured as an escape from postwar Nagasaki. In a single gesture, this moment of repeated affirmation and infelicitous phrasing signals the unreliability of Etsuko's narrative, the exoticism of its rhetoric, and the foreignness of her perspective. The emphatic nostalgia of Etsuko's language records her failing effort to make England correspond to the place she allowed herself to imagine. For her, "England" remains an optimistic fiction from a Japanese past.

That familiar category, "unreliable narrator," would seem to characterize the first-person protagonist in every one of Ishiguro's six novels to date. Throughout Ishiguro's work, the signs of this unreliability are often indistinguishable, as they are in *Pale View*, from the details that make a speaker seem foreign to the novel's discourse. To consider this connection, one might observe that unreliable narrators typically articulate values or interpretations jarring to the reader's expectations.[35] That is, the unreliable narrator is one whose values are visible, for the category functions only if readers can recognize the speaker's perspective as radically different from their own. The *unreliable* narrator emerges in a contested or troubled identification between narrator and reader. In this sense, unreliable narrators are an effect of cultural and conventional disjunction: we know that the narrator's world is not ours, not because we perceive the content of this difference, but because we perceive the fact of difference at all. This difference is marked: unlike the "reliable" narrator, the unreliable narrator is perceived as *being* the story rather than merely *having* one.

Unreliable narrators regularly project their stories into the lives of the people they describe. One thinks of Nelly Dean in *Wuthering Heights* or Charles Kinbote in *Pale Fire*, both of whom liked to imagine the considerable effect of their influence in the choices made by others. This desire, which the narrators hardly realize, is part of the story these novels tell. Ishiguro's narrators, though they also offer information about themselves that they do not know or do not say they are providing, importantly reverse the usual projective process: rather than claim all stories as their own, they try to propose that their own stories are always someone else's. The anxiety and disappointment they detail, they assure us, do not belong to them. For the reader, Ishiguro registers this disavowal through the displacement or abstraction of pronouns. Floating worlds, unreliable and gestural, are thus articulated in and as floating words. This analogy between the processes of culture and the processes of the novel is one of the aspects of Ishiguro's work that seems most continuous with earlier modernist fiction. Ishiguro's aberrant grammar has the effect not of substitution but of comparison and reflection: individual people and distinctive loyalties, no longer subordinated by time and moral certainty, become less individuated and less distinctive, competing truths rather than continuous ones.

For example, in *Remains of the Day*, Stevens translates personal choices into universal rhetoric by addressing his own morality as a matter of English "dignity." When the housekeeper Miss Kenton accuses him of complacency towards the Jewish maids who were fired, Stevens denies indifference, replying: "Naturally, one disapproved of the dismissals. One would have thought that quite self-evident" (154). Ishiguro has the wit to notice that the choice of "one" over "I" unites an "impersonal" grammar with the rhetoric of English impersonality. Stevens's language seems at once natural—what a butler sounds like—and yet tactical. "One" negates the claim to personal feeling Stevens's statement would otherwise offer, and it is stilted, an attempt to sound like the gentleman that Stevens, in his indifference and in his status as a butler, fails to be. "One" cannot be said to replace "I" exactly, since "one" leaves open the possibility that "I" is implied; moreover, we might notice that "I" is everywhere dependent on Stevens's fantasy about what "one" would do.

Reading this last scene, it is important to see the "I" that "one" at once effaces and putatively includes. A narrator is unreliable if he or she blithely conflates a unique and subjective experience with a generic and objective fact: Stevens allows "one's" disapproval to compensate for *his* silence. The reader's assumption that a statement has a universal application rather than an individual specificity is an everyday force of habit, certainly a valid expectation for readers trained, as we are, in the traditional model of sympathetic reading. However, an unreliable narrator, for whom our expectations fail to function, makes this habit visible. For Ishiguro, the realization that a speaker has fused a story about him- or herself with a story about someone else revises the status of linear past and discernable narrator, as well as the status of blame, guilt, and loyalty. Readers are no longer confident of knowing a fact or a character when they see one.

One learns from a slippery pronoun in *Pale View of Hills* that Etsuko may be revealing information about herself when she says she is telling a story about Sachiko, a woman she knew in Nagasaki. At the time Etsuko met Sachiko, about three decades before the novel opens, the latter woman was planning to marry an American soldier stationed in Japan for the postwar occupation. Sachiko was hoping to leave Nagasaki with her future husband and her daughter, and this is not unlike the (not shown, little discussed) trajectory we know Etsuko follows, as she marries an Englishman and takes her daughter abroad. In a scene she describes from memory, Etsuko tries to convince Sachiko's daughter, Mariko, that a departure for America will "turn out well," though at the last moment she shifts from "you" to "we": "if you don't like it over there, we can always come back" (173). This is the text's first explicit signal that the girl Etsuko calls

Mariko in her memories might be Keiko, Etsuko's daughter who hangs herself in England many years later. The narrator shifts to "we," but the girl is still called "Mariko" as the chapter closes. It is hard to tell where Etsuko's past begins and Sachiko's narrative ends, or whether Sachiko is really there at all.

An Artist of the Floating World complicates this structure of displaced narrative by recounting and layering, in a palimpsest of memories, several stories at once. Toward the end of the novel, Ono describes a long-past confrontation with Mori-san that took place in "that same pavilion" (175, 177) where, he tells us, a later conversation with his own student, Kuroda, also unfolded. The later scene is never explicitly narrated in the novel. In the earlier scene, Ono tells Mori-san that he needs to leave the "floating world" and its art for "something more tangible than those pleasurable things that disappear with the morning light" (180). Mori-san, who has already confiscated Ono's new "experimental" paintings, demands the last of Ono's unfinished work, the "one or two" canvases Ono did not store with the others (178). Eventually, when Ono demurs, Mori-san offers a cutting response. As Ono reports this exchange, he interrupts his account to acknowledge that Mori-san's language might in fact be his own, the phrases he later used in a similar exchange with Kuroda; Ono is not sure what he has remembered and what he has projected backward.

The retrospective tense that tells us that the earlier scene with Mori-san is at an end—"I still turn over in my mind that cold winter's morning"—also indicates that the much later scene with Kuroda has already taken place as well (180). "That" recalls "that same pavilion" and links the two events (175): the "arrogance and possessiveness" Ono seems to attribute to Mori-san seamlessly becomes the very attitude he adopted towards Kuroda (180). In this transition, Ono's narrative jumps ahead. He is now visiting Kuroda's home where imperial police have taken the younger artist into custody and burned his paintings because Ono, angry at his student's turn away from nationalist themes, has fingered him as a political traitor. There is "the smell of burning," a smell we associate with a childhood memory Ono relates at the beginning of the novel, in which his father, trying to urge a more "useful" profession, destroys all of his son's early paintings but the "one or two" Ono has hidden (43–47). Ono later associates this same smell with the damage to his adult home and the death of his wife in the war, as well as with the death of his son, Kenji, who was a soldier in the Japanese army ("'The smell of burning still makes me uneasy,' I remarked. 'It's not so long ago it meant bombings and fire'" [200]). The repetition of phrases, "the smell of burning" and those "one or two" paintings withheld from father and teacher by son and student (43, 178), implies that Ono's discussion with Mori-san and the episode with his father stand in for a scene we will never see: Ono's rejection and betrayal of Kuroda, who is subsequently tortured as a government traitor. Rather than shift from personal to impersonal as in *Remains*, or from "you" to "we" as in

Pale View, Ono's telltale, demonstrative pronoun—"that same pavilion"—merely floats, leaving the reader to imagine a scene that is not or cannot be given and to measure the nearness of artistic and political treason.

The betrayal of Kuroda seems to be the political kernel or "primal scene" of Ishiguro's novel, even though it is difficult to separate this scene, which we never see, from all of its echoes throughout the text: we come to know the betrayal of Kuroda—a betrayal prompted by Ono's inability to tolerate Kuroda's independence—only in so far as Ono compares it to other, represented betrayals in his life.[36] As the novel continues, the later scenes offer new interpretations of early ones: the scenes that seem like echoes, that seem like pale views of the narrator's past, introduce some information for the first time. In retrospect, the given scene with Mori-san and the implied scene with Kuroda lend a political tone to the scene with Ono's father, which constitutes the first betrayal in the novel: as Kuroda is imprisoned for refusing to be "useful" to the militarist regime, so Ono's father, who punishes his son for choosing art over business, seems to enforce a similar orthodoxy (46). The novel not only refuses to separate politics and art but suggests that art is both political and politicized when its values (decadence, imagination, nonconformity) are among those that politicians seek to suppress. For the novel, the refusal to inhabit, to affirm, or to represent "the real world"—as Ono's imperialist mentor demands, as Ono's father demanded before him—is its own political act (172).

From the novel's later point of view, patriarchy is legible as an element of fascism, and this implication is present in the relationship between Ono and his father, in the relationship between Ono and his children, and in the metaphors of obedience that Ishiguro uses to describe Japan's postwar relationship to the United States (185). Ishiguro presents Ichiro's reluctance to watch a film about a destructive monster as an alternative to the heroic nationalism that Ono cultivated in his son, who died while an eager soldier in the war.[37] To his daughter, Setsuko, who does not want Ichiro to acquire the values passed down to her brother, Ono responds, " 'You know, I remember your mother protesting in just the same way when I decided to let Kenji have a taste of sake at this age. Well, it certainly did your brother no harm' " (157). In turn, Setsuko reminds her father that his past attitudes, both in relation to his wife and in relation to his son, were not, from a postwar perspective, for the best: " 'There is no doubt Father devoted the most careful thought to my brother's upbringing. Nevertheless, in the light of what came to pass, we can perhaps see that on one or two points at least, Mother may in fact have had the more correct ideas' " (158). Ishiguro would have his readers see, as Ono begins to see, that what is "correct" has changed: Ono needs to betray his past—to display it, to question it, and to turn away from the values of absolutism—in order to live responsibly in the present. Ishiguro demonstrates in these examples that people may commit treason not only because they do not embrace the values of their government but also because the values that once seemed loyal can become disloyal, from the perspective of a new leader or a new teacher or a new parent: Ono's past activities, which once seemed like "the best of things," now seem, even to him, like "things best forgotten" (94); those whom Ono has called "victims of the occupying forces" (88) are now called "war criminals" (56). The lesson here is not that new loyalties must replace old ones but that all-encompassing forms of loyalty have to become more discriminating in some ways and less discriminating in others: it is not enough to follow the American generals instead of the Japanese emperor, Ishiguro suggests; instead, Ono has to learn to distinguish attitudes of loyalty, conflicting loyalties (to country, children, friends, art), and the interest that any given loyalty serves.

✳ ✳ ✳

That the violence Ono attributes to his father and his teacher may be his own violence, that the absolute allegiance that they demanded may be what he also required: these alter the lessons of the novel and establish betrayal as an essential aspect of the novel's instruction. Ono tells a number of stories, but his subsequent unreliability, our sense that he has evaded both scrutiny and responsibility, obscures the content and the characters that he has led his readers to discern. The telling of stories turns out to be the subject as well as the strategy of Ishiguro's novel. As reliable and unreliable narration are usually distinguished, one is either the master of a narrative, one who possesses knowledge, or one *is* the narrative, one about whom knowledge is generated. In *Artist*, however, the narrator's inability or unwillingness to maintain these distinctions, to make it clear for the reader whose experiences he is describing, produces several histories and several perspectives. We know Ono through his relation to others, through the words he recalls as other people's words, through the actions we must guess by implication. His stories—abstract, indirect, partial—constitute the substance of the storyteller, but they may fail to produce an authoritative plot, definitive self, or coherent community. Kathleen Wall has suggested, writing about *Remains of the Day*, that, "changes in how subjectivity is viewed will inevitably be reflected in the way reliable or unreliable narration is presented" (22). As Ishiguro accommodates and theorizes such changes, his narratives estrange and challenge the theory as well as the content of national identity. What readers confidently label "foreign" or "Japanese" in Ishiguro's work may be an attempt to reify a process of classification that his work aims to obstruct.

Confidence and labeling are themselves primary topics in Ishiguro's novels, and that primacy is nowhere more apparent than in the first paragraph of his very first book. *A Pale View of Hills* begins:

Niki, the name we finally gave my younger daughter, is not an abbreviation; it was a compromise I reached with her father. For paradoxically it was he who wanted to give her a Japanese name, and I—perhaps out of some selfish desire not to be reminded of the past—insisted on an English one. He finally agreed to Niki, thinking it had some vague echo of the East about it.

(9)

Ishiguro's oeuvre opens with an echo: Niki, a name that is not "a Japanese name" but merely sounds like one. "Niki" imitates what is already an imitation. It is an echo of an echo, a "vague" repetition of an abstracted place, "the East." The narrator wishes to forget the past, but the "compromise" name intones, in its more-than-Englishness, the nagging effect of reminder—not Japan but its reverberating, persistent memento. The novel thus opens with an empty gesture of several sorts: the father does not speak Japanese, but he wants to give his daughter a Japanese name; the compromise name is English in origin but sounds Japanese, though only to an English father. The echo represents another (though the first) structure of failed consolation, where what is missing is always out of reach, in the previous city, in the past, in a fantasy of transparent proper nouns.[38]

Ishiguro's novels associate loyalty with what seem to be two very different impulses: fascism, on the one hand, and multiculturalism, on the other. Above all, this may be Ishiguro's treason. In *Artist*, oaths of loyalty recapitulate an undernoticed coercion: even after the war, when Ono finally announces that his past influence is "best erased and forgotten," he observes his son-in-law's father watching him "like a teacher waiting for a pupil to go on with a lesson" (123). The new loyalty enforces old positions: no longer a sensei, Ono must be a student. The postwar slogans of the American occupation ("our country has finally set its sights on the future" [186]) echo the polished assurance of prewar imperialism ("Japan must go forward" [169]). Ishiguro uses this repetition with very little difference to make allies of American democracy and Japanese militarism, both certain of progress and continuity. He replaces continuity with transience: less heroic and less affirmative, Ishiguro's progress is visible in Ono's daughters, who no longer obey; in Ono's grandson, who is allowed to admit fear; and even in Ono, who seems to learn that fleeting moments may be more valuable, and more reliable, than permanent monuments. Committed to change but also to conflict, Ishiguro commits to treason: his floating worlds betray their narrators, and they everywhere betray "us."

5

RUSHDIE'S MIX-UP

*The trouble with the Engenglish is that their hiss hiss history happened overseas,
so they dodo don't know what it means.*

—SALMAN RUSHDIE, *THE SATANIC VERSES*

KAZUO ISHIGURO SHOWS that the rhetoric of misunderstanding, often a result of cross-cultural or cross-generational encounters, tends to erase social
conflict and political history: his characters find it easier to describe a passive
state of confusion than to say that they disagreed in the past or that they no longer agree in the present. By allowing the past to irrupt into the present, Ishiguro suggests that treason—the willingness to test and change allegiances—is
a principle of critical cosmopolitanism and political transformation. Salman
Rushdie, too, is interested in misunderstandings and mistakes, though he tends
to approach them synchronically rather than diachronically. Whereas Ishiguro
revives the modernist critique of progress and heroism, which I've associated
with Conrad and Woolf, Rushdie emphasizes the aleatory, the trivial, and the
playful, modernist strategies that I've associated with Joyce. Like Joyce, Rushdie proposes that ordinary social and semantic mistakes—mix-ups—can create
opportunities for effective, if sometimes impermanent agency.

Whiskey Sisodia's parodic, stuttering slur about "the Engenglish"—that they
are confused about their identity because their past is defined by an empire they
never understood and no longer possess—became in the 1990s a kind of wry
slogan for postcolonial criticism: Homi Bhabha embraced the spirit of Sisodia's
claim for his theory of "DissemiNation" and cultural hybridity;[1] Ian Baucom
later reproduced Sisodia's remark, taken from Salman Rushdie's *Satanic Verses*
(1988), as the opening sentence of his book on Englishness and empire.[2] Bhabha
and Baucom use Sisodia's comment to pursue a similar line of argument: Sisodia demonstrates in Bhabha's essay that "the national narrative is a site of ambivalent identification" (167)—over-here is mixed-up with over-there—while

he confirms in Baucom's account that empire is "less a place where England exerts control than the place where England loses command of its own narrative of identity" (3). For Bhabha and Baucom, Rushdie's parody registers a mix-up of place: English history is defined by events that "happened" somewhere other than England; the conquered territories on which English culture was imposed also served to change what English culture is.

An Indian film producer living in London, S. S. "Whiskey" Sisodia, whose name voices his favorite drink ("Scotch and Sisodia"), likes to announce "The Trouble With The English" in a litany of jibes meant to reverse the usual anti-immigrant litany directed against British Indians and other minorities. In the slogan about English history, Sisodia conveys a witty, generalized indictment, while disrupting the rhetoric of impersonal generalization; eminently quotable, Sisodia's edgy one-liner offers an implicit parody of racist iteration and habitual abuse. As the slogan is repeated, "England loses command" in the present as well as in the past because the glory of over-here, maintained through the kinds of comments that Sisodia imitates, is diminished by the perspective of "overseas," which Sisodia interposes by "hissing" at history and by comparing the English to a "dodo," proverbially foolish and extinct. Sisodia's critique is in good part a slogan about slogans, a rallying cry about the nature of xenophobic rallying.

It is important to notice that in Sisodia's comment there are, really, two mixups, and they are not equivalent: there is the confusion that Sisodia describes (the effect of colonialism) and also the confusion that Sisodia introduces (the effect of anticolonial critique). "The English" may be mixed-up, but so is Sisodia's language: he stutters; he combines an attack on colonialism with the rhetoric of colonialist attack; and he introduces an additional layer of commentary by mixing into his intentional statement what seem to be unintentional sounds or partial words. Rushdie is widely associated with the indiscriminate celebration of mixing or hybridity, in part because his novels seem to perform this celebration, in their exuberant combination of genres and cultural references, and in part because his essays call for "*mélange*" as a practice both of cultures and of writing.[3] In this chapter, I will be focusing on Rushdie's later novels and stories, where he presents examples of mixing that are ambivalent at best—street encounters between immigrants and nativist thugs, the hybridity of U.S. capitalism, the racism of a British consulate—and thus asks his readers to make distinctions among social contexts and social actors that are not all the same. In the passage from *The Satanic Verses*, Rushdie is suggesting that some kinds of mixing, such as Sisodia's, are critical and oppositional, whereas other kinds, such as British colonialism, are not. I argue that Rushdie uses the mix-up to introduce new experiences of contemporary immigration and also to distinguish between the cosmopolitanism of exploitative fusion, on the one hand, and the cosmopolitanism of tactical syncretism, on the other.

In his writing about immigration, Rushdie tests different models of cosmopolitanism by manipulating new and old slogans, clichés, aphorisms, epithets, proverbs, and mottos of national culture. Mixing up everyday language, Rushdie's characters resist generalizations by inserting new perspectives and by reflecting on the language of assimilation. In *The Satanic Verses*, Sisodia's remark functions as *critique* as well as *correction* because it redescribes "the English" while also changing the conditions of description. Cultural axioms must be resisted, Rushdie proposes, not only because they are fundamental to racist paradigms but also because racist paradigms are fundamental to them. Since axiomatic thought tends to affirm consistent differences, Rushdie argues, it cannot constitute a practical or even ethical model for antiracist literature. Rushdie abjures correctness; only cultural mix-ups, he contends, will make things right.

Rushdie's contention, that correctness does not constitute an ethical model for antiracist or multicultural literature, echoes Kazuo Ishiguro's project in the present and recall James Joyce's in the past. Rushdie's position does not contribute easily or even principally to a politics of collective action, and some critics have attributed his mix-ups not to analytic purpose but to professional convenience and social accommodation.[4] Timothy Brennan has described Rushdie as a preeminent example of "convenient" cosmopolitanism.[5] Rushdie's work is convenient, Brennan argues, because it does not exhibit sufficient antagonism: according to Brennan, Rushdie fails to project the traditions, behaviors, and tastes appropriate to his origins, offering the West "a flirtation with change" rather than a confrontation with difference.[6] I argue that Rushdie uses strategies of flirtation and mix-up to offer an alternative to the opposition between accommodation and antagonism. But he is not offering a heroic alternative: national distinctiveness and cultural assertion are the purposeful targets, rather than the accidental or collateral victims, of Rushdie's fiction.

Rushdie emphasizes the contingent, the popular, and the trivial rather than the traditional, the correct, and the necessary. His rejection of decorum and correctness may seem like a truism of late modernity, but Rushdie suggests that such values persist or have resurfaced not only in new forms of racism and fundamentalism but also in forms of "planetary humanism," such as multiculturalism and some brands of cosmopolitanism. Flirting, mixing things up, Rushdie imagines new opportunities for agency and intimacy within the imposed conditions of cultural encounter. The psychoanalyst and cultural critic Adam Phillips promotes flirtation as a social affect that makes room for new, not yet imagined relationships.[7] Phillips argues, "flirting may not be a poor way of doing something better, but a different way of doing something else" (xxii). Rushdie refuses to make absolute political distinctions, not least because he rejects absolutism's tone: he values commitments that are various, momentary, and even contradictory. Rushdie's emphasis on less ambitious forms of agency shares in Virginia Woolf's effort to understand ordinary actions politically and in the efforts of cosmopolitan theorists who have argued for an internationalist ethics of the everyday.[8]

Rushdie's literary mix-ups are "tactics" of countercultural bricolage.[9] Michel de Certeau's immigrant-tactician, "a North African living in Paris or Roubaix (France)," resembles many of Rushdie's characters (*Practice of Everyday Life*, 30). The North African, de Certeau explains, mixes up French culture by mixing himself in:

> [He] insinuates *into* the system imposed on him by the construction of a low-income housing development or of the French language the ways of "dwelling" (in a house or in a language) peculiar to his native Kabylia. He superimposes them and, by that combination, creates for himself a space in which he can find *ways of using* the constraining order of the place or of the language. Without leaving the place where he has no choice but to live and which lays down its law for him, he establishes within it a degree of *plurality* and creativity. By an art of being in between, he draws unexpected results from his situation.
>
> (30; EMPHASIS IN ORIGINAL)

Like Rushdie, de Certeau recognizes and values the small degrees of resistance that make room for plurality, creativity, and transformation. In some ways, de Certeau is an analogue for Rushdie: they are both itinerant ethnographers, and both emphasize the experience of immigration. Indeed, de Certeau's theory of everyday life is in many ways modeled on immigrant life, and in this sense his art—"being in between"—is also Rushdie's. Yet whereas the sociologist's tactics are ephemeral, Rushdie's create artifacts. For Rushdie's characters, creativity is often temporary, but for Rushdie there is production: his "use" of British culture has changed the British novel, making its norms more visible and also more variable.

✳✳✳

The Satanic Verses marks a significant shift in Rushdie's career from narratives of decolonization in India and Pakistan to narratives of immigration in Britain and the United States. Writing in the *New York Times Magazine* in January 1989, Gerald Marzorati calls *The Satanic Verses* "the first major novel of the new England, an England with more than two million immigrants, one in which it is no longer clear, exactly, what 'English life' comprises, what 'being English' means";[10] Timothy Brennan, in his book-length study of Rushdie's work, describes *The Satanic Verses* as "the most ambitious novel yet published to deal with the immigrant experience in Britain";[11] and Ian Baucom, linking the novel's tactics to the South London antiracism riots, which the novel describes, argues that *The Satanic Verses* serves to "re-create England through an act of disorderly conduct" (*Out of Place*, 200). In his writing, Rushdie is indeed "disorderly," because he refuses to make sharp distinctions among national cultures and political regimes: he is critical of India and Pakistan but also of Britain; of the after-effects of colonialism but also of the present-effects of immigration; of British racists but also of Islamic fundamentalists. Rushdie's disorderly conduct has brought controversy as well as acclaim: for arguing that mistakes are a norm not only of British culture but of Islamic culture as well, Rushdie was condemned to death for blasphemy by the Ayatollah Khomeini of Iran; the Iranian government continued to support the death sentence, announced in February 1989, until 1998.[12]

Writing about immigration, Rushdie develops the mix-up as an analytic strategy of social confusion and cultural mélange. He elaborates this strategy in his volume of stories *East, West* (1994) and then turns to reflect on its efficacy in his novel about New York City, *Fury* (2001). To be sure, the mix-up is also a feature of Rushdie's early work: in *Midnight's Children* (1981), Rushdie's celebrated novel about India after the British Empire, the narrator is swapped with another infant at birth and then raised by his adopted parents; this private mix-up prefigures the novel's several mistakes, or modifications, of political history. *Midnight's Children* presents cultural mix-ups as accidents of colonialism; in the later work, however, mix-ups become postures of immigrant culture. In the remainder of this chapter, I will identify those protocols of flirtation and incorrectness that Rushdie articulates first in *The Satanic Verses* and then displays most fully in the urban scenes—sidewalks, public buildings, auctions, and apartment houses—of *East, West* and *Fury*.

In their treatment of cultural traditions, including those traditions to which Rushdie does not belong, Rushdie's mix-ups seek to disrupt "the stultifications of excessive respect."[13] Rushdie argues that respect, because it privileges distance and consistency, is not an effective strategy of antiracism or intercultural exchange. Rushdie's critique of respect leads him to adopt a playful, comic tone, even and especially when he describes the effects of ethnic violence and social antagonism. Rushdie works to oppose these effects by creating unexpected alliances, both among characters and among cultural traditions; he generates new intimacies in the transient encounters and everyday mixing of metropolitan immigration.

Rushdie's persistent, exuberant humor differentiates his writing from the lighter, more ironic humor of Kazuo Ishiguro and from the more reflective, melancholic novels of W. G. Sebald. But Rushdie shares with Ishiguro and Sebald the effort to write British novels while rewriting what it means to be British.

While Rushdie was born in India, his family migrated to England when he was fourteen and then to Pakistan two years later; he was educated in England from the age of thirteen; he has written his novels, full of references to British and U.S. and Indian culture, while living in England or the United States; he is a British citizen who today resides both in New York and in London. Rushdie is part of a "we" who are not English and thus can speak of them, "hiss" at them, and criticize their racist attitudes; however, he is also part of a "we" who take part in English culture, who have occupied places where English history "happened," and who now occupy England. Since moving to the United States, Rushdie has also become part of a "we" who sometimes live in Britain but do not wish to be confused with all Britons or with the glorified Britannia imagined by Anglophilic Americans.[14] Writing in 1988, the year that Rushdie published *The Satanic Verses*, Stuart Hall observed two versions of "difference" within "the new ethnicities" of late-twentieth-century Britain: "the 'difference' which makes a radical and unbridgeable separation" (the *we* who are not English) and the "'difference' which is positional, conditional, conjunctural" (the *we* who are heterogeneous and sometimes part of *they*).[15] The latter "difference," Hall acknowledged, shares in Jacques Derrida's concept of *différance* and thus resists any position that is not conditional and unfixed ("The New Ethnicities," 162). Like Hall, who advocates a combination of differences, Rushdie seeks to retain the oppositional energy that is generated by separatist difference and yet also to occupy a conditional difference that is less rigid in its distinctions. Rushdie's writing is not separate from the British tradition, but it is often critical of that tradition. And it does articulate specific experiences of travel and transience.

We can see this double aspiration in Rushdie's tactics of nicknaming, such as those emplyed in Sisodia's motto, which create new communities while bringing visibility to the several communities to which any one person belongs. As I have noted in previous chapters, modernist writers often use stutters or stammers to register antagonisms within a civic rhetoric that claims to be uniform and consistent; the stutter represents the discrepancies within collective assertion; it registers a protest that is otherwise prohibited. Sisodia's stutter, for example, serves to dislodge "the English" from one place and from one historical perspective; the stutter helps to remind readers that Sisodia is in some ways foreign to the language of generalization and in other ways entangled with the culture and language he disdains.[16] "The English," Sisodia's comment suggests, are less homogenous than they—and he—think they are, and also they are less homogenous than the system of racist aphorism generally proclaims. By speaking of "the English" rather than, say, "the British," Sisodia is invoking "the particularly closed, exclusive and regressive form of English national identity," to use Stuart Hall's formulation, that distinguishes between British citizens, who may be black or white and whose backgrounds may be Indian or Scottish, and

Englishmen, who are meant to be white, native to England, and culturally homogenous ("The New Ethnicities," 161). Writing about the history of race in Britain, Robert Young contends, " 'British' is the name imposed by the English on the non-English."[17] This imposition serves, Young argues, at once to mask and to mark the English conquest of Scotland, Wales, Ireland, India, Africa, and the Caribbean (*Colonial Desire*, 3). Purposefully, Sisodia is using an exclusive name to send up exclusivity: he is suggesting that exclusivity no longer exists in contemporary London and that exclusivity was, in the past, a function of political idiom rather than genuine distinction. Put another way, Sisodia suggests that English exclusivity was a ruse: it masked the heterogeneity of British national and international culture.

As Sisodia's stutter makes "the English" more diverse, Rushdie's own stutter, in an interview from 1989, transforms the collective voice—"we"—into a perspective that is at once more intimate and less consistent than it was before. Rushdie's locution, what seems like an infelicitous repetition, produces an aberrant grammar: "We are increasingly becoming a world of migrants, made up of bits and fragments from here, there. We are here. And we have never really left anywhere we have been."[18] The content of *we* changes in this passage, and this change records a diversification not only of national cultures but of rhetoric as well. Because "we are here," Rushdie proposes, the impersonal, universal *we* (the community of all persons) of the first sentence becomes the specific *we* (the community of migrants) of the last. Rushdie's transformation implies that local collectivity—"we"—has a new temporality: "here" now includes, and will keep including, the "bits and fragments" of places that are spatially but not culturally distant.

In his own voice and in Sisodia's, Rushdie is resisting authenticity, whose rhetoric of accuracy and distinctiveness was crucial to debates about immigration and antiracism in the 1980s.[19] Immigrant writers were asked to choose between one and several traditions: would they immerse their work in the homogeneous tradition of a particular, oppositional culture or in the intermingled traditions of a mongrelized Britain? As Jeremy Waldron observes in a retrospective essay, the structure of this choice assumed that there were, in the 1980s, homogenous traditions to choose. Like Rushdie, Waldron rewrites the question, shifting his emphasis from a choice among two existing *versions* of culture (homogeneous and mixed) to a choice among two existing *theories* of culture (homogenous and mixed): Waldron does not ask, is it more or less authentic to choose a separate tradition; instead, he asks, do distinct, separate traditions exist?[20] For his part, Rushdie argues that there is no correct tradition to choose, and indeed he comes to reject correctness altogether. Instead, Rushdie adopts several mixed-up traditions: he calls himself an Indian or Indo-British writer; he calls himself a writer of English literature; he even calls himself a British writer because he is contributing to the diversity of British culture.[21] At one point, Rushdie asserts that he is "an international writer," but this does not mean that he has relinquished the other titles or that he claims no national affiliations.[22] Rushdie adopts neither an uncommitted cosmopolitanism, belonging to nowhere at all, nor a cosmopolitanism committed to everywhere, on the model of "worldwide allegiance."[23] Mixing things up, Rushdie generates an attitude of cosmopolitanism that involves eclecticism, flirtation, courtship, nicknaming, and strategic assimilation.

✳✳✳

In *The Satanic Verses*, Rushdie creates the Bombay doctor and art critic Zeeny Vakil, whom the narrator describes as "a rash, bad girl" (52). Zeeny becomes the lover of Rushdie's protagonist Saladin Chamcha, né Salahuddin Chamchawala, an Anglophile immigrant born in Bombay and transplanted to London; Zeeny aspires to "reclaim" Saladin from England, where he values "warm beer, mince pies, common-sense" (175), and a white, English wife with a "right-wing voice" (182). Impious in her appropriations, Zeeny's badness exaggerates Rushdie's own and offers an alternative to Saladin's assimilation:

> She was an art critic whose book on the confining myth of authenticity, that folklorist straightjacket which she sought to replace by an ethic of historically validated eclecticism, for was not the entire national culture based on the principle of borrowing whatever clothes seemed to fit, Aryan, Mughal, British, take-the-best-and-leave-the-rest?—had created a predictable stink, especially because of its title. She had called it *The Only Good Indian*. "Meaning, is a dead," she told Chamcha when she gave him a copy. "Why should there be a good, right way of being a wog? That's Hindu fundamentalism. Actually, we're all bad Indians. Some worse than others.
>
> (52)

This passage offers a medley of mix-ups: free indirect discourse mixes-up Zeeny's perspective ("the confining myth of authenticity") with the narrator's, or Rushdie's; Zeeny mixes up racist axioms ("take-the-best-and-leave-the rest"; "the only good Indian"; "wog") and an antiracist argument; Zeeny's book title invokes Columbus's mix-up, in which he misidentified and misnamed indigenous Americans, whom he called "Indians"; Zeeny's antiracist racist slogan, "the only good Indian," mixes up time and place by associating several very different conquests (Columbus's mistake; the genocide of Indians in the U.S.; contemporary Hindu fundamentalism in India); the book title mixes up bigotries, comparing the cowboy racism of the American West (designating good and bad Indians) to the fundamentalism of contemporary India; in a rhetorical mix-up, Zeeny reverses the American quip ("the only good Indian is a dead Indian") to argue, chiastically, "a dead Indian is the only good Indian."

The most important aspect of Rushdie's mix-ups is their visibility. The rhetorical clothes that Zeeny puts on, contemporary as well as historical, look "borrowed," since eclecticism only looks like eclecticism if the act of combination can be perceived. In an essay whose title is an assertion, "'Commonwealth Literature' Does Not Exist" (1984), Rushdie first voices the theory that he will later attribute to Zeeny. In the essay, Rushdie promotes "eclecticism" as "the ability to take from the world what seems fitting and to leave the rest" (67). Rushdie presents the mix-up as a literary as well as cultural style, something like collage, and he suggests that it is the cultural style of every culture from which he takes. Rushdie objects to the category of Commonwealth literature because it tends to assume, he argues, that writers are defined by their country of origin and must produce literature that is recognizably and exclusively national. Rushdie proposes, instead, that his work reflects many national cultures and, moreover, that national cultures are mixed-up cultures. He describes India as a "*mélange* of elements as disparate as ancient Mughal and contemporary Coca-Cola American. To say nothing of Muslim, Buddhist, Jain, Christian, Jewish, British, French, Portuguese, Marxist, Maoist, Trotskyist, Vietnamese, capitalist, and of course Hindu elements" (67). Mixing India with other national traditions that are similarly mixed, Rushdie's international writing becomes a mélange of a mélange, not a representative democracy of distinguishable parts but a jumble of parts that are themselves already jumbled. Defending *The Satanic Verses* as a celebration of "our mongrel selves," Rushdie appropriates racist metaphors by affirming the impurity of metropolitan culture.[24]

The description of Zeeny's badness demonstrates one of Rushdie's most common and effective strategies: a purposeful, often shocking use of racist aphorisms. This strategy is effective not because Rushdie makes the aphorisms less bad but because he draws attention to the function of propriety within racism. By refusing to reproduce that propriety, by refusing to be good, Rushdie opposes racism as a system of moral distinctions. Rushdie's strategy reflects a substantive choice about how literature can contribute to a vital and flexible democratic culture, and it marks a shift in antiracist, multicultural writing from the affirmation of new, more proper descriptions to the critique of description as a precondition for political and social recognition.[25] For this reason, Zeeny does not replace the bad with the good. Instead, she makes the slur worse by multiplying the objects of its aggression: she uses a racist generalization and call to violence ("the only good Indian is a dead Indian") that originates in the American West to critique generalization and violence in South Asia. The call to violence, which could have been applied by the British to Indians like Zeeny, was in fact applied by American settlers to American Indians, whom Columbus misnamed as—and mistook for—Indians from South Asia. The allusion to Columbus serves to suggest that international conquest, despite claims to rationality and cultural progress, is a tradition of mistakes. By reproducing the slur, Rushdie asserts a strategic continuity between old and new: he argues, in effect, that Western civilization is mixed-up from the start. The difference between Columbus's mistake and Rushdie's mix-up is significant, however, because it is the difference between generalization and eclecticism. Columbus assumes that all brown people are the same, that there must be only one "new world," whereas Rushdie disaggregates general categories, such as "the Indian," by historicizing the use of names.

In its historical allusions, Zeeny's title suggests that that the idea of the "good Indian" and the idea that there is "only" one kind of Indian are limited and now outdated strategies of affirmation. Instead of replacing one description with another, Zeeny offers a history of racist description. By neutralizing the rhetoric of good Indians, Zeeny aims to short-circuit present as well as past justifications for violence. Rushdie's association of colonialist and anticolonialist projects is risky, particularly since it is produced through the repetition of a racist joke. Rushdie retells the racist joke in order to display the social process that makes people into categories. The joke resists its own generalizing statement because it invokes several kinds of Indians (the Indians of 1492; the Indians of the American West; the Indians of contemporary India) and because the one who tells the joke is also an object of the joke, making "only" one into at least two.[26] Like her use of the joke, Zeeny's adoption of the slogan "take-the-best-and-leave-the-rest" serves to diversify objects ("the best") and reorient agency. Zeeny repeats a familiar mantra of colonialist exploitation as a motto of self-determination, decentralizing the perspective of judgment (what counts as best?) and including "the West" among the elements from which "the rest," now, can choose. "Taking" in this context has changed, since the initial appropriation assumed unanimity in the evaluation of desirable and useful resources, whereas the second appropriation, Rushdie's, asserts the contingency of preference.

Zeeny's question to Saladin Chamcha—"Why should there be a good, right way of being a wog?"—emphasizes in its invocation of a racist epithet ("wog") that reclaiming a "way of being" means refusing a condition of confinement, as well as a condition of degradation. Zeeny's question expresses two sentiments: "we're all 'wogs' to the English" *and* "'we' who choose to call ourselves 'wogs' are not all the same, as the epithet 'wog' was meant to suggest." Repeating the epithet, Zeeny creates a new usage for "wog" and also recalls the racism of previous usage: she argues that "wog" is the name for any Indian identity based on confinement and also that Indians can only escape this confinement by being a "wog" in as many different ways as possible. For Zeeny, being a bad "wog" is the best way to avoid being a "wog" in the older sense—an object of racist generalization—at all. Writing about the epithet "queer," Judith Butler makes a similar argument: "a word that wounds," she proposes, becomes an instrument of resistance if one "destroys the prior territory of [the word's] operation."[27] That territory, in Zeeny's case, is the system of authoritative names. Butler recommends "a repetition in language that forces change," though she acknowledges that the repetition is dangerous: linguistic security, assumed in the original use of the slur, is no longer available once the system of authority is destroyed (*Excitable Speech*, 163). To create a community in opposition to the slur, Butler argues in a separate essay, one must contest past uses as well as the structure of those uses: this means recognizing that categories of identity tend to generalize and that a new, oppositional use of an epithet will need to promote division rather than conceal it.[28] Reproducing the degraded word and asserting its divisiveness, Zeeny opposes bigotry by affirming the diversity of "wogs."

The title of Rushdie's novel, "the satanic verses," aspires to this kind of affirmation: reclaiming the "satanic" for antiracism, Rushdie implies that models of the good have been part of racism's problem. For this reason, Rushdie opens his novel with two models of the bad, a star of Bombay film who impersonates Hindu gods and a star of British radio who impersonates frozen vegetables; the actors, Indian immigrants, drop from the sky over the southern coast of England. Gibreel Farishta (in English, "Gabriel Angel") and Saladin Chamcha (approximately, "Muslim Sycophant") are the only two survivors of a hijacked jet, full of immigrants from India to Britain, which explodes over the "English Sleeve" (5) and casts them down to the sand where William the Conqueror had arrived 900 years before. From the beginning of the novel, England is a culture whose boundaries are permeated by mythic arrivals: "the English Sleeve" recalls, in its translated mixture of English Channel and *La Manche* (the sleeve), the history of France in England and the foreign conqueror who made England what it is today. Rosa Diamond, an Englishwoman longing for "the dear, dead days," imagines when she sees Gibreel and Saladin washed up on the beach that they might be the ghosts of Norman invaders (130). Rushdie revisits the myths of English history to show that the old England is defined by the arrival of new Englanders; Rosa Diamond mistakes two Indian immigrants for the historical invaders who would restore England to a past free of Indian immigrants; in Rushdie's novel, ground zero for an idealized, English past is an event of immigration.

The Satanic Verses introduces its pastiche of cultures (Hindu gods and English vegetables, Indian immigrants and French invaders) in a mix-up of cultural artifacts (songs), each of which expresses disdain for the kind of cultural mixing in which Rushdie has made them participate. The first chapter brings together two of the novel's many "satanic verses," whose mutual topic is the inviolability and separateness of cultures. As Gibreel and Saladin float miraculously from sky to ground, Gibreel, postcolonial nationalist, sings an English translation of a popular Hindi song: "O, my shoes are Japanese. These trousers English, if you please. On my head, red Russian hat; my heart's Indian for all that" (5). Saladin, Anglophile collaborator, sings back fragments of "Rule, Britannia": "Mr Saladin Chamcha, appalled by the noises emanating from Gibreel Farishta's mouth, fought back with voices of his own. What Farishta heard wafting across the improbable night sky was an old song, too, lyrics by Mr James Thomson, seventeen-hundred to seventeen-forty-eight" (5–6). Rushdie reproduces in his style of narration the style of schoolboy recitation, dates and all, that Saladin would have learned in his English public school. Thomson's poem attributes its well-known chorus to angelic verse: "And guardian angels sung this strain: / 'Rule, Britannia, rule the waves;/ Britons never will be slaves.'"[29] Saladin's version emphasizes and confirms the "rule" of Britain in his enunciation and exaggeration of English vowels:

> Chamcha carolled through lips turned jingoistically redwhiteblue by the cold, 'arooooose from out the aaaazure main.' Farishta, horrified, sang louder and louder of Japanese shoes, Russian hats, inviolately subcontinental hearts, but could not still Saladin's wild recital: 'And guardian aaaaangels sung the strain.'
>
> (6)

Saladin's recital is "wild" in good part because he is playing angel to his oppressor, helping to guard Britannia against people like himself. The third verse of "Rule, Britannia," not reproduced in Rushdie's novel, articulates explicitly the politics of isolation that Saladin is invoking:

> Still more majestic shalt thou rise,
> More dreadful, from each foreign stroke:
> As the loud blast that tears the skies,
> Serves but to root thy native oak.
> "Rule, Britannia, rule the waves;
> Britons never will be slaves."

In the context of colonialism, "Rule, Britannia" invisibly transforms the British enslavement of other nations into Britain's struggle for freedom; foreign encounters make Britain truer to itself. Just so, in his explosive arrival, Saladin reinforces Britannia's majesty by embracing British isolation.

Gibreel and Saladin sound the lyrics of authenticity and unchanging national identity in two versions of cosmopolitanism: Gibreel's traveling nationalism, accessorized but unaffected by other cultures, and Saladin's old-fashioned assimilation, which relinquishes all to English mastery. Unlike Zeeny who sees "borrowing" as a process of identity in the making, Gibreel invokes his shoes, trousers, and hat merely to dress up a given identity that never changes. Similarly, Saladin, who wants to join the unprofaned Britannia of imperialist song, approves Thomson's assurance that foreign elements, repelled by Britain's might, lend strength to British insularity. At the beginning of the novel, Gibreel and Saladin represent two models of transformation: Rushdie attributes the first model to Ovid, in which one may look different but in essence remain the same, and the second model to Lucretius, in which one becomes something completely different, leaving all past characteristics behind (276–77). *The Satanic Verses* embraces neither model. Rushdie suggests, instead, that Gibreel and Saladin participate in the same superficial multiculturalism: Gibreel buys globally, but thinks only locally; Saladin impersonates, besides frozen peas, a world of voices, including "Russian, Chinese, Sicilian, the President of the United States," but he has no voice of his own. Using his many voices and computer-generated effects, Saladin plays an ever-transforming alien, "Maxim Alien," on British television, allegorizing foreignness as science fiction so that "picture postcard" England can remain natural, familiar, and real (60–63). Playing the greatest of aliens, Saladin becomes a "maxim," an abstract emblem of "overseas."

At the end of *The Satanic Verses*, Rushdie suggests that mixed-up identities need to acknowledge their disparate materials, including the materials of the past. Whereas Gibreel Farishta is unable to live with his many selves and commits suicide in the closing pages, Saladin Chamcha comes to accept his selves more fully, by giving up the "old and sentimental echo" of England and of India (547). Saladin sells his father's house in Bombay and relinquishes his Anglicized name, which he had adopted while a schoolboy in England. Throughout most of his novel, Rushdie uses nicknames to question the authority of cultural traditions: he renames Muhammad and gives the names of Muhammad's wives to prostitutes in a brothel. Applying these names, Homi Bhabha has argued, Rushdie "[violates] the system of naming" and thus makes "contingent and indeterminate" the shared perspective of an entire community.[30] However, I want to distinguish between renaming and nicknaming: the latter is informal, unofficial, and improper—not a new proper name but an intimate, only partial appellation. For Rushdie, the problem with Saladin's shortened name is not its incorrectness but its invisibility. To the English, "Saladin Chamcha" conveys no characteristics; it makes the bearer, literally, a sycophant, someone who is happy to fit in. While nicknames register a diversity of selves, Saladin's contracted name conceals his history and his various affiliations.

Giving up an old, static version of India, Saladin, now "Salahuddin," embraces a new, changing India by taking part in a demonstration for national integration. Salahuddin swaps the symbolic history of his nation and family house for the quotidian present of personal intimacy and a rented apartment. Zeeny's final statement in the novel is addressed to Salahuddin: "My place . . . Let's get the hell out of here" (547). Assenting, Salahuddin chooses cultural as well as romantic flirtation: his embrace of Zeeny is also his embrace of an "actually existing place" (541)—someone's apartment rather than someone's nation—where belonging will be negotiated on a smaller, less axiomatic scale. By challenging shared perspectives, including the meaning of "place," Rushdie's work creates a model of cosmopolitan affiliation that is critical of national paradigms but nevertheless specific and collective.

***

The final lines of *The Satanic Verses* propose that seduction is not a failing but a tactic of immigrant culture. Rushdie's novel resolves in flirtation, which it offers as a more practical, more dynamic negotiation of cultural difference than antagonism or respect. In *East, West*, the collection of short stories that he published in the wake of the *Satanic Verses* debacle, Rushdie makes this argument from the beginning: he uses flirtation to resist aphoristic truths about immigration, gender, and citizenship and to imagine transient communities based on mistakes, mix-ups, and experimentation. Rushdie's stories display a new range of social relationships, which are produced in urban settings such as consulates and apartment houses; in these settings, Rushdie explores the manners of immigration as they are embedded and negotiated in the proverbs, jingles, and clichés of popular culture.

The characters in *East, West* are always being tested: whether they receive a British passport, whether they are welcomed in England, depends on whether they manage the requisite form. Do they speak standard English? Do they affect the requisite gratitude? Does their behavior correspond to their interlocutors' expectations? Unable to avoid these tests but unwilling to accept them, Rushdie's characters get their answers wrong, often purposefully. Rushdie suggests in these stories that immigrants can use mix-ups against the aggressive rhetoric of "the immigrant's mistake." This rhetoric assumes that the speech and behavior of immigrants are incorrect and in need either of correction or exclusion; it assumes also that culture is unchanging and unchangeable. As a writer and an immigrant, Rushdie is adding to what British literature can contain, by mixing in or mixing up different cultural traditions within a single literary text; moreover, he is criticizing the standards by which correctness is measured.

East, West begins with "Good Advice Is Rarer Than Rubies," a story about a potential immigrant from Pakistan to England who does not, in fact, want to immigrate: the story is about the assumption that the West is more desirable than the East and about the assumption by Pakistani men that young women must want to marry and live in England.[31] While *The Satanic Verses* focuses on the axiomatic language of doctrine, slogans, mottos, patriotic jingles, and aphoristic slurs, "Good Advice" focuses on proverbs, such as the one in the story's title. It is important to notice that proverbs constitute a special genre of truism: they may seem to invoke social orthodoxy, but they are suppler and more ambiguous than other kinds of sayings. Rushdie uses proverbs in this story to create opportunities for flirtation and for mixing up clichés.

The main character, Miss Rehana, has come to the British consulate to apply for a visa so that she can join her fiancé in England; her fiancé is a much older Pakistani man to whom she was engaged as a child by her parents. A Pakistani advice expert, who makes his living by defrauding women in search of visas, approaches Miss Rehana to offer his services: he offers what he calls "good advice," to which Miss Rehana replies, offering the first of several proverbs, "Good advice is rarer than rubies."[32] Within the story, "good advice" is like a proverb: the meaning depends on the interpretation. Miss Rehana knows that there may be several points of view, but the advice expert, Muhammad Ali, does not know this, either about proverbs or about life: he mistakes the regular arrival of women like Miss Rehana—every "last Tuesday of the month" (5)—for the predictability of their knowledge and desires. Making a characteristic into a category, the advice expert assumes that Miss Rehana is one of many helpless "Tuesday women": he does not imagine for a moment that Miss Rehana might be less than helpless, nor does he imagine that she would not wish to go to England and marry her fiancé. Like the British officers within the consulate, Muhammad Ali assumes that Miss Rehana would lie or falsify papers in order to leave.

There are several initial hints in the story that those who assert their possession of knowledge are rather more mixed up than they realize: while Miss Rehana is described as "munching chili-pakoras contentedly," Muhammad Ali, who eats nothing and is not in search of a visa, feels the effects of nervousness; her eyes, Rushdie explains, "did bad things to his digestive tract" (6). Muhammad Ali is the conman, but Miss Rehana has all the confidence. Like the British officers, Muhammad Ali is ignorant of his ignorance. Later in the story, the advice expert claims to have produced in Miss Rehana "a captive audience," even though it is he who is captivated by *her* (9). These reversals of rhetoric and control intimate the "topsy-turvey" tactics that Miss Rehana will employ at the end of the tale (15).

As in *The Satanic Verses*, where Rushdie mixes up Islamic fundamentalism and English nationalism, in *East, West*, he brings together Pakistani sexism and British racism, clichés about marriage and clichés about immigration. "Good Advice" is placed in Rushdie's collection at the head of a section called "East," but the title invokes a proverb whose origins derive from both East and West, popular and classical traditions: the Book of Job meets the Pakistani marketplace. Rushdie provides an implicit critique of cultural axioms by showing that family matters at home are embedded in international matters abroad: in the story, sexuality and marriage are international as well as domestic concerns. Rushdie introduces and then mixes up the following assumptions: people in the East really want to be in the West (all Pakistanis want to go to England); the West understands the East (the British consulate officials are smarter than the "Tuesday women"); all women want to get married; all women who come to the consulate are "crooks and liars and cheats" (9); "mistakes" are always accidents.[33]

The genre of the axiom structures the expectations of characters and readers alike. In the course of the story, however, Miss Rehana transforms cultural axioms—the East's desire for the West, for example—into tactics of social manipulation. The advice expert gives Miss Rehana what he calls "good advice": how to convince the immigration officers that she knows her fiancé well, even though she does not know him at all. Miss Rehana takes this advice and makes it good for *her*: that is, she uses it to give the most incorrect answers possible. Returning outside after her interview, she reports, " 'I got all their questions wrong. Distinguishing marks I put on the wrong cheeks, bathroom décor I completely redecorated, all absolutely topsy-turvy, you see' " (15). Miss Rehana stays in Pakistan, where she is happy in her job as a governess, by purposefully making the mistakes that all would-be immigrant women, so it is thought, would make by accident. The consulate officials think that Miss Rehana is a liar because she has pretended to know her fiancé better than she does; in fact, Miss Rehana is a liar because she has pretended to pretend. It is the consulate officials, rather than the immigrant petitioner, who are mistaken.

"Good Advice" is a story about the East that seeks to make both Western and Eastern readers reconsider what they think the East wants, who they think the East is, and whether they think the people of the East all want the same thing. By disrupting "shared standpoints" about the good, Miss Rehana also disrupts shared assumptions about marriage, immigration, and gender. She introduces a world of partial alliances and partial deviations: Muhammad Ali and Miss Rehana agree that the consulate officials ask offensive questions, but they do not agree, for example, whether "one's parents act in one's best interests" (14).

On the chance that the reader has missed Rushdie's point, he provides a final clue to the narrative in a moment of anxious correctness. This moment is apparent only in retrospect, from the later knowledge of topsy-turvy intentions. Before entering the consulate, the advice expert offers to examine Miss Rehana's application to see if her answers will do. She asks him—the narrator reports a note of anxiety in her voice—"Is it OK?" (8). The expert responds, "Tip-top. All in order." Miss Rehana thanks him for his advice. Reading the story for the first time, one assumes that Miss Rehana wants to be right; reading for the second time, however, it seems more likely that correctness is not her aim. Miss Rehana is anxious, not to pass the test, but to fail it. When she turns her tip-top answers upside-down in the interview, she suggests that correctness—what's "OK"—is a variable standard, both within national cultures and between one culture and another. Rushdie suggests, finally, it is more important to know which values correctness serves than to know which value is correct.

If Rushdie's collection begins with the surprise of purposeful mistakes, it ends by promoting mistakes as a principle of transnational culture.[34] The last section of the book brings together East and West in three stories about Indian immigrants in England. In each of the stories, Rushdie introduces an image of mixed-up culture: in the first story, it is harmony; in the second, it is federation; in the last, it is courtship. Whereas Rushdie presents the first two images as unfulfilled, unrealistic aspirations (both lead to violence), he presents courtship as a successful, if provisional tactic (a refuge from violence that might help to change the conditions that allow violence to operate). Courtship seems to work because, unlike harmony and federation, it constitutes an informal process rather than a finished object; it demonstrates a commitment to change rather than a commitment to stability. The last story, called "The Courter," describes several images of courtship: the literal courtship between an Indian ayah and an apartment house porter from Eastern Europe; the figurative courtship in the characters' speech between English and Hindi and between the standard English of India and the standard English of England; the courtship of Asian and European cultures that makes up the game of chess;[35] and the courtship of black culture and white culture that makes up popular music in the 1960s, when the story is set. Rushdie promotes courtship against the isolation of racism and xenophobia; he argues that national rituals and local artifacts are the products of past assimilation.

In its title and in its strategies, "The Courter" invokes Lewis Carroll's "portmanteau," a figurative suitcase that creates new words by bringing together, accidentally, two or more unrelated words; the new words are mixed-up objects, in which assimilation is visible and jarring.[36] Lewis Carroll is an important figure for Rushdie, who values, as Carroll did, the liberating pleasures of nonsense and private language; both Rushdie and Carroll focus on childhood, a condition in which identities are not yet settled or socialized. Besides the portmanteau, Rushdie invokes Carroll's "wonderland," his character "the Dodo," his obsession with chess, and even Carroll's real name (Charles Dodgson) to describe the alternative, made-up culture of an immigrant apartment house in London. Like Carroll, Rushdie makes linguistic tactics out of linguistic mistakes, new words out of mispronunciations.[37] Rushdie's linguistic playfulness detaches persons and things from confining interpretations. Derek Attridge has argued about portmanteau words that they help to show "that meaning is an *effect* of language, not a presence within or behind language, and that the effect is unstable and uncontrollable."[38] For Attridge, the portmanteau word is a norm of language because "every word in every text is a portmanteau, a combination of sounds that echo through the entire language and through every other language, and back through the history of speech" ("Unpacking the Portmanteau," 154). Attridge is arguing that all language is a mix-up, that combinations go unnoticed only because they are unrecognized. Rushdie has a more specific concern: he aims to represent the social and political conditions that make mix-ups hard to see; to do this, he makes mix-ups on purpose.

In "The Courter," immigration creates portmanteaux, mixing by mistake or without intention one culture into another. The portmanteau facilitates not the combination of two meanings into one but a playful encounter, a flirtation. Rushdie uses the semantic mix-up as a principal device within a story about courtship and immigration, but the mix-up of words also generates the story from the beginning. "The Courter" is about naming, renaming, and nicknaming, and it is also about name-calling. Set in an immigrant apartment house on the west side of London, the story tells how the narrator, like Rushdie an immigrant from Bombay, became a British citizen in the 1960s. The title of the story is the name given to the apartment-house porter by the narrator's Indian ayah. The ayah's mispronunciation of English—her Ps come out as Cs—transforms the porter into a "courter," a kind of courtier, by mistake. The porter, who is also an immigrant from the East, but from Eastern Europe, decides to embrace the new name: " 'Courter, courter, caught.' Okay. People called him many things, he did not mind. But this name, this courter, he would try to be" (177). Mixing up porter and courtier, a doorman or bag carrier and a royal attendant or wooer, Rushdie brings together ordinary culture and literary tradition, labor and aristocracy, West Kensington apartment house and European chivalry. Rushdie makes up a new word; the new word, however, implies that carrying and flirting, travel and courtship are—have always been—related endeavors, that there is no contact without exchange.

By assimilating the porter to her own style of speech, the ayah establishes new intimacies between East and East (Europe and India) and between East and West (India and London). Through tactics of assimilation and poaching, the ayah and the porter, initially mixed up by the strangeness of London, develop agency and comfort by doing the mixing themselves: the porter renames the front stairs to make the ayah's climb less difficult—he calls them the "Kensington Ghats," after the Ghats (mountains) of India (175); the ayah and the porter go out on dates to department stores, where they pretend to choose furniture and curtains for "imaginary homes"; they create domestic routines within the "cramped lounge" of the porter's tiny apartment (188); they fancy themselves and their employers as characters in "The Flintstones," taking the name "Rubble" and giving the name "Flintstone" to the narrator's parents; they make chess their "private language" (194), transforming "the great formalisation of war [into] an art of love" (196). Nicknaming functions as a practice of assimilation because it allows characters to personalize and to appropriate. Besides the porter and the ayah, the children in the apartment house also make up names: the narrator and his siblings give nicknames to all of the apartment house residents (179–81); they call the porter "Mr. Mixed-Up," because they cannot pronounce his Eastern European name and because he seems confused by his surroundings (179); they call their ayah "Jumble-Aya," because she, too, seems mixed-up (181);[39] they call a retired colonial administrator "the Dodo," after the extinct bird and the foolish character in Lewis Carroll's fiction (191). Many of the characters in Rushdie's story have more than one nickname, and the point of the story is not to choose among them. The proliferation of nicknames within the apartment house serves to resist the social limitations imposed by racist and xenophobic name-calling, which is directed at the immigrant characters by outsiders, such as English thugs and politicians. Whereas the racists in the story demand correctness, even while making mistakes, the immigrants create a community by mixing up cultures at will.

The violence of correctness is an important and literal element in Rushdie's narrative, and it becomes increasingly intense and explicit as the story develops. This violence ranges from the porter's intimation that he has been called by names he does not like but has accepted (177); to a slap in the face, when the narrator's father, shopping for baby supplies, asks a salesgirl if she has any "nipples" (the word refers only to the tops of baby bottles in Indian English) (183); to a rant about "immigrants" by an English politician on television (189); to a racist diatribe, shouted by local thugs who mistake the narrator's mother and ayah for two other Indian women (204); and, finally, to a stabbing, in which the porter is attacked when he rushes over to protect the ayah from the thugs (206). The private language of the story is disrupted, permanently and violently, by the attack at the end. The characters' intimate and playful names are replaced by a single nasty epithet, which not only precedes the knifing but also, to the thugs, seems to justify it. One of the thugs, who is convinced that the mother and ayah are the relatives of an Indian resident whom they have come to assault, react to the women's claims of "mistaken identity" with further generalization: "'Fucking wogs,'" he said. 'You fucking come over here, you don't fucking know how to behave. Why don't you fucking fuck off to fucking Wogistan? Fuck your fucking wog arses. Now then,' he added in a quiet voice, holding up the knife, 'unbutton your blouses'" (204). Even though the thug believes that there is, in this case, no "mistaken identity," his rhetoric suggests that, in effect, there can be no "mistake," because he believes that all Indian immigrants are the same ("wogs"), that all of them behave in the same way, and that none of them behave correctly. The evaluation of correctness belongs to the racist with the knife. The racists hate the immigrants for making social blunders, whose offensiveness, they say, justifies physical harm; however, they later describe their own blunder as an "honest mistake" (205). The honesty of the thugs' mistake depends on the assumption that all Indians are, in fact, indistinguishable. Like Columbus's mistake in *The Satanic Verses* and like the mistake of the consulate officials in "Good Advice," the so-called honest mistake is an effect of racism: it is a result of generalization rather than intimacy, and it serves to reinforce exclusion and correctness. In contrast, the immigrants' mistakes, once they become Rushdie's mix-ups, create new communities and new intimacies.

Rushdie delays the comparison between nicknaming and racist name-calling until late in his story. At the beginning, the porter chooses the role he will play, adopting a local idiom against the confining idioms of xenophobia; made-up names, such as the porter's, turn the apartment house into a home. However, when the nicknames are gone, effaced by violence, the story's figurative mix-ups dissolve into literal confusion: the flirtation between the ayah and the porter ends; the ayah returns to Bombay; the narrator's family leaves England for Pakistan. Some time after these departures, the narrator returns to the apartment house, where he finds a new porter in residence. At the door of the porter's lounge, "a stranger answered" (211). The narrator asks, "Where's Mixed-Up?" The man, a "stranger" to the narrator and to the story's idiom, responds: "I don't know anything about any mix-up." In Rushdie's narrative, rhetorical flirtation is extinguished by physical antagonism, even if the idioms of that antagonism—xenophobic name-calling—are resisted by the story's transformation of standard Britishness. Rushdie's proliferation of nicknames, in the apartment house and in his writing, helps to create new examples of British culture and also to change the rules of inclusion. He deploys the mistakes of immigration as the mix-ups of critical cosmopolitanism.

✳ ✳ ✳

More than fifteen years after he published *The Satanic Verses* and a decade after *East, West*, there are signs that Salman Rushdie has entered the late afternoon, perhaps the early evening, of his career. For one thing, he has taken to writing about the Upper West Side, that zone of Manhattan comfort and liberal respectability. For another, he has begun to parody not only his life but his literary devices as well. In *Fury*, the novel about New York that he published in 2001, Rushdie imagines an unimaginative copywriter—a novelist of the one-liner—who has designed a culturally eclectic but terribly boring slogan for American Express. The copywriter shows this slogan to his neighbor, an immigrant (like Rushdie) who has moved from Bombay to London to a "comfortable Upper West Side sublet" in New York City (*Fury*, 29).

Above several images of cities photographed at sunset, the copywriter has printed the following motto: "The sun never sets on American Express International Banking Corporation." The motto is a cosmopolitan mix-up: the copywriter brings together semantic elements from different national traditions (an aphorism of the British Empire and an advertisement for an American company), and the elements are themselves international (artifacts of colonialism and globalization). However, the motto is also mixed up in another sense, and this is the parody: the advertisement implies a limited future for the company that it means to advance. The slogan claims that American Express has as many outposts and as much longevity as the British Empire had in the past, and it also proposes that U.S. imperialism has one-upped the British product, which no longer sees the light of day. These assertions are not quite compatible: the copywriter, who knows little about history and even less about politics, seems to fancy the British Empire as a heroic role model for corporate America; he does not realize that images of conquest are unlikely to generate, in fact have never generated, universal or permanent appeal.

The copywriter has a problem with generalization: not only does he assume that national aphorisms command unequivocal interpretations, but he assumes also that English-sounding immigrants, like his neighbor, must be wholly and proudly British. The copywriter figures that the neighbor, who sounds British to him, can—or would—speak for British patriotism. Whereas Rushdie has written in the past about the problems of cultural exclusiveness—Britain's refusal to acknowledge its mix-up with India, for example—he now acknowledges that inclusiveness is not always desirable. The mix-up depends on the mixer, and on the political and economic contexts of multinationalism.[40] " 'Is it okay?' " the copywriter asks the so-called Britisher: " 'There's no offense intended. That's what I want to be sure of. That the line [in the advertisement] doesn't come across as an insult to your country's glorious past' " (36).

Rushdie's adman is concerned about the ethics of cultural borrowing. He is wondering whether "it's okay," as he puts it, to insert what he takes to be a lofty British aphorism into a low, or popular, American slogan. He is concerned about showing cultural respect. What is interesting about this scene, as a comment about anxious internationalism, is Rushdie's sense that borrowing is not, or is no longer, the relevant subject for ethical dispute: it does not really matter either to the British-sounding neighbor or to Rushdie that the copywriter is mixing traditions. What does matter is the copywriter's generalization, both about global expansion and about immigrants. The worst insult, Rushdie is arguing, is the copywriter's assumption that all immigrants with an English accent would wish to defend Britain's glories; or that all immigrants with an English accent would think that there are any glories to defend.

Rushdie asks his readers to notice, as the copywriter does not, that the problem with the slogan is not its mix-up of national cultures, or of epic diction and commercial jargon, but rather its failure to acknowledge both the history and the critique of global conquest. Rushdie implies, finally, that the copywriter's mistake is more accurate than his intention: American capitalism, exemplified by the slogan, shares in the generalizations of Britain's triumphalist past. The copywriter's unintended offensiveness, for all its naïveté, reflects a systematic blindness that is comparable to the "honest mistake" of the thugs in *East, West.* Writing against aphoristic truths, Rushdie demonstrates the interpretive conflicts that corporate slogans and national axioms do not otherwise promote. Through his parody of mix-ups, Rushdie argues that the mixing of national traditions is now (and has long been) a tradition of global capitalism; he reminds us, that is, that a critical cosmopolitanism will need to reflect on the uncommon histories of international contact. To produce models of culture that are less consistent and also less invisible, Rushdie generates aesthetic and cultural mistakes: inadvertent double meanings; the mispronunciation of words; lightness of tone where seriousness seems to be required. These mix-ups are critical to the extent that they diffuse prior gestures of correctness. For Rushdie, that persistent question—"Is it okay?"—is never the right one.

6

Un inglese, he said, and looked across at me with what I took to be a touch of contempt.

—W. G. SEBALD, *VERTIGO*

W. G. SEBALD'S novels gather disparate stories of migration and globalization, but he does not mix up so much as assemble, display, and loosely hold together. While his narratives wander globally, through England and much of continental Europe, Ireland, the United States, China, Peru, the Congo, and Palestine, they concentrate episodically on individual journeys, conversations with friends, small regions such as Suffolk, and the transnational itinerary of commodities such as silk and herring. Sebald's revival of modernist strategies is most obvious in his emphasis on perception, but it is also present in his emphasis on renaming (think of Joyce) and diversion (think of Woolf), and especially in his emphasis on reputation and patterns of recognition (think of Conrad, whom Sebald discusses explicitly). His method generates new histories of thinking and acting beyond the nation, and it asks us to compare the different interests that transnational thought and action have served. But it also generates the failure to historicize and the failure to compare: analogies, metaphors, and accidents create elements of disorder and irrelevance within narratives of causality and accountability. Sebald imposes a sense of vertigo by forestalling common knowledge about places, catastrophes, commodities, literary and political celebrities, and works of art. Through strategic gestures of adding and withholding information, Sebald construes less conclusive and more limited postures of cosmopolitanism.

One of the earliest and most influential appreciations of Sebald's work comes from Susan Sontag, who attributes the difference between Sebald's reputation in the United States and his reputation in Germany to the circumstances of his novels' translation.[1] In English, Sontag observes, Sebald's career began with

The Emigrants, a novel that tells of Jewish emigrants whose families were mur-
dered by the Nazis and who themselves escaped this end by moving to England
or the United States.[2] Whereas English readers received Sebald as a chronicler
of the Holocaust, Sontag explains, his career began in German with *Vertigo*, a
novel that gives most of its attention to the narrator's post-Holocaust travels
in Austria, Italy, and Germany, and to the lives of much earlier writers and
travelers such as Stendhal and Kafka.[3] Sontag observes that readers' expectations about a book can trump or even determine its perceived quality, and she
speculates that U.S. readers may be disappointed by *Vertigo*, whose publication
in English occasioned her essay. But Sontag does not acknowledge, at least not
here, that desire may inform disappointment.[4] "Americans," Sontag explains in
a subsequent essay, "prefer to picture the evil that was *there*, and from which
the United States—a unique nation, one without any certifiably wicked lead-
ers throughout its entire history—is exempt."[5] Not only do U.S. readers expect
Sebald's novels to focus on the Holocaust, Sontag's later comment implies, they
have a decided preference for the topic because it distracts them from the more
proximate evil of U.S. slavery. Among many English-language readers, the Holocaust precludes irony or political ambiguity, and indeed Sontag, who made
a career out of arguing that critical writing should abstain from interpretation
and especially from metaphor, celebrates, in her earlier essay, Sebald's freedom
"from all-undermining or undiginified self-consciousness" ("A Mind," 41).[6] In
the United States, and to some extent in Britain, a book about the Holocaust
can seem "noble," a term Sontag uses twice to describe Sebald's work ("A Mind,"
41, 47). In Germany, it is difficult to imagine this response; in fact, the question
of whether Sebald's books are marred by a lack of self-consciousness or irony
has been a source of some debate among scholars of German literature.[7]

Sebald's novels are interested in these contextual differences: they remind
us often that they are written, and need to be read, within and across several
political histories, even while they complicate and often unsettle what those
political histories are. To be certain, this is one kind of self-consciousness in
which Sebald's novels are, indeed, engaged. Among German readers, novels
that discuss the murder and deportation of Jews alongside Belgian or British imperialism, or alongside the Allied firebombing of German cities, may
resemble too closely the efforts of Holocaust deniers or apologists who have
tried to diminish the Nazi genocide by comparing it to other, implicitly worse
crimes.[8] Among British and U.S. readers, however, novels that discuss, along
with the Holocaust, European imperialism and the Allied air war can serve to
correct an uncritical self-righteousness about German violence and British or
U.S. liberalism. Neil Levi and Michael Rothberg have observed that "the assertion of the Holocaust's uniqueness has a different resonance in the land of
the perpetrators, Germany, than it does in the United States, a nation that has

its own, frequently disavowed, violent origins and history."[9] For his part, Sebald aggressively rejects the denial or minimization of Nazi genocide,[10] but he does pursue both panoramic and microscopic views of that genocide: the panoramic view involves historicism and comparison, while the microscopic view involves speculation and idiosyncratic observation. Sebald is eager to avoid or undo what Roland Barthes calls "myth": the ossification of the past into repeated but unanalyzed stories, and the assumption that underwrites ossification, that these stories need no analysis.[11] Myth, Barthes explains, is "the decorative display of what-goes-without-saying" (11); it presents "a world which is without contradictions because it is without depth, a world wide open and wallowing in the evident, it establishes a blissful clarity: things appear to mean something by themselves" (143). Sebald suggests that irrational perception—the disruption both of bliss and of clarity—is necessary for and often prompts the analysis of naturalized histories. It does this by introducing not yet relevant details and by retracting details that are too well known.

In an essay on the air war, published in English after his death, Sebald objects to "vague generalizations," those numerical abstractions and potted histories that allow people to come to terms with the past ("AW" 4). He objects, that is, not only to a kind of knowledge ("generalizations") but also to an attitude of knowing. Some fifteen years earlier, in an article on which the later essay seems to have been modeled, Sebald suggests that those who write about twentieth-century Germany should aim to convey an uncomforting style: "a sense of reality that appears foreign."[12] For this, Sebald recommends "the attitude of an agency that simply presents a report" ("BH" 77), which he will contrast with a narrative style that involves "bringing order to the discrepancies in the wide field of reality" (85). Sebald wants his stories to seem unfinished, so that readers will have to attempt their own order, or reckon with disorder. He proposes that a materialist history of European culture, a history attentive to the economic conditions and political contestation of values and norms, requires not only the first-person stories of natives and visitors but also the panoramic stories of economic relations and the researched or imagined stories of microscopic details. Adding panoramic and microscopic accounts (what he calls "synoptic and artificial" views ["AW" 25–26]) to eyewitness testimony, he argues, creates more authenticity because less coherence. Sebald thus combines the immigrant archives and aerial vision of the late twentieth century—what we know now that we could not know before—with the critical protocols and speculative postures of early-twentieth-century modernism.

Sebald's combination of panoramic and microscopic views produces a relentless vertigo: whereas the panoramic view gathers context and locates agency, the microscopic view introduces details that resist any one context and often seem to point to a context that eludes specification. The panoramic view displays historical processes, and it expands transnationally the analysis of local events such as exploitation in the Congo or the production of silk in Milan. Eva Hoffman, a memoirist who was born in Poland and now lives between Boston and London, likewise values the panoramic view because it displays the transnational conditions and consequences of the Holocaust.[13] A daughter of Holocaust survivors, Hoffman distinguishes between "writers" and "carriers": a "writer" is someone who makes a narrative of "what happened," whereas a "carrier" transports "the cargo of awesome knowledge . . . carefully, with all the iterated accounts literally intact" (*After Such Knowledge*, 14–15). She explains:

> It was not that the mythical vision of the world I had put together from scraps of story and imagery was untrue. The mythology, after all, derived from reality. It was just that I knew it *as* mythology and had no way of grasping it as actuality. It would take me a long time to discover and put its real-world components together. But as I was growing up, I had no comprehension of the background to the war or its course, of the circumstances visited upon Poland during the cataclysm, or the contemporaneous situation within which our lives unfolded in postwar Cracow.
>
> (16; EMPHASIS IN TEXT)

Hoffman wants to supplement the close-up "reality" of individuals' stories with the panorama of "real-world components" (the history of prewar Europe, the treatment of Poland by Germany and the Allies, and the political and social conditions of Cracow after the war). Like Sebald, she uses these components to introduce cause and complicity and to keep familiar stories from being reified into "icons and sagas" (12).

Sebald worries, however, that panoramic views can promise too much and offer too few distinctions. Narrative and visual panoramas may convey the familiarity and omniscience of the realist novel, which Sebald aims to avoid, rather than the foreignness and uncertainty of the report ("BH" 77). A museum diorama of the Battle of Waterloo, for example, gives the false impression that everything can be seen:

> We, the survivors, see everything from above, see everything at once, and still we do not know how it was. The desolate field extends all around where once fifty thousand soldiers and ten thousand horses met their end within a few hours. The night after the battle, the air must have been filled with death rattles and groans. Now there is nothing but the silent brown soil. Whatever became of the corpses and moral remains? Are they buried under the memorial? Are we standing on a mountain of death? Is that our ultimate vantage point? Does one really have the much-vaunted historical overview from such a position?
>
> (R 125)

Preferring a more transient vision, Sebald suggests that aerial and documentary views need to be supplemented by speculative descriptions.[14] Writing of the firebombing of Dresden, Sebald values subjunctive observation: what someone might have seen if someone could have seen it. He will imagine the destruction not only of buildings, trees, and inhabitants but also of "domestic pets" and "fixtures and fittings of every kind" ("AW" 25). The destruction of objects at once numerous and absurdly various must have led to "paralysis of the capacity to think and feel," Sebald conjectures. By including these objects in his narrative, Sebald hopes to rectify that paralysis (by asking readers to think and feel about loss, including the loss of rationality) and also to imitate it (by asking readers to learn about details whose significance cannot be rationalized). And as he asks his readers to think of pets and fixtures when Dresden burned to the ground, so he focuses in his stories of Jewish emigration and Nazi occupation on the loss of everyday practices, like driving on the left, and of personal possessions, like "Grandfather's pair of budgerigars," whose impoundment by customs officials at Dover conveyed, for one family, "the whole monstrosity of changing countries under such inauspicious circumstances."[15] With these details, Sebald aims both to narrate and to describe, and thus to produce an unsettling, ironic cosmopolitanism.[16]

Amitava Kumar, an Indian expatriate and a U.S. theorist of immigration whose multigenre, artificial memoirs resemble Sebald's, has proposed that the mixing of journalism and literature, analysis and speculation provides a necessary alternative to "the language of government agencies."[17] Kumar calls his first book a "forged passport" because it "will help you enter only the zones of a particular imagination" (ix). Instead of a government passport, which "chooses to tell its story about you," Kumar produces his own "passport," choosing the story he wants to tell. His amalgam of snapshots, anecdotes, and political analysis is meant to add, he writes, "a stubborn density, a *life* to what we encounter in newspaper columns as abstract, often faceless, figures without histories" (xi; emphasis in text). Details are "stubborn," Kumar suggests, when they resist abstraction and enumeration. While panoramic views offer the kinds of analysis that can inform social policy and claims of political responsibility, artificial views emphasize idiosyncrasy and fantasy. In his recent anthology of writing by those he calls Indian expatriates, Kumar includes stories of "imaginary journeys" and portable objects alongside stories about Indians who have traveled abroad.[18] He includes these additional writings, he explains, in order to represent several realities: the reality of journeys from one place to another that people actually take; the reality of places transformed by the journey of transnational capital (for example, the arrival of Tropicana orange juice to a small town in northern India); and the reality of imagined journeys to places memorized but never touched.[19]

Sebald's modulation among different realities points to an ambivalence that pervades his work: he is committed to a materialist analysis of the present, which means insisting on causality and human agency; at the same time, he is suspicious of systemization, integration, and order, which means insisting on those accidental phenomena that escape intention and understanding. On the side of materialist analysis, Amir Eshel and others have identified Sebald's "Benjaminian gaze," and Sebald himself invokes Benjamin's image of the "angel of history" in one of his late essays.[20] The Benjaminian imprint is visible in Sebald's effort to display the acts of barbarism and exploitation that underwrite monuments of European civilization.[21] It is also visible in the resemblance between his narrators' meanderings and the practice of *flânerie*, and in his way of approaching the present through the irruption of details from the past.[22] There is also what I will call his "Horkheimian gaze": Sebald's insistence on comparison and distinction among various acts of international violence. This means he will describe specific acts and actors, expanding the Benjaminian gaze from continental Europe to Britain, South America, and Africa, extending his research synchronically as well as diachronically.[23] Both of these "gazes" establish Sebald's connection to the philosophical tradition of German critical theory and to a critical cosmopolitanism, influenced by that theory, that considers the political histories of national boundaries and international contacts. Sebald may focus his novels on the lives of individuals, but he attributes the suffering of those individuals to social and political systems: institutions such as trading companies, governments, and customs offices, and traditions of knowledge such as geography, political science, and military history. This version of critical cosmopolitanism assumes that demystification and enlightenment are possible, and also desirable.

But in Sebald's novels, the Benjaminian gaze is prompted by episodes of intellectual and physical collapse—that is, by the failure to think critically. Sebald's narrators, who share many of their author's biographical details—sometimes his name—often express a sense of uneasiness, discomfort, and even panic that Sebald calls "vertigo." In the novel of that title, the narrator is distressed by the "vague apprehension" of famous historical figures, Dante and Kafka, whom he thinks he has seen, though he knows it is impossible, in the streets of Vienna and on a bus traveling from Verona (*V* 35, 88–89). The most literal account of vertiginous thinking comes from Great-Uncle Adelwarth, who reports in *The Emigrants* that "memory . . . makes one's head heavy and giddy, as if one were not looking back down the receding perspectives of time but rather down on the earth from a great height, from one of those towers whose tops are lost to view in the clouds" (*E* 145). A narrator who is literally paralyzed "when confronted with the traces of destruction, reaching far back into the past," echoes this sentiment in Sebald's subsequent novel, *The Rings of Saturn* (*R* 3). And in *Austerlitz*, the novel that Sebald published before his death in 2001, vertigo is caused by the recovery of "forgotten things" (*A* 151) and by the hint of things that cannot be recovered, such as a family's vanished life (*A* 297).

For characters, episodes of collapse create time to speculate and research and the occasion for accidental encounters. In this way, vertigo motivates thought rather than simply preventing it: the experience of anxiety and the process of recuperation lead to impractical, unplanned adventures. This is especially true in *Austerlitz*, whose story is inaugurated and on the whole structured by a fortuitous encounter between the narrator and his eponymous friend. At the beginning of the novel, the narrator recalls a trip he made from England to Belgium in the mid-1960s. On his arrival at Antwerp Centraal Station, feeling uneasy for reasons he cannot explain, he decides to visit a zoo that is adjacent to the terminal (*A* 3). Walking through the rooms of a Nocturama, a darkened space designed for nocturnal animals, the narrator regains his composure but changes the way he sees: adjusting his eyes to the dim interior, he takes notice of the "sombrous lives behind the glass" (*A* 4). When the narrator returns to the train station, he observes shadowy details that he had missed on his initial visit: the imperialist façade, with its "verdigris-covered Negro," and the various travelers, who "wore the same sorrowful expression as the creatures in the zoo" (*A* 6–7). Newly attentive, the narrator notices Austerlitz, whom he meets for the first time on that day and who, he learns, is writing a book about "the architectural style of the capitalist era," in particular "the compulsive sense of order and the tendency towards monumentalism evident in law courts and penal institutions, railway stations and stock exchanges, opera houses and lunatic asylums" (*A* 33). Austerlitz recounts the shadowed history of Antwerp station, whose patron, King Leopold II, used the profits of colonial enterprise abroad to erect magnificent public buildings at home (*A* 9). The narrator's vertigo leads him to the unintended juxtaposition of zoo and railway station and to the subject (Austerlitz) of the novel; it reorients his attention from practical matters to ornaments and objects; and it extends the range of his analysis by introducing thoughts of captivity and exploitation in Africa to experiences of travel and modern architecture in Europe.

Of course, new information is not always enabling. It can create uncertainty about knowledge and about the political meanings of knowledge, and it may induce in the reader a kind of critical breakdown. Sebald produces this effect not only by adding details but also, as I've suggested, by withholding them. Amir Eshel has shown that the proliferation of details in Sebald's narratives leads to a "suspension" or slowing down of time.[24] But by withholding some (well-known) details and providing others (that are less well known), Sebald is not only delaying and diverting the progress of knowledge but also drawing our attention to those processes of editing, contracting, and encoding that limit what we can see. In Sebald's novels, adding and withholding involve a formal device I call "unassimilation," which refers to the literal de-Anglicization of proper nouns and also to the less-literal disaggregation of collective experiences. Unassimilation does not return names to an original state of propriety: rather, it displays the history of translation, it uncontracts that history, by situating individuals, places, and even novels within several national, subnational, or transnational traditions. Unassimilation in some ways contributes to Benjaminian and Horkheimian endeavors because it expands the reader's knowledge of places, people, and events. But in other ways it resists these endeavors by establishing less definitive classifications. When he speaks of "the camps where untold numbers of people were burnt" ("AW" 71), for example, Sebald will list where those people came from, not to emphasize the universality of suffering so much as to emphasize the variety: "people from Berlin and Frankfurt, from Wuppertal and Vienna, from Würtzburg and Kissingen, from Hilversum and The Hague, Naumur and Thionville, Lyon and Bordeaux, Kraków and Łódź, Szeged and Sarajevo, Salonika and Rhodes, Ferrara and Venice—there was scarcely a place in Europe from which no on had been deported in those years" ("AW" 72–73). Lists of this sort, and there are many in Sebald's writings, are striking because they enumerate (there are many places), they overwhelm (there are *so* many places), and they create new, smaller lists (some of these places are metropolitan cities; some are provincial centers).

Sebald extends unassimilation not simply to the characters and events within his novels but to the geographies, cultures, and languages that allow us to place his novels within specific national traditions. Sebald asks us to consider how the political meanings and ethical consequences of his work are shaped by its multiple contexts of production, circulation, interpretation, and translation. *The Rings of Saturn* conveys this multiplicity most directly by reminding us, several times, that there are two different names for the body of water that the narrator sees along the beaches of Suffolk (*R* 46, 67, 78, 225). Sometimes, the narrator will speak of the North Sea and sometimes of the German Ocean. When he speaks of the North Sea, he identifies the eastern boundary of the British Isles. When he speaks of the German Ocean, a name seldom used after the nineteenth century, he registers a perspective: a view from the past and from the continent. Sebald's narrator does not seem to be conscious of this oscillation, but it allows Sebald to show that reputations influence even the facts of geography. Sebald suggests that national borders are no more evident or unchanging than national identities.[25] Introducing obsolete, uncommon, or foreign names, Sebald makes his readers see transiently. He makes them learn about the German resorts that once flourished along now-decrepit English beaches, consider the Allied bombing of civilians in German cities as well as the German massacre of Jews in concentration camps, and recognize England as an east as well as a west, in some ways distinct from and in some ways continuous with Europe.

Sebald changes the names of historical figures whose stories have come to represent, sometimes automatically, a collective past that is known rather than analyzed. By withholding familiar details, Sebald moves celebrities from the world of myth into the world of fiction; he makes them *writable*, rather than merely recognizable.[26] This transformation has three principal aims: to make readers perceive familiar stories analytically rather than automatically; to reverse and thereby display the processes of translation, immigration, and assimilation in which past experiences are often lost; and to introduce political contexts for which celebrated figures are not yet known. Sebald's novels present characters whose change of name reflects the desire to avoid or to retain anonymity.[27] Sometimes Sebald restores anonymity to well-known figures, as in *Vertigo*, which begins with an anecdote about "Marie Henri Beyle," a young officer in Napoleon's army and later a great novelist, whose *nom de plume*—Stendhal—Sebald will never invoke (*V* 4); or as in *Rings*, which describes a "young French nobleman," a "*vicomte*," who has fled to England during the French Revolution and who is only later identified as the Vicomte de Chateaubriand, the French author and diplomat (*R* 250). In one case, Sebald frustrates anonymity by reproducing it: in *Rings*, he alludes to "a young Viennese officer" who helped to round up Bosnians, Jews, and Serbs during the Second World War and later became Secretary General of the United Nations, but the words "Kurt Waldheim" will never appear in the text (*R* 97–99). Emphasizing or imposing anonymity, Sebald transforms concrete monuments into dynamic anecdotes that can be seen and interpreted in the context of other anecdotes.

Introducing details that are not yet or no longer known, Sebald both extends and disorients the modern experience of place. On the one hand, he wants to create a more expansive sense of the past by describing "forgotten things" and "almost unperceived" events;[28] on the other hand, he wants to suspend or delay the acquisition of knowledge by introducing objects and experiences that seem to thwart classification. The difference between these projects, the effort to establish more inclusive, more accurate strategies of description and the effort to unfix, even disable social categories, is regularly understood as the difference between modernism and postmodernism.[29] I have been arguing in this book, however, that the two efforts coexist, if uncomfortably, at both the beginning and the end of the twentieth century: the tension between them is a hallmark of critical cosmopolitanism.

***

Since Sebald lived in England as a German citizen, composed his novels in German, criticized other Germans for remaining silent about the air war and about the Holocaust, and often seemed to be responding to the writing of German predecessors, it makes sense that scholars and reviewers have thought about his work in the context of German literature. Martin Swales has shown that Sebald's prose reflects a German narrative tradition that is concerned with "the complex and ceaseless interplay of materiality and mentality."[30] One can see this tradition in Sebald's efforts both to describe everyday details and, at the same time, to attribute to those details "signification beyond common perception" ("Theoretical Reflections," 26). Amir Eshel has shown that Sebald's suspicion of ordering and his insistence on the value of metaphor follows "the credos of the West German documentary literature of the 1960s and 1970s," and that there are several German precedents for situating a critique of Nazi ideology within a broader critique of European modernity. And Andreas Huyssen has argued that Sebald's work identifies with and tries "to compensate for an undeniable German deficit of memory and experience."[31]

In the remainder of this chapter, I will be speculating about the Britishness of Sebald's novels. I do this neither to ignore the place of those novels in German literary history nor to suggest they have failed to achieve a fully "German" sensibility.[32] Rather, I want to consider how Sebald animates problems of national classification in general and the problem of his own classification in particular. In the context of British literary history, Sebald's analysis of imperialism appears not simply as an analogue for fascism but as an investigation of liberalism and other ideologies that have claimed to oppose tyranny. An emphasis on Britain, where Sebald's narrators live as tourists and residents, foregrounds Sebald's preoccupation with social and ethical marginality and with the geographical margins of Europe. Sebald discusses these issues most explicitly in *The Rings of Saturn*, where the eastern edges of Britain, he suggests, include Bombay and Hong Kong as well as Lowestoft and Norwich. Walking through Suffolk, the narrator of *Rings* describes the many voyages between periphery (Lowestoft) and periphery (Hong Kong) that defined the region in the past, and he suggests that Britain's coast may have many peripheries within it: peripheral communities like crumbling seaside towns; peripheral citizens like homosexuals and invalids; and peripheral experiences like the loss of pet birds in the customs hall at Dover. Whereas Kazuo Ishiguro, Salman Rushdie, Timothy Mo, and other immigrants to Britain wrote in the 1980s about Orientalism and colonialism, about the sites of U.S. and European imperialism, and about the immigration of Japanese, Pakistanis, and Chinese after the Second World War, Sebald wrote in the 1990s about the relationship between colonial exploitation and European architecture, about the small coastal towns of England, and about the prewar immigration of Poles, Germans, and Czechs, many of whom were Jews. Sebald brings the British novel back to Europe, one might say, but he does so by way of Asia, the Caribbean, and Africa: his novels extend the strategies of postcolonial critique, the analysis of "the East" as an imagined geography and cultural stereotype, to the analysis of "the West," its national histories, mythologies, and borders.

The Caribbean-born, British-raised novelist and critic Caryl Phillips, who lives in New York, could have included Sebald among his anthology of "extravagant strangers," those writers (he includes William Thackery and George Orwell as well as T. S. Eliot, Joseph Conrad, David Dabydeen, and Ben Okri) who were not born in Britain but whose work "contains a formal response to Britain's perception of herself."[33] Sebald is not a native of Britain, but he resembles the group of British-born contemporary writers who, as Phillips tells it, "explore primary historical ruptions in British society—both past and present—around issues of gender, class and sexuality" and who produce "post-consensus fictions" ("Extravagant Strangers," 294). Sebald's project shares in recent efforts to "provincialize Europe,"[34] to raise "questions about the coherence, presumed originality, and boundednesss of the modern, Western, Euro-American nation as a historical form,"[35] and to consider the "mostly unacknowledged traffic" between Europe and the non-European world.[36] A German native who lived in England for the last thirty years of his life, Sebald emphasizes the foreign entanglements both of his own endeavor and of those past endeavors, such as Joseph Conrad's, whose example he follows and reimagines.

The Rings of Saturn is Sebald's most British novel in setting and in subject, and in its effort to consider what passes for British today. One object that passes, Sebald suggests in an important episode, is *Heart of Darkness*; he will present the novel as a product not simply of Britain but of Poland, Belgium, and the Congo. Another is that trope of little England, the country house, whose "bygone paraphernalia," Sebald writes of one example, seems to have been gathered on "a tour of duty to Nigeria or Singapore" (*R* 35). Visiting Somerleyton Hall, with its stuffed polar bear in the entrance, "one is not quite sure," the narrator reports, "whether one is in a country house in Suffolk or some kind of no-man's land, on the shores of the Arctic Ocean or in the heart of the dark continent" (*R* 36). Sebald oscillates between peculiar detail (a stuffed polar bear, a camphorwood chest) and panoramic history: he reports the account of a Dutch acquaintance, who remarks that English country houses are more impressive than those in other European nations because the profits of colonialism were used in England to build rural estates, whereas in Holland they financed great buildings in the cities (*R* 193); the Dutchman adds that important art museums in both nations, the Tate Gallery in London and the Mauritshuis in The Hague, whose buildings contain and also constitute national treasures, "were originally endowed by the sugar dynasties or were in some other way connected with the sugar trade" (*R* 194).

Sebald uses the panoramic view to make two related points about British national monuments: they are built from the materials of other cultures, objects gathered abroad that serve as art or ornament at home; and they are built with the capital accrued from the exploitation of those cultures, the profits of sugar and slavery. The panoramic view allows Sebald to show, in the Benjaminian fashion I have discussed above, that the accomplishments of English civilization—the novel, the country house, and the art museum—were nourished by acts of exploitation and violence. The panoramic view also makes a point about geography: the monuments that define what seems to be a specific and exceptional nation owe many of their characteristics to the cultures that nation has conquered, destroyed, or excluded; for this reason, so-called national monuments must be seen as international artifacts, products of many cultures and of the sometimes violent contact among those cultures. The microscopic view, while it provides the details that allow Sebald to make these arguments, introduces residual uncertainties and a jolt of obliviousness about exploitation: the narrator will ponder the question of an object's origins without resolving it ("Nigeria or Singapore"?), and he will suggest that the country house, whatever its provenance, retains aesthetic or allegorical value, at least to him ("how fine a place the house seemed to me," the narrator relates, "now that it was imperceptibly nearing the brink of dissolution and silent oblivion" [36]).

Yet another object that passes for British, Sebald suggests, is his narrator, who takes after the author and whose Englishness is recognized in *Vertigo* by an Italian waiter quoted in my epigraph: "*Un inglese*, he said, and looked across at me with what I took to be a touch of contempt" (*V* 79). It is important to observe, of passing in general and of this incident in particular, that the waiter's recognition is not simply false: in Sebald's novels, national identities change over time and across contexts; the narrator is not quite an Englishman—he carries a German passport—but he speaks English, lives in England, and perhaps sounds English to an Italian. On a visit to a German town, later in the same novel, the narrator is taken for an "English foreign correspondent," and the epithet seems to fit (*V* 192). Of course, when we speak of people or objects that pass, we usually mean that they do not belong to the ethnicity or race or nation whose characteristics they appear to share: Sebald's novels only *pass* because they are not, in fact, British.[37] Yet Sebald seems to be working with rules of belonging that are somewhat more fluid, or at least more ambivalent than this view of passing would suggest: what is passing to some—being a resident but not a native of Britain, for example—is belonging to others; it depends which attributes (language, custom, citizenship, residency) are necessary and which merely incidental. Sebald proposes that immigration confers new, often provisional identities; that immigrants do not move between homogeneous and wholly distinct national cultures; and that the national or regional identity of an author and even of a novel depends not simply on the language of initial production but on the conditions of translation, circulation, and sympathy.

The Rings of Saturn is full of people who visualize Germany while residing in England and whose views create less unanimous, less official geographies. Sebald tells of Michael Hamburger, who left Berlin in 1933, at the age of nine, and whose "hallucinations and dreams . . . often take place in a setting reminiscent partly of the metropolis of Berlin and partly of rural Suffolk" (*R* 179). "For instance," Hamburger explains, "I may be standing at a window on the upper floor of our house, but what I see is not the familiar marshes and the willows thrashing as they always do, but rather, from several hundred yards up, acres and acres of allotment gardens bisected by a road, straight as an arrow, down which black taxis speed out of the city in the direction of the Wannsee" (*R* 179–80). In its Englishness and in its fantasy of aerial perspective, Hamburger's view of Berlin is similar to the one imagined by William Hazel, an English gardener who learned the terrain of Germany, he explains, by memorizing a military relief map. Looking at the map, the narrator reports, Hazel thought of the bombing raids that were "launched on Germany from the sixty-seven airfields that were established in East Anglia after 1940" (*R* 38). Every evening, Hazel remembers, "I watched the bomber squadrons heading out over Somerleyton, and night after night, before I went to sleep, I pictured in my mind's eye the German cities going up in flames, the firestorms setting the heavens alight, and the survivors rooting in the ruins" (*R* 38). The Germany that Hazel imagines is not equivalent to the map; rather, the map allows Hazel to envision an itinerary of destruction, a relationship between English airfields and German ruins. Hazel's story, focused on the Allied destruction of German cities, offers a counterpoint to Hamburger's story, about the Nazi destruction of Jewish life in Berlin. These are different points of view, ethically and historically, and they allow Sebald to suggest that various instances of travel, from England to Germany and from Germany to England, have transformed the geography of Europe, supplementing government maps and empirical measurements with snapshots, anecdotes, and informal affiliations. Falling asleep, dreaming, hallucinating: in these semiconscious states, Michael Hamburger and William Hazel are able to think globally and locally at the same time.

✳ ✳ ✳

In *Rings*, Sebald introduces this mixing of perspectives (local and global) and genres (empirical and imagined) with three epigraphs that he places at the beginning of the German edition.[38] Printed in different languages (English, French, and German) and taken from disparate sources (a seventeenth-century treatise, a nineteenth-century letter, and a twentieth-century scientific essay), the epigraphs reflect variously on the failure to see morally, empirically, or sympathetically. In each case, failure seems to be unavoidable and in some way valuable. The second epigraph, about the entanglement of good and evil, comes from *Areopagitica*, John Milton's treatise against literary censorship; the third, about the orbiting ruins that create the appearance of Saturn's rings, comes from an article in a German encyclopedia.[39] And the first epigraph, the one in French, comes from a letter written by the young Joseph Conrad to his aunt Marguerite Poradowska. Conrad's words, like those in the other epigraphs, prepare and even seem to rehearse the concerns of Sebald's novel: we learn right away of the need to pardon or excuse "ces âmes malheureuses qui . . . regardent sans comprendre l'horreur de la lutte, la joie de vaincre ni le profond désespoire des vaincus."[40]

While I don't think that Sebald agrees with Conrad, that one must above all excuse those who fail to understand, he shares Conrad's interest in the causes and opportunities of blindness. Not only in his epigraphs but also in an important chapter of *Rings*, Sebald will cite Conrad's words, as well as his works, strategies, and personal history. In obvious ways, Sebald resembles Conrad, in his experience of immigration, in his late career as a novelist in Britain, in his analysis of European colonialism, and in his consistent generosity toward those who fail to see. But Sebald will display an analytic difference between Conrad's narratives and his own, adding perspectives that Conrad was unable or unwilling to offer and introducing political choices that helped to determine, in the early days of modernism, what could be looked at and what could be understood. Sebald articulates these differences by telling a story of Conrad's life alongside a story about Conrad's acquaintance, the Anglo-Irish statesman Roger Casement, a colonial administrator and critic of colonialism who was executed for high treason in 1916.

Moving almost invisibly among several genres—letters, anecdotes, statistics, novels, government reports, and photographs—Sebald's story of Conrad and Casement brings together entries from Conrad's diary, passages from *Heart of Darkness*, an economic analysis of Belgian colonialism, a story about the narrator's trip to Brussels in December 1964, Casement's detailed version of Belgian labor policies in the Congo, pages from Casement's "black diary" in which he recorded his sexual encounters with men, and a panoramic account of European colonialism that connects events in the Congo to those closer to home. The structure of the novel's ten chapters is suggestive about the structure of this single chapter. The parts are held together by the narrator's "pilgrimage"—he is walking along the coast of Suffolk, from one town to another—and by the reappearance of physical materials, such as silk. However, these materials have both empirical and metaphorical trajectories: describing the production and circulation of silk, Sebald considers the economic history of European smuggling and global trade, on the one hand, and analytic paradigms of mourning, prophecy, and transformation, on the other.[41] The persistence of metaphor means that the reader must assemble the novel's pieces, but the pieces create an unfinished work. Late in his novel, Sebald offers a metaphor for this metaphor in his description of "a bridal gown made of hundreds of scraps of silk embroidered with silken thread" (*R* 212). The gown, produced by three sisters who live on a neglected family estate in Ireland, is made up of "remnant fabrics," pieces of other garments, which, like Sebald's narratives, have been stitched together and then elaborated ("embroidered") with new, intricate designs. The gown bears the traces of its composition, though Sebald suggests that the mixing of colors and fabrics and the superimposed stitching makes the new garment all the more original. The story of the gown and the three sisters reminds us that Sebald is inventing as well as assembling, and that we are meant to invent, too.

In his account of Conrad and Casement, Sebald's method involves both more sewing and more embroidering than the narrator at first acknowledges. Most of the chapter presents the narrator's efforts to "reconstruct" a television documentary about Casement's life. But since the narrator has not in fact seen the documentary—he fell asleep while watching—the so-called reconstruction is the product not of memory but of research and speculation. Sebald's conceit allows him begin his story with Conrad and to approach Britain from the marginal perspectives of Poland, the Congo, and Ireland. He speaks first of Conrad's experience of Russian imperialism, in part to emphasize, by the later contrast with Casement, the versions of imperialism that Conrad does not consider and in part to draw connections among various forms of "tyranny," Russian, Belgian, and British (*R* 104).

Like many other characters in Sebald's text, the author of *Heart of Darkness* goes by more than one name: initially, he is called by his English pen name, Joseph Conrad, but more often he is called by one of his Polish names, Konrad Korzeniowski. There are stylistic affinities between Sebald's novel and Conrad's—for example, Sebald's unassimilation of Conrad's name echoes Conrad's strategy "delayed decoding," and Sebald's use of embedded narrators evokes Conrad's similar conceit in *Heart of Darkness*.[42] In Sebald's text, Conrad becomes the object of his own celebrated techniques. Withholding what readers conventionally know about Conrad, Sebald focuses attention on Korzeniowski's movement among several national cultures and on the production of his British self. By reminding readers that Conrad began his life among those who were "suffering the humiliation of foreign rule" (*R* 105), as Conrad seems to put it, Sebald will have us connect the occupation of Poland by Russia to the occupations of the Congo by Belgium and of Ireland by Britain; and he will have us connect Korzeniowski's early experience of border crossing, living in Polish Russia, with his later experiences as a French seaman and a British novelist.

Sebald uses Conrad's critique of Belgium in *Heart of Darkness* to establish an expansive critique of Britain in his own novel. If Conrad is critical of liberal nationalism, as Pericles Lewis has shown, Sebald goes further in describing the illiberal actions that liberal nationalism has helped to obscure.[43] He does this by integrating language from Conrad's fiction with a report on Conrad's experience, so that it is Korzeniowski as much as Conrad's fictional narrator Marlow who observes "black shadows," worked nearly to death, building the Congolese railroad (*R* 120). Sebald attributes to Korzeniowski the observation that the "bombastic" architecture of Brussels, where he went to visit his aunt, seemed like "a sepulchral monument erected over the hecatomb of black bodies" (*R* 122). Conrad speaks of "black shadows," but it is Sebald, not Conrad, who will mention bodies and who will introduce Belgian architecture to the story of African colonies; moreover, it is Roger Casement who will speak explicitly about Belgian atrocities and who will draw connections between Belgian colonialism in the Congo and British colonialism in Ireland. Sebald turns to Casement to supplement Conrad's account because Casement "could tell things that he, Korzeniowski, had long been trying to forget" (*R* 127). Some of the things that Casement could tell about the Congo include "an exact account of the utterly merciless exploitation of the blacks" (*R* 127). But Casement does not stop there: he also describes British exploits in "the jungle areas of Peru, Colombia, and Brazil that resembled those in the Congo in many respects"; and British culpability in Ireland, where "in recent times more than a million Irish had died of starvation" (*R* 128–29).

It is significant that Sebald is adding concrete details. However, it is also significant that Sebald does not correct Conrad's silences by offering non-European voices, such as those that might belong to those "black bodies" that the British and the Belgians exploited. And he does not correct Casement, who expressed racist stereotypes in private even while he opposed exploitation in public.[44] Instead, he will focus on "liberal" forms of tyranny: he will describe Britain's treatment of Casement, whose execution for treason during the First World War, after a failed attempt to enlist German support for the Irish uprising, was hastened by evidence of his homosexuality. Sebald notices that those who might have sympathized with Casement, for his willingness to criticize European exploitation and for his defense of Ireland, were unwilling to support him once his private diaries had been circulated by British officials.

At the start of *The Rings of Saturn*, one is tempted to see Conrad as Sebald's double, and in some ways he is. But in other ways, Casement is the closer relation. Whereas Conrad carefully manages proximity and detachment, Casement fails to balance or withhold his passions. Allied at one time or another with Britain, Germany, Belgium, and Ireland, Casement is a perpetrator who is also a victim: he helped to administer colonial governments in the Congo and South America, and yet his public criticism of those governments helped to prompt international outrage against economic and environmental exploitation; he offered military support to Germany during the First World War but did so to help the cause of Irish independence from Britain. In this political history, Sebald sides with the anti-imperialist, homosexual traitor, noting that Casement's inability to separate what Cynthia Enloe has called "the personal and the international" was both his downfall and his greatest resource; it was Casement's personal experience of marginality, Sebald proposes, that made him attentive to international suffering.[45] Because he had to reflect on his own embodiment, Sebald suggests, Casement was better able to notice and less eager to ignore the bodies of others.

In Sebald's texts, the experience of marginality generates a kind of vertigo that is politically useful in two ways: it makes people more aware of their own materiality (their physical bodies but also the particularity of their views); and it makes people question the comforts of inclusiveness. Massimo Leone has observed that, medically speaking, vertigo involves the negative perception of one's own equilibrium. This means, he proposes, that vertigo "could be an occasion (or a voluntary strategy) through which the human body seeks to develop a full awareness of itself."[46] That is, it could be an occasion to reflect not only on disequilibrium but also on those states of being that go unperceived. Vertigo is in this sense a process or a strategy of estrangement. As an ethical paradigm, vertigo can inspire what Michael Rothberg has called "puzzlement": not the comprehension or reconciliation of multiple views, but "the apprehension of the simultaneously global and local dimension of intersecting histories."[47] Writing of W. E. B. Du Bois's effort to think simultaneously about Nazi terror and U.S. racism, Rothberg suggests that puzzlement can acknowledge "the perils of transcultural movement" while valuing "the idea that only by passing through such perils can the traveler gain insight into the world."

There are at least three models of cosmopolitanism that one should see in Sebald's work. One is the effort to consider how the lives of people in one place rely on, exploit, or benefit the lives of people elsewhere. This is an old model of cosmopolitanism: it emphasizes the value of recognizing and feeling attachments across national divides. This effort is "critical," in the sense of demystifying, because it displays economic patterns, systems of exploitation, and political responsibilities that were not previously visible. Yet Sebald combines the traditional model with two others: first, there is the effort to compare, distinguish, and judge among different versions of thinking beyond the nation—among, say, Conrad's, Casement's, the version that animates British imperialism, the version that animates anti-imperialist nationalisms, and so on. And, second, there is the effort to generate, instead of judgment and order, an ethos of embodied uncertainty that is sometimes at odds with political action and the affects of critical theory. By refusing to praise Conrad or to bury him, by reproducing Conrad's strategies of display but also adding to them, by speculating as well as documenting, by placing the conflict between personal freedoms and collective actions at the heart both of modernism and of cosmopolitanism, Sebald asks us to consider that a critical cosmopolitanism will have to reflect not only on social uses and political interests but also on intellectual protocols and analytic styles.

Peter Craven has attributed to Sebald the conviction that no memory is "so trivial or intolerable that it cannot become the subject of art."[48] I would offer something stronger: triviality and intolerability, because they test the formal and ethical limits of inclusion, are the conditions of Sebald's art. Bringing the margins of British history to the center of his narratives, Sebald enhances and disables the place of national fiction; its constituency and its borders, he affirms, are vertiginous at best.

INTRODUCTION

1. *Granta*'s "Best of Young British Novelists" awards are limited to writers under forty who are citizens of the United Kingdom, though the winners need not be residents; one of the 2003 winners lives permanently in the United States, while another was born and in part raised in Pakistan; see Ian Jack, "Introduction," *Granta* 81 (Spring 2003): 10. The Whitbread Award for "contemporary British writing" does not require citizenship in the United Kingdom but does require at least three years residency. The Man-Booker Prize is awarded for the best full-length novel written in English by a citizen of the Commonwealth or the Republic of Ireland. In May 2002, the sponsors of the Booker proposed that novels written in English by U.S. citizens also should be considered, but this proposal was later retracted to protect what Lisa Jardine, a Booker judge and professor of English, called the "voice of the Commonwealth." Robert McCrum, "The World of Books: Parochial, Smug, Ill-Informed. And That's Just the Critics," *The Observer*, 26 May 2002, 18.

2. *Austerlitz* was published almost simultaneously in German (Munich, March 2001) and in English (New York and London, October 2001); Sebald's other books were published first in German and only later in English.

3. For an account of modernist literary styles used to articulate a fascist politics, see Jessica Berman, *Modernist Fiction, Cosmopolitanism, and the Politics of Community* (Cambridge: Cambridge University Press, 2001), 21, 139.

4. For a more modest or "strategic" type of "planetary humanism," see Paul Gilroy, *Against Race: Imagining Political Culture Beyond the Color Line* (Cambridge, Mass.: Harvard University Press, 2000), 356. Gilroy's project sounds more like critical cosmopolitanism when, in his more recent work, he distinguishes between a planetary humanism based on "mundane encounters with difference" and "recipes

for good governance that have been pronounced from up above." Paul Gilroy, *After Empire: Melancholia or Convivial Culture?* (London: Routledge, 2004), 75. For other versions of "cosmopolitan universalism," see Ross Posnock, *Color and Culture: Black Writers and the Making of the Modern Intellectual* (Cambridge, Mass.: Harvard University Press University Press, 1998), 21; and Martha Nussbaum, "Patriotism and Cosmopolitanism?" in *Respondents, For Love of Country: Debating the Limits of Patriotism,* ed. Joshua Cohen (Boston: Beacon Press, 1996), 2.

5. Edward W. Said, "Heroism and Humanism," *Al-Ahram Weekly Online,* no. 463 (6–12 January 2000), http://weekly.ahram.org.eg/2000/463/op10.htm; Jacques Lezra, "Unrelated Passions," *differences: A Journal of Feminist Cultural Studies* 14, no. 1 (2003): 83–84; Benjamin Lee, "Critical Internationalism," *Public Culture* 7, no. 3 (Spring 1995): 591; Melba Cuddy-Keane, "Modernism, Geopolitics, Globalization," *Modernism/Modernity* 10, no. 3 (2003): 546.

6. Immanuel Kant, "An Answer to the Question: 'What is Enlightenment?'" in *Kant: Political Writings,* 2nd ed., ed. Hans Reiss, trans. H. B. Nisbet (Cambridge: Cambridge University Press, 1991), 56.

7. Immanuel Kant, "An Answer to the Question," 54–60; "Idea for a Universal History with a Cosmopolitan Purpose" in *Kant: Political Writings,* 2nd ed., ed. Hans Reiss, trans. H. B. Nisbet (Cambridge: Cambridge University Press, 1991), 49; and "Perpetual Peace: A Philosophical Sketch" in *Kant: Political Writings,* 2nd ed., ed. Hans Reiss, trans. H. B. Nisbet (Cambridge: Cambridge University Press, 1991), 108, emphasis in original.

8. I'm thinking here of Bruce Robbins's "cosmopolitics," of Melba Cuddy-Keane's "critical globalization," of James Clifford's "discrepant cosmopolitanism," and of Homi K. Bhabha's "vernacular cosmopolitanism," as well as of Walter Mignolo's own "critical cosmopolitanism." Below, I discuss these formulations in greater detail.

9. Max Horkheimer, "Traditional and Critical Theory," in *Critical Theory: Selected Essays,* trans. Matthew J. O'Connell et al. (New York: Herder and Herder, 1972), 188–243. For recent efforts to historicize and offer alternatives to the contemporary norms of "critical reading," see Eve Kosofsky Sedgwick, "Paranoid Reading and Reparative Reading; or, You're So Paranoid, You Probably Think This Introduction Is About You," in *Novel-Gazing: Queer Reading in Fiction,* ed. Eve Kosofsky Sedgwick (Durham, N.C.: Duke University Press, 1997), 1–37; Jordana Rosenberg, "The Bosom of the Bourgeoisie: Edgeworth's *Belinda," ELH* 70 (2003): 575–96; and Michael Warner, "Uncritical Reading," in *Polemic: Critical or Uncritical,* ed. Jane Gallop (New York: Routledge, 2004), 13–38.

10. Warner, "Uncritical Reading," 17. For an analysis of these efforts to replace reason with ethos, see Amanda Anderson, "Argument and Ethos" in *Polemic: Critical or Uncritical,* ed. Jane Gallop (New York: Routledge, 2004), 103–34.

11. Theodor W. Adorno, "Critique," in *Critical Models,* trans. Henry W. Pickford (New York: Columbia University Press, 1998), 284, 287. Stuart Hall, "What Is This 'Black' in Black Popular Culture?" in *Black Popular Culture,* ed. Michele Wallace and Gina Dent (Seattle: Bay Press, 1992), 24, 27.

12. Warner, "Uncritical Reading," 17; Rosenberg, "Bosom of the Bourgeoisie," 592. Also, see Sharon Marcus's discussion of sentimentality in "Anne Frank and Hannah Arendt, Universalism and Pathos," in *Cosmopolitan Geographies: New Locations in Literature and Culture*, ed. Vinay Dharwadker (New York: Routledge, 2001), 92.

13. Sianne Ngai, *Ugly Feelings* (Cambridge, Mass.: Harvard University Press, 2005), 5.

14. For an extended discussion of cosmopolitanism's negotiation between distance and proximity, see Amanda Anderson, *The Powers of Distance: Cosmopolitanism and the Cultivation of Detachment* (Princeton, N.J.: Princeton University Press, 2001). I am grateful to Sianne Ngai for helping me to think about "suspended agency" as a condition of postmodernity (*Ugly Feelings*, 32).

15. Walter D. Mignolo, "The Many Faces of Cosmo-polis: Border Thinking and Critical Cosmopolitanism," in *Cosmopolitanism*, ed. Carol A. Breckenridge et al. (Durham, N.C.: Duke University Press, 2002), 170–74.

16. Sheldon Pollock, Homi K. Bhabha, Carol A. Breckenridge, and Dipesh Chakrabarty, "Cosmopolitanisms," in *Cosmopolitianism*, ed. Breckenridge et al. (Durham: Duke University Press, 2002), 3.

17. It is important to see that the opposite of "critical cosmopolitanism" is not really "uncritical cosmopolitanism," since even a cosmopolitanism that does not reflect on its historical uses or on the varieties of critique will still involve the effort to display and often to judge economic patterns, systems of exploitation, and political responsibilities that were not previously visible. For this reason, I will refer, after Horkheimer, to "traditional cosmopolitanism."

18. In formal terms, scholars have disagreed about which literary techniques are sufficient or necessary to properly modernist texts. For a helpful discussion of this disagreement, see Brian Richardson, "Remapping the Present: The Master Narrative of Modern Literary History and the Lost Forms of Twentieth-Century Fiction," *Twentieth Century Literature* 43, no. 3 (Autumn 1997): 291–309. I share Richardson's sense that "modernist" writing can be identified in the early as well as the late twentieth century. However, I will not be attempting to choose among competing definitions of modernist form. Instead, I will be base my use of the term "modernist" on two assumptions: (1) that texts may include both modernist and postmodernist elements; and (2) that a more capacious definition of literary modernism allows us to notice contradictory impulses within responses to modernity and globalization.

19. The question of whether an "English literary history" (defined by language and subject matter) or a history of "British literature" (defined by sites of production) is more attentive to the experience of minority cultures, the history of colonialism, the variety of spoken or written languages used in Britain, and the history of writing and reading in English deserves much more attention than I will give it here. For a defense of "English literary history," see Jonathan Bate, general preface to *The Oxford English Literary History*, in *The Internationalization of English Literature*, vol. 13, ed. Bruce King, in *The Oxford Literary History* (Oxford: Oxford University Press, 2003), viii–x. For a defense of a history of "British literature," see David

Damrosch, preface to *The Longman Anthology of British Literature*, vol. 2 (New York: Longman, 1999), xxxiii–xxxvii.

20. For the relationship between "the personal" and "the international," see Cynthia Enloe, *Bananas, Beaches, and Bases* (Berkeley: University of California Press, 1990), 196–97; Bruce Robbins cites Enloe in *Feeling Global: Internationalism in Distress* (New York: New York University Press, 1999), 172.

21. Dilip Parameshwar Gaonkar, "On Alternative Modernities," in *Alternative Modernities*, ed. Dilip Parameshwar Gaonkar (Durham, N.C.: Duke University Press, 2001), 13–14.

22. Michel Foucault, "What Is Enlightenment?" in *The Foucault Reader*, ed. Paul Rabinow, trans. Catherine Porter (New York: Pantheon, 1984), 39, 42.

23. Susan Stanford Friedman, "Definitional Excursions: The Meanings of Modern/ Modernity/Modernism," *Modernism/Modernity* 8, no. 3 (September 2001): 505; Dipesh Chakrabarty, *Provincializing Europe: Postcolonial Thought and Historical Difference* (Princeton, N.J.: Princeton University Press, 2000), 181, 187.

24. Terry Eagleton, *Exiles and Émigrés* (New York: Schocken, 1970); George Steiner, *Extra-Territorial: Papers on Literature and the Language Revolution* (New York: Atheneum, 1971); Michael Seidel, *Exile and the Narrative Imagination* (New Haven, Conn.: Yale University Press, 1986); Caren Kaplan, *Questions of Travel: Postmodern Discourses of Displacement* (Durham, N.C.: Duke University Press, 1996), 102. For an effort to shift the metaphor from "exile" to "diaspora," see Nico Israel, *Outlandish: Writing Between Exile and Diaspora* (Stanford, Calif.: Stanford University Press, 2000).

25. For important accounts of the expansion and centrality of place in twentieth-century British fiction, see Ian Baucom, *Out of Place: Englishness, Empire, and the Locations of Identity* (Princeton, N.J.: Princeton University Press, 1999); and Simon Gikandi, *Maps of Englishness: Writing Identity in the Culture of Colonialism* (New York: Columbia University Press, 1996). For more recent work on this subject, see Bruce King, ed., *The Internationalization of English Literature*, vol. 13 of *The Oxford Literary History* (Oxford: Oxford University Press, 2003); John Clement Ball, *Imagining London: Postcolonial Fiction and the Transnational Metropolis* (Toronto: University of Toronto Press, 2004); and Bishnupriya Ghosh, *When Borne Across: Literary Cosmopolitics in the Contemporary Indian Novel* (New Brunswick, N.J.: Rutgers University Press, 2004).

26. In recent years, scholars have sought to diversify modernism's internationalism. Edward Said and Simon Gikandi have argued that the intellectual and economic movement between metropolitan centers in Europe and the United States and the centers of empire in India, East Asia, and Africa was crucial to the modernist imagination. Edward W. Said, *Culture and Imperialism* (New York: Knopf, 1994); and Gikandi, *Maps of Englishness*. Earlier accounts of internationalism have been supplemented as well by a move toward greater specificity and plurality in the definition of the term: scholars now acknowledge the very different internationalisms, both biographical and literary, of T. S. Eliot, Henry James, James Joyce, Joseph Conrad, and others. See Alex Zwerdling's discussion of Eliot and

James in *Improvised Europeans: American Literary Expatriates in London* (New York: Basic Books, 1998).

27. Michael H. Levenson, "Does *The Waste Land* Have a Politics?" *Modernism/Modernity* 6, no. 3 (September 1999): 1–13.

28. Virginia Woolf, "Modern Fiction" (1925), in *The Common Reader* (New York: Harcourt, 1984), 150, 152; "Mr Bennett and Mrs Brown" (1924) in *The Captain's Death Bed and Other Essays* (New York: Harcourt, 1978), 94–119.

29. I take the phrase "inadequacy and indispensability" from Antoinette Burton's discussion of the usefulness of "the nation" as a disciplinary paradigm in "Introduction: On the Inadequacy and Indispensability of the Nation," in *After the Imperial Turn: Thinking With and Through the Nation*, ed. Antoinette Burton (Durham, N.C.: Duke University Press, 1999), 1–26; she takes her use from Chakrabarty's discussion of the Enlightenment in *Provincializing Europe*. My sense of the tension between expanding and disabling traditions has been enriched by these formulations.

30. Pollock et al., "Cosmopolitanisms," 10.

31. For an example of universal cosmopolitanism, see Nussbaum, "Patriotism and Cosmopolitanism?" 4. For plural cosmopolitanisms, see Pollock et al., "Cosmopolitanisms," 1–14. For a discussion of the popular tradition, see Mica Nava, "Cosmopolitan Modernity: Everyday Imaginaries and the Register of Difference," *Theory, Culture, and Society* 19, no. 1–2 (2002): 81–99.

32. See Amanda Anderson, "Cosmopolitanism, Universalism, and the Divided Legacies of Modernity," in *Cosmopolitics: Thinking and Feeling Beyond the Nation*, ed. Pheng Cheah and Bruce Robbins (Minneapolis: University of Minnesota Press, 1998), 268.

33. James Clifford, *The Predicament of Culture: Twentieth-Century Ethnography, Literature, and Art* (Cambridge, Mass.: Harvard University Press, 1998), 95.

34. Homi K. Bhabha, "Editor's Introduction: Minority Maneuvers and Unsettled Negotiations," *Critical Inquiry* 23, no. 3 (Spring 1997): 434; James Clifford, *Routes* (Cambridge, Mass.: Harvard University Press, 1997), 31.

35. Bruce Robbins, "Introduction, Part 1: Actually Existing Cosmopolitanism," in *Cosmopolitics: Thinking and Feeling Beyond the Nation*, ed. Pheng Cheah and Bruce Robbins (Minneapolis: University of Minnesota Press, 1998), 2; Kwame Anthony Appiah, "Cosmopolitan Patriots," *Critical Inquiry* 23, no. 3 (Spring 1997): 617–39; Anderson, "Cosmopolitanism, Universalism," 268–69, 285; Bruce Robbins, *Secular Vocations* (London: Verso, 1993), 181.

36. Matthew Arnold, for example, supports cosmopolitanism as a "commingling of cultures" (this is Amanda Anderson's phrase) and as the transcendence of provinciality, rather than as a change in what culture means (Anderson, *The Powers of Distance*, 94).

37. To be sure, modernist writers were preoccupied with national traditions and public rituals in the troubled political and economic climate of the 1930s, as Esty shows, but I argue that the manners and rituals of English society were a principal subject for modernist writing in previous decades as well. Jed Esty, *A Shrinking Island:*

Modernism and National Culture in England (Princeton, N.J.: Princeton University Press, 2004), 40.

38. My argument about the critique of heroic nationalism in some modernist works has been enriched by Christopher Reed's account of "housework" modernism in *Bloomsbury Rooms: Modernism, Subculture, and Domesticity* (New Haven, Conn.: Yale University Press, 2004), 5.

39. Jennifer Wicke has described the "socialist individualism" of Bloomsbury as "Wildeanism lived in a coterie fashion," "a design for living" that the Bloomsberries would live and others could emulate: Jennifer Wicke, "*Mrs. Dalloway* Goes to Market: Woolf, Keynes, and Modern Markets," *Novel* 28, no. 1 (Fall 1994): 9. Similarly, in *Bloomsbury Rooms*, Reed argues that "Bloomsbury artists' thirty-year project to make modern rooms to suit their ideals for modern life attests to the persistence within modernism of subcurrents associated with the suppressed categories . . . [of] decoration, leisure, pleasure, femininity, sensuality" (277).

40. Sarah Cole, *Modernism, Male Friendship, and the First World War* (Cambridge: Cambridge University Press, 2003); Susan Stanford Friedman, "Geopolitical Literacy: Internationalizing Feminism at 'Home'—The Case of Virginia Woolf," in *Mappings: Feminism and the Cultural Geographies of Encounter* (Princeton, N.J.: Princeton University Press, 1998), 107–31.

41. Chantal Mouffe, *The Democratic Paradox* (London: Verso, 2000), 101.

42. For work on the gender of modernity, see Janet Wolff, "The Feminine in Modern Art: Benjamin, Simmel, and the Gender of Modernity," *Theory, Culture, and Society* 17 (2000): 37; Rita Felski, *The Gender of Modernity* (Cambridge, Mass.: Harvard University Press, 1995); on Woolf's "alternative discourse of feminist action and power . . . which seeks to intervene directly in the political life of Britain," see Berman, *Modernist Fiction*, 117.

43. Virginia Woolf, *Three Guineas* (1938), in *A Room of One's Own and Three Guineas*, ed. Michèle Barrett (London: Penguin, 2000), 234.

44. Jean-François Lyotard, *The Postmodern Condition: A Report on Knowledge*, trans. Geoff Bennington and Brian Massumi (Minneapolis: University of Minnesota Press, 1984), 81.

45. Decadence is an affect of cosmopolitanism, but it is a product of cosmopolitanism as well: consider, for example, Oscar Wilde's *Salomé*, an Orientalist drama about perverse desire and embodied display, composed by an Irishman acting out French symbolism in imperial London. Judith R. Walkowitz, "The 'Vision of Salome': Cosmopolitanism and Erotic Dancing in Central London, 1908–1918," *American Historical Review* 108, no. 2 (April 2003): 337–76. Arguing for "the utopian exemplarity of 'excessive' pleasure—including the pleasure of 'excessive' interpretation—in a cultural order intensively involved in the regulation and distribution of *sufficient* pleasure," Joseph Litvak introduces sophistication's decadence as a strategy of social critique. Joseph Litvak, *Strange Gourmets: Sophistication, Theory, and the Novel* (Durham: Duke University Press, 1997), 7.

46. One thinks of the Auden generation, of the Beat poets, and of contemporary novelists such as Jeanette Winterson and Alan Hollinghurst, among others. This

legacy is the subject of Alan Sinfield, *The Wilde Century: Effeminacy, Oscar Wilde, and the Queer Moment* (New York: Columbia University Press, 1994); its effects on the literature of the First World War is discussed by Samuel Hynes in *A War Imagined: The First World War and English Culture* (London: The Bodley Head, 1990), 16–17.

47. Some of the recent scholarship on modernism has sought to remedy this absence: while Amanda Anderson has emphasized the "strongly individualist elements" within the tradition of cosmopolitanism, including the "appeal to self-cultivation" in Oscar Wilde's work (*The Powers of Distance*, 31–32), Heather Love has argued that, "as a form of aesthetic and moral apostasy, modernism joins the image of revolt to the image of abject failure." Heather K. Love, "Forced Exile: Walter Pater's Queer Modernism" in *Bad Modernisms*, ed. Douglas Mao and Rebecca L. Walkowitz (Durham: Duke University Press, 2006), 19–43. For a critique of the assumption that the heroic model of modernism is the general model and for an analysis of the military metaphor, see Reed, *Bloomsbury Rooms*, 2, 11.

48. Mica Nava, "Cosmopolitan Modernity"; Monica L. Miller, "The Black Dandy as Bad Modernist," in *Bad Modernisms*, ed. Douglas Mao and Rebecca L. Walkowitz (Durham: Duke University Press, 2006), 179–205; Arjun Appadurai, *Modernity at Large: Cultural Dimensions of Globalization* (Minneapolis: University of Minnesota Press, 1996); Amitava Kumar, *Away: The Indian Writer as Expatriate* (New York: Routledge, 2004).

49. Like Joyce, some scholars now affirm ambivalence and conflict as necessary, sometimes useful conditions of cosmopolitan thought. The advocates of this position include anthropologists and literary scholars, as well as political theorists such as Chantal Mouffe, who argues for a model of radical democracy "that recognizes us as divided subjects and does not dream of an impossible reconciliation." Chantal Mouffe, "Which Ethics for Democracy?" in *The Turn to Ethics*, ed. Marjorie Garber, Beatrice Hanssen, and Rebecca L. Walkowitz (New York: Routledge, 2000), 94. Also see Robbins, *Feeling Global*, 4, 17; James Clifford, "Mixed Feelings" in *Cosmopolitics: Thinking and Feeling Beyond the Nation*, ed. Pheng Cheah and Bruce Robbins (Minneapolis: University of Minnesota Press, 1998), 368–69. See Enda Duffy's discussion of the "aggressive" qualities of postcolonial *flânerie* in *The Subaltern* Ulysses (Minneapolis: University of Minnesota Press, 1994), 63.

50. Vinay Dharwadker, introduction to *Cosmopolitan Geographies: New Locations in Literature and Culture*, ed. Vinay Dhardwadker (New York: Routledge, 2001), 2.

51. Samuel Scheffler, "Conceptions of Cosmopolitanism," *Utilitas* 11, no. 3 (November 1999): 255–76.

52. Of course, some might say that Tagore is hardly a critic of Eurocentrism. For this argument, see my "Cosmopolitan Ethics" in *The Turn to Ethics*, ed. Marjorie Garber, Beatrice Hanssen, and Rebecca L. Walkowitz (New York: Routledge, 2000), 221–30. Amit Chaudhuri argues that "some Orientals (Tagore, say) both were and were not Orientalists": Chaudhuri, "In the Waiting-Room of History," *London Review of Books*, 24 June 2004, 5.

53. Nussbaum, "Patriotism and Cosmopolitanism?" 8.

54. Eurocentrism aside, learning French and reading English poetry are valorized by the cosmopolitan character Nikhil not as strategies of "worldwide allegiance" (Nussbaum's phrase) but as strategies of individualism. Chakrabarty has pointed to the complexity of Tagore's status not only within nationalism but also within modernism (*Provincializing Europe*, 158–171).

55. These echoes of modernism in contemporary cosmopolitanism are faint in some accounts, particularly in Nussbaum's, which explicitly rejects versions of cosmopolitanism not committed to direct ethical action, but they are more distinct in those accounts that are committed to what I am calling "critical cosmopolitanism." See Chakrabarty's critique of the "waiting-room" theory of modernization in *Provincializing Europe*, 6–8 and passim.

56. Robbins, *Feeling Global*, 15.

57. This term was used as the title of a collection of essays edited by Robbins and Pheng Cheah in 1998. In "The Village of the Liberal Managerial Class," in *Cosmopolitan Geographies: New Locations in Literature and Culture*, ed. Vinay Dharwadker (New York: Routledge, 2001), 15–32, published three years after *Cosmopolitics*, Robbins admires the selective cosmopolitanism of Kazuo Ishiguro's fictional butler, Stevens, whose "detached professional affectivity removes him sufficiently from the national passions raging around him that he can play his small part in what turns out to have been a plausible, even visionary project, a project to avoid Hitler's rise to power and the catastrophe of World War II" (30).

58. In the later essay, Robbins argues that "an internationalist antiglobalization politics" will have to emerge out of ordinary moments of "hesitation," which he describes in two ways: as "the effort to perceive one's place in [the division of labor]" and as a "limited moment of ethically inspired consumer consciousness." Bruce Robbins, "The Sweatshop Sublime," *PMLA* 117, no. 1 (January 2002): 86, 89, 94.

59. Robbins, *Feeling Global*, 119, 23.

60. Dharwadker aims to expand "the analysis of cosmopolitanism from its usual setting in post-Enlightenment modernity and contemporaneity back toward late-medieval Europe and the classical Latin Middle Ages, even while redistributing its points of critical departure out from the north and the west to the south (Africa) and the east (Asia)" (Dharwadker, introduction, 2–3). Walter D. Mignolo aims to "reconceive cosmopolitanism from the perspective of coloniality"; he calls this new perspective "critical cosmopolitanism" ("The Many Faces of Cosmo-polis," 159). Clifford invokes "discrepant cosmopolitanisms" to characterize the range and specificity of different "diasporic articulations" in *Routes*, 36.

61. I am grateful to Vinay Dharwadker and Lucienne Loh for helping me to think about these distinctions.

62. Cuddy-Keane, "Modernism, Geopolitics, Globalization," 553. I take this to be part of Dipesh Charkrabarty's point, in *Provincializing Europe*, when he distinguishes between the democratic project of representing "minority histories" and what he sees as the more radical, analytic project of using these histories to "raise . . . fundamental questions about the discipline" (97–98). Mignolo will describe this as changing "the terms, not just the content of the conversation" (*Local Histories,*

Global Designs: Coloniality, Subaltern Knowledges, and Border Thinking [Princeton, N.J.: Princeton University Press, 2000], 70), whereas Gaonkar will propose that "alternative modernities" are characterized by "an attitude of questioning the present" ("On Alternative Modernities," 13).

63. See Goankar, "On Alternative Modernities," 20–21.

64. For the argument that cosmopolitanism should be rejected even in its renovated forms, see David Parker, "Diaspora, Dissidence, and the Dangers of Cosmopolitanism," *Asian Studies Review* 27, no. 2 (June 2003): 164. For the argument that cosmopolitanism should be retained as an analytic paradigm but dissociated from "class, hierarchy, and affluence," see Dharwadker, introduction, 11. Cuddy-Keane makes a point related to mine when she argues that "cultural globalization" need not be identified solely with "economic imperialism, leaving, as the only alternative, the oppositional stance of *anti*-globalization" ("Modernism, Geopolitics, Globalization," 541). Antoinette Burton displays the political ambiguities of twentieth-century cosmopolitanism in her elegant analysis of the "quasi-colonial postcolonial cosmopolitan" career of Santha Rama Rau ("The Postcolonial Careers of Santha Rama Rau," work in progress, 9).

65. Stefan Collini, "On Variousness; and on Persuasion," *New Left Review* 27 (May/ June 2004): 96. Caroline Levine makes a powerful argument for the politics of suspenseful narration in *The Serious Pleasures of Suspense* (Charlottesville: University of Virginia Press, 2003).

66. Raymond Williams, "Metropolitan Perceptions and the Emergence of Modernism," in *The Politics of Modernism: Against the New Conformists*, ed. Tony Pinkney (London: Verso, 1989), 38–39.

67. Fredric Jameson, "Modernism and Imperialism," in *Nationalism, Colonialism, and Literature*, ed. Terry Eagleton, Fredric Jameson, and Edward W. Said (Minneapolis: University of Minnesota Press, 1990), 60.

68. Fredric Jameson and Jed Esty have asked us to notice that even those modernist texts that seem to have little or no thematic engagement with imperialism, such as E. M. Forster's *Howard's End*, are marked by the influence of British imperial relations: Jameson, "Modernism and Imperialism." Esty argues not only that "we must recognize imperialism as a significant context even for modernist works that seem insulated from imperial concerns" but also that "several of modernism's aesthetic hallmarks . . . can be understood as formal correlates to high imperialism" (*A Shrinking Island*, 6, 30).

69. For a similar argument, see Collini, "On Variousness," in which he contends that establishing "limits to classifying presumption" can contribute to and even provoke "public discourse" (91). See Foucault's account of the dandy, who possesses the "spectator's posture" of the *flâneur* but also "transfigures the world" and takes himself "as object of a complex and difficult elaboration" ("What Is Enlightenment?" 40–41).

70. Laura Chrisman argues that "some modernist writings do contain direct representations of colonized peoples" and that, even in those modernist texts that do not contain such representations, this absence is not "automatically

inevitable." Chrisman, "Imperial Space, Imperial Place: Theories of Empire and Culture in Fredric Jameson, Edward Said, and Gayatri Spivak," *New Formations* 34 (Summer 1998): 66. Moreover, I share Chakrabarty's sense that the description of "colonized daily life," what Chakrabarty calls the view of "India" rather than of "Europe," is important but insufficient for a radical analysis of imperialism and global relations because, as he argues, seeing the world from the margins means analyzing the strategies of description that have been part of imperialist discourse and whose extension to colonized peoples, while necessary to the political efforts of anticolonialism, cannot fully disrupt the structure of privileged sight. This is what Chakrabarty means when he says that within traditional historiography, " 'Europe' remains the sovereign, theoretical subject of all histories, including the ones that we call 'Indian,' 'Chinese,' 'Kenyan,' and so on" (*Provincializing Europe*, 27). He adds, in his discussion of "minority histories," that the addition of minority perspectives does not necessarily "change the nature of historical discourse" (98).

71. Fredric Jameson, "Modernism and Imperialism," 48. In chapters 4 and 6, I discuss other affects of critical thinking such as treason, which can suspend triumphalist progress in its forceful articulation of nonalignment, and vertigo, which introduces new objects of attention and new, comparative modes of attentiveness.

72. Clifford describes the charge of "cultural inventiveness" in "Mixed Feelings," 366. Timothy Brennan attributes "self-indulgence" to cosmopolitan writers and critics in *At Home in the World: Cosmopolitanism Now* (Cambridge, Mass.: Harvard University Press, 1997), back cover. Aijaz Ahmad condemns "postmodern" international writers for validating "the pleasures of . . . unbelonging": Aijaz Ahmad, *In Theory* (London: Verso, 1992), 157–58.

73. Even today, as Joan W. Scott has argued, an emphasis on "experience" in the disciplines of history and literary studies has had the positive value of expanding and diversifying accounts of the world but the negative value of establishing and requiring the "prior existence of individuals" whose assumption of self and cognition of experience are not addressed: Scott, "Experience," in *Feminists Theorize the Political*, ed. Judith Butler and Joan W. Scott (New York: Routledge, 1990), 27. On the literature of experience, see Henry Louis Gates Jr., " 'Authenticity,' or the Lesson of Little Tree," *The New York Times Book Review*, 24 November 1991.

74. J. Middleton Murry, "The Classical Revival," *The Adelphi* 3, no. 9 (February 1926): 589–91.

75. J. Middleton Murry, *The Problem of Style* (London: Oxford University Press, 1921), 23.

76. Edward Garnett, unsigned review of *The Secret Agent*, by Joseph Conrad, *Nation*, 28 September 1907. Reprinted in *Conrad: The Critical Heritage*, ed. Norman Sherry (London: Routledge & Kegan Paul, 1973), 191–93.

77. "Cosmopolitan Art—a Friendly Dispute Between Selwyn Image and Lewis F. Day," *The Art Journal* 18 (December 1902): 374–75.

78. I take my understanding of indexical meaning from John Kerkering's excellent account in *The Poetics of National and Racial Identity in Nineteenth-Century American Literature* (Cambridge: Cambridge University Press, 2003), 19–20.

79. Robert Lynd, review, *Daily News*, 10 August 1908, 3. Reprinted in *Conrad: The Critical Heritage*, ed. Norman Sherry (London: Routledge & Kegan Paul, 1973), 210–12.

80. W. J. Turner, "Stravinsky in London and Paris," *The New Statesman*, 31 July 1920, 475.

81. Theodor W. Adorno, *Minima Moralia: Reflections from a Damaged Life*, trans. E. F. N. Japhcott (London: Verso, 1978), 101.

82. For example, see the presentation of these essays in Ernst Bloch et al., *Aesthetics and Politics* (London: Verso, 1980).

83. Jean-Paul Sartre, "What is Literature?" (1947), in *"What is Literature?" and Other Essays*, trans. Steven Ungar (Cambridge, Mass.: Harvard University Press, 1988), 230.

84. Theodor W. Adorno, "Commitment," in *Notes to Literature*, vol. 2, ed. Rolf Tiedemann, trans. Shierry Weber Nicholsen (New York: Columbia University Press, 1992), 81.

85. Jean-Paul Sartre, "Black Orpheus" (1948), in *"What is Literature" and Other Essays*, trans. Steven Ungar (Cambridge, Mass.: Harvard University Press, 1988), 302.

86. Sartre, "Black Orpheus," 293–94.

87. In *The Emigrants*, Sebald tells stories of the Holocaust and Jewish emigration that are interspersed with references to butterflies and to Vladimir Nabokov, author and famous lepidopterist. W. G. Sebald, *The Emigrants*, trans. Michael Hulse (New York: New Directions, 1996).

88. John R. Reed, *Decadent Style* (Athens: Ohio University Press, 1985), 37; and Alfred Garvin Engstrom and Clive Scott, "Decadence," in *The New Princeton Encyclopedia of Poetry and Poetics*, ed. Alex Preminger and T. V. F. Brogan (Princeton, N.J.: Princeton University Press, 1993), 275.

89. Walter Pater, *The Renaissance* (New York: Modern Library, 1919), 197.

90. Michel de Certeau, *The Practice of Everyday Life* (1974), trans. Steven Rendell (Berkeley: University of California Press, 1984), xii–xv.

91. Anderson, *The Powers of Distance*, 148–49.

92. Theodor W. Adorno, "Resignation," in *Critical Models: Interventions and Catchwords*, trans. Henry W. Pickford (New York: Columbia University Press, 1998), 289–93.

93. For a discussion and defense of the "poetic" aspect of de Certeau's theory, see James Donald, *Imagining the Modern City* (Minneapolis: University of Minnesota Press, 1999), 17.

94. Pheng Cheah and Bruce Robbins, eds., *Cosmopolitics* (Minneapolis: University of Minnesota Press, 1998); Ghosh writes of "literary cosmopolitics" in *When Borne Across*.

95. Jane Gallop, *Anecdotal Theory* (Durham, N.C.: Duke University Press, 2002), 2–3.

96. Stuart Hall, "The New Ethnicities" (1988), in *Ethnicity*, ed. John Hutchinson and Anthony D. Smith (Oxford: Oxford University Press, 1996), 161–64.

97. Traditionally, as David Damrosch explains, "world literature" referred to "an established canon of European masterpieces." Damrosch seeks to change that

definition in *What Is World Literature?* (Princeton, N.J.: Princeton University Press, 2003), 4.

98. In her introduction to *After the Imperial Turn*, Antoinette Burton articulates the hope that "foregrounding Britain will be viewed as a strategic maneuver designed not to reinstantiate it but, rather, to subject its presumptive centrality to interrogation" (2). I share that aspiration.

99. My argument about the function of these tactics is indebted to Raymond Williams's methodology in *Keywords*. Of course, there are some significant differences between his methodology and mine: I have not presented a cultural history or genealogy of "naturalness" or "treason"; moreover, Williams analyzes a broad range of sources, including newspapers, speeches, poems, and pamphlets, while I have restricted my analysis to narrative fiction and criticism of that fiction. Raymond Williams, *Keywords: A Vocabulary of Culture and Society* (New York: Oxford University Press, 1983), 15.

100. For a discussion of "the politics of comparison," see R. Radhakrishnan, *Theory in an Uneven World* (Oxford: Blackwell, 2003), 77–78.

101. Carolyn Dever, *Skeptical Feminism: Activist Theory, Activist Practice* (Minneapolis: University of Minnesota Press, 2003), 4–5.

102. Cynthia Enloe, *Bananas, Beaches, and Bases*, 196–97.

1. CONRAD'S NATURALNESS

1. Of course, one does not "choose" one's culture outright, as Homi K. Bhabha has observed, because culture is the condition from which choices are made. For an excellent account of cultural indeterminacy in the early twentieth century, see Deborah Cohen, "Who Was Who? Race and Jews in Turn-of-the-Century Britain," *Journal of British Studies* 41 (October 2002): 460–83, esp. 469. For a discussion of "cultural choice" in the late twentieth century, see Homi K. Bhabha, "On Cultural Choice," in *The Turn to Ethics*, ed. Marjorie Garber, Beatrice Hanssen, and Rebecca L. Walkowitz (New York: Routledge, 2000), 181–82.

2. See Deborah Cohen, "Who Was Who?" 478–80; Bernard Gainer, *The Alien Invasion: The Origins of the Aliens Act of 1905* (London: Heinemann, 1972), 106–28; and Jonas Barish, *The Anti-Theatrical Prejudice* (Berkeley: University of California Press, 1981), 467.

3. F. R. Leavis, *The Great Tradition* (London: Chatto and Windus, 1960), 17–18.

4. There are many different accounts of what makes up Conrad's foreignness: see Jeffrey Meyers, *Joseph Conrad* (New York: Charles Scribner, 1991), 355; Frederick R. Karl, *Joseph Conrad: The Three Lives* (New York: Farrar, Straus and Giroux, 1979); Geoffry Galt Harpham, *One of Us: The Mastery of Joseph Conrad* (Chicago: The University of Chicago Press, 1996); Yves Hervouet, *The French Face of Joseph Conrad* (Cambridge: Cambridge University Press, 1990); and Adam Gillon, "Joseph Conrad: Polish Cosmopolitan," in *Joseph Conrad: Theory and World Fiction*, ed. Wolodymyr T. Zyla and Wendell M. Aycock (Lubbock: Texas Tech University Press, 1974), 41–69.

5. Nico Israel describes this tendency in *Outlandish: Writing Between Exile and Diaspora* (Stanford, Calif.: Stanford University Press, 2000), 23–26.

6. Writing of "ethnographic self-fashioning," James Clifford compares Conrad to the anthropologist Bronislaw Malinowski; here, I am comparing Conrad to aesthetes and dandies such as Oscar Wilde. See James Clifford, "On Ethnographic Self-Fashioning: Conrad and Malinowski," in *The Predicament of Culture* (Cambridge, Mass.: Harvard University Press, 1988), 92–113.

7. Fredric Jameson, "Romance and Reification: Plot Construction and Ideological Closure in Joseph Conrad" in *The Political Unconscious: Narrative as a Socially Symbolic Act* (Ithaca, N.Y.: Cornell University Press, 1981), 206–80.

8. For leading me to think about dandyism as a characteristic of books as well as of people, I am grateful to Monica L. Miller, "The Black Dandy as Bad Modernist," in *Bad Modernisms*, ed. Douglas Mao and Rebecca L. Walkowitz (Durham, N.C.: Duke University Press, 2006), 179–205. Jessica R. Feldman presents dandyism "as an expression of anti-essentialism" that extends from nineteenth-century London or Paris into figures of display in twentieth-century culture. See Feldman, *Gender on the Divide: The Dandy in Modernist Literature* (Ithaca, N.Y.: Cornell University Press, 1993), 5. Many critics now treat dandyism as a cultural tactic that is available to immigrants as well as to locals. For this trend, see Susan Fillen-Yeh, ed., *Dandies: Fashion and Finesse in Art and Culture* (New York: New York University Press, 2001).

9. See Edward W. Said, *The World, the Text, and the Critic* (Cambridge, Mass.: Harvard University Press, 1983), 106; and Harpham, *One of Us*, 147. On the preoccupation with art and literary decadence, see Ellis Hanson, *Decadence and Catholicism* (Cambridge, Mass.: Harvard University Press, 1997), 2.

10. See Richard Ellmann, "Introduction: The Critic as Artist as Wilde," in *The Artist as Critic*, ed. Richard Ellmann (Chicago: University of Chicago Press, 1982), xi.

11. Oscar Wilde, "The Decay of Lying" (1889), in *The Artist as Critic: Critical Writings of Oscar Wilde*, ed. Richard Ellmann (Chicago: University of Chicago Press, 1982), 290–319.

12. Amanda Anderson focuses on the epigram as a strategy of ethical detachment and participant observation in *The Powers of Distance: Cosmopolitanism and the Cultivation of Detachment* (Princeton, N.J.: Princeton University Press, 2001), 147–75. For previous studies that consider Conrad in the light of Wilde, see Paul Kirschner, "Wilde's Shadow in Conrad's 'The Return,'" *Notes and Queries* 40 (December 1993): 495–96; and Joseph William Martin, "The Shock of Trifles: Decadence in the Novels of Joseph Conrad" (Ph.D. diss., Purdue University May 1990).

13. Patrick Brantlinger, "*Heart of Darkness*: Anti-Imperialism, Racism, or Impressionism?" in *Case Studies in Contemporary Criticism: Heart of Darkness*, ed. Ross C. Murfin (Boston: Bedford, 1996), 281.

14. Joseph Conrad, *The Secret Agent* (1907), ed. Martin Seymour-Smith (London: Penguin, 1990), 129.

15. Conrad to Hugh-Durand Davray, January 1908, *The Collected Letters of Joseph Conrad*, ed. Norman Sherry (Cambridge: Cambridge University Press, 1983), 4:28–29.

16. Robert Lynd, review, *Daily News*, 10 August 1908, 3; reprint, in *Conrad: The Critical Heritage*, ed. Norman Sherry (London: Routledge & Kegan Paul, 1973), 210–12.

17. Hugh Walpole, *Joseph Conrad*, rev. ed. (London: Nisbet & Co., 1924), 19.

18. Anonymous, unsigned review of *The Secret Agent*, by Joseph Conrad, *Times Literary Supplement*, 20 September 1907, 285; reprint, in *Conrad: The Critical Heritage*, ed. Norman Sherry (Cambridge: Cambridge University Press, 1983), 185.

19. Edward Garnett, unsigned review of *The Secret Agent*, by Joseph Conrad, *Nation*, 28 September 1907. Reprint, in *The Critical Heritage*, ed. Norman Sherry (Cambridge: Cambridge University Press, 1983), 191–93.

20. Unsigned review, *Glasgow News*, 3 October 1907, 5. Reprinted in *The Critical Heritage*, ed. Norman Sherry (Cambridge: Cambridge University Press, 1983), 195–97.

21. Arthur Symons, "Conrad," in *Dramatis Personae* (Indianapolis: Bobbs-Merrill, 1923), 1, 20.

22. Joseph Conrad, "Author's Note," in *A Personal Record* (1912), reprint, in *The Mirror of the Sea; and A Personal Record* (London: J. M. Dent, 1968), iii–vi.

23. Geoffrey Galt Harpham has called *The Secret Agent* Conrad's "most consciously 'created' work," and he presents the novel's preface as the author's sincere account of composition. Although I share Harpham's sense of the novel's exceptional deliberateness, I see Conrad's preface as yet another creation. Harpham, "Abroad Only by a Fiction: Creation, Irony, and Necessity in Conrad's *The Secret Agent*," *Representations* 37 (Winter 1992): 79–81.

24. Conrad, *The Secret Agent*, 173.

25. Joseph Conrad, *Heart of Darkness* (1899), in *"Heart of Darkness" and Other Tales*, ed. Cedric Watts (Oxford: Oxford University Press, 1990), 140–41.

26. Joseph Conrad, *The Nigger of the "Narcissus"* (1898; New York: Norton, 1979), 148. See Ian Watt, *Conrad in the Nineteenth Century* (Berkeley: University of California Press, 1979), 88; Michael Fried, *Realism, Writing, Disfiguration: On Thomas Eakins and Stephen Crane* (Chicago: University of Chicago Press, 1987), esp. 114–15.

27. See Joseph Conrad, *Lord Jim* (1900; New York: Norton, 1968), 27 and passim; and Joseph Conrad, *Nostromo* (1904; London: Penguin, 1983), 124 and passim.

28. See Oscar Wilde's quip, in the preface to *The Picture of Dorian Gray*: "It is the spectator, and not life, that art really mirrors." Oscar Wilde, preface to *The Picture of Dorian Gray*, in *The Artist as Critic: Critical Writings of Oscar Wilde*, ed. Richard Ellmann (Chicago: University of Chicago Press, 1982), 236.

29. Roland Barthes, "The Reality Effect," in *The Rustle of Language*, trans. Richard Howard (Berkeley: University of California Press, 1989), 148.

30. Nicholas Dames has observed that it is hard to find any narrative detail whose meaning, when one looks hard enough, is entirely "useless." Within the world that Conrad describes, the ink and stamps are "useless" because the characters do not notice them; they have no denotative content. For the reader, however, the stamps and the ink have use because they participate in a genre of pretense. Conrad suggests that it is part of England's fiction to make its own foreignness as irrelevant as possible. See Nicholas Dames, "Brushes with Fame: Thackeray and the Work of Celebrity," *Nineteenth Century Literature* 56, no. 1 (2001): 23–51.

31. Roland Barthes, *S/Z*, trans. Richard Miller (Oxford: Blackwell, 1992), 54–55.

32. Jesse Matz observes, also reading Watt, that the "coding" does not occur in the "impression" but in the "explanation which follows the impression ... so that what Watt calls 'delayed decoding' might be more appropriately be called 'delayed *encoding*.'" See Jesse Matz, *Literary Impressionism and Modernist Aesthetics* (Cambridge: Cambridge University Press, 2001), 144–45. Bruce Johnson makes a similar point when he argues, "The meaning we see in an apparently discreet moment or event depends on the conceptual and emotional 'net' we use to capture it." I share Matz's and Johnson's claims about Conrad's aesthetic strategies, but for me these strategies exist to promote, above all, a less natural idea of culture. By displaying the process of "encoding," Conrad suggests not only that reputation (Johnson's "net") precedes and guides identity but also that a change in perception can lead to a change in how culture is understood. See Bruce Johnson, "Conrad's Impressionism and Watt's 'Delayed Decoding,'" in *Conrad Revisited: Essays for the Eighties*, ed. Ross C. Murfin (Tuscaloosa: University of Alabama Press, 1985), 52, 60.

33. Oscar Wilde, *The Importance of Being Earnest* (1895), in *The Importance of Being Earnest and Other Plays*, ed. Peter Raby (Oxford: Oxford University Press, 1995), 266. Noting the echo of Wilde in Conrad, Joseph Martin observes of *The Secret Agent* that "theatricality of one sort or another underlies virtually every character and every relationship in the novel" ("The Shock of Trifles," 103).

34. Francesca Coppa argues that Wilde's plays function as epigrams because they master the conventions of late-nineteenth-century theatre just as Wilde's phrases master the language of social ritual. Coppa defines "epigram" as the citation and negotiation of one or more previous formulations of knowledge. See Francesca Coppa, "'I Seem to Recognize a Device That Has Done Duty in Bygone Plays': Oscar Wilde and the Theatre of Epigram," in *Reading Wilde, Querying Spaces: An Exhibition Commemorating the Hundredth Anniversary of the Trials of Oscar Wilde* (New York: Fales Library, New York University, 1995), 11–19.

35. Oscar Wilde, "Decay of Lying," 1086.

2. JOYCE'S TRIVIALITY

1. Vincent J. Cheng, *Joyce, Race, and Empire* (Cambridge: Cambridge University Press, 1995), 2.

2. Enda Duffy, *The Subaltern Ulysses* (Minneapolis: University of Minnesota Press, 1994); Derek Attridge and Marjorie Howes, eds., *Semicolonial Joyce* (Cambridge: Cambridge University Press, 2000).

3. Joseph Valente, "James Joyce and the Cosmopolitan Sublime," in *Joyce and the Subject of History*, ed. Mark A. Wollaeger, Victor Luftig, and Robert Spoo (Ann Arbor: University of Michigan Press, 1996), 61–62.

4. Vincent J. Cheng, "'Terrible Queer Creatures': Joyce, Cosmopolitanism, and the Inauthentic Irishman," in *James Joyce and the Fabrication of Irish Identity*, ed. Michael Patrick Gillespie (Amsterdam: Rodolfi, 2001), 32.

5. For an important exception that is focused on Joyce's resistance to nationalism,

see David Lloyd, *Anomalous States: Irish Writing and the Post-Colonial Moment* (Dublin: The Lilliput Review, 1993).

6. Andrew Gibson, *Joyce's Revenge: History, Politics, and Aesthetics in* Ulysses (Oxford: Oxford University Press, 2002), 1–20.

7. Benedict Anderson, *Imagined Communities* (1983; reprint, London: Verso, 1991), 44; Arjun Appadurai, *Modernity at Large: Cultural Dimensions of Globalization* (Minneapolis: University of Minnesota Press, 1996), 176; Lauren Berlant, *The Anatomy of National Fantasy: Hawthorne, Utopia, and Everyday Life* (Chicago: University of Chicago Press, 1991), 217.

8. Etienne Balibar, "The Nation Form: History and Ideology," in *Race, Nation, Class,* ed. Etienne Balibar and Immanuel Wallerstein, trans. Chris Turner (London: Verso, 1991), 94; Ernest Renan, "What is a Nation?" in *Becoming National: A Reader,* ed. Geoff Eley and Ronald Grigor Suny (New York: Oxford University Press, 1996), 41–55; M. M. Bakhtin, *The Dialogic Imagination: Four Essays,* ed. Michael Holquist, trans. Caryl Emerson and Michael Holquist (Austin: The University of Texas Press, 1981), 16. Appadurai has proposed that local neighborhoods are often at odds with nation-states "because the commitments and attachments (sometimes mislabeled 'primordial') that characterize local subjectivities are more pressing, more continuous, and sometimes more distracting than the nation-state can afford" (191).

9. See my discussion of this issue, in relation to African American culture and the Harlem Renaissance, in "Shakespeare in Harlem: *The Norton Anthology,* 'Propaganda,' Langston Hughes," *Modern Language Quarterly* 60, no. 4 (December 1999): 495–519.

10. See, for example, Adorno's aphorism "Morality and Style" in *Minima Moralia: Reflections from a Damaged Life,* trans. E. F. N. Jephcott (London: Verso, 1978), 101. For a seminal discussion of how habitual attention is created and resisted in literature, see Victor Shklovsky, "Art as Technique" (1917), in *Russian Formalist Criticism: Four Essays,* ed. and trans. Lee T. Lemon and Marion J. Reis (Lincoln: University of Nebraska Press, 1965), 3–24.

11. Theodor W. Adorno, "The Position of the Narrator in the Contemporary Novel," in *Notes to Literature,* vol. 1, ed. Rolf Tiedemann, trans. Shierry Weber Nicholsen (New York: Columbia University Press, 1991), 31–32.

12. Adorno, "The Position of the Narrator," 31.

13. Raymond Williams, *Culture and Society, 1780–1950* (New York: Harper & Row, 1958), 289–92. For Williams, vagrancy is exile without "principle." Joyce's view of exile emphasizes freedom from those institutionalized principles—nation, empire, church—that keep cultures from changing. For example, see Stephen Dedalus's speech about "silence, exile, and cunning" in Joyce, *The Portrait of the Artist as a Young Man* (1916; reprint, New York: Penguin, 1999), 212.

14. James Joyce to Grant Richards, 5 May 1906, in *Selected Letters of James Joyce,* ed. Richard Ellmann (New York: Viking Press, 1979), 82.

15. Joyce to Richards, 23 June 1906 and 20 May 1906, in *Selected Letters,* 88–90.

16. Joyce to Richards, 5 May 1906, in *Selected Letters,* 83.

17. S. P. B. Mais, "An Irish Revel: And Some Flappers," *Daily Express*, 25 March 1922, reprint, in *James Joyce: The Critical Heritage*, ed. Robert H. Deming (New York: Barnes and Noble, 1970), 1:191.

18. Valéry Larbaud, "James Joyce," *Nouvelle Revue Française* 18 (April 1922): 385–405, reprint, in *James Joyce: The Critical Heritage*, ed. Robert H. Deming (New York: Barnes and Noble, 1970), 252–62; references in my text refer to the *Critical Heritage* printing. John Middleton Murry, "Mr. Joyce's *Ulysses*" (1922), in *Defending Romanticism: Selected Criticism of John Middleton Murry*, ed. Malcolm Woodfield (Bristol: The Bristol Press, 1989), 117–20. Murry's review was first published in the *Nation and Athanæum* in April 1922, but citations in the text are to the reprinted version. See, also, Richard Ellmann, *James Joyce* (New York: Oxford University Press, 1959). For an excellent account of early-twentieth-century debates about the meanings of "Europe," see Luisa Passerini, *Europe in Love, Love in Europe: Imagination and Politics Between the Wars* (New York: New York University Press, 1999).

19. Larbaud introduces Miró and Gomez by full name, as recent arrivals on the European scene. Gabriel Miró (1879–1930), known as a novelist of poetic, impressionist style, was critical of religious institutions; Ramón Gómez (1888–1963) was an avant-garde writer, best known for his literary gatherings, his biographies of Ruskin and Wilde, and his Wildean epigrams, which he called *greguerías*. See Philip Ward, ed., *The Oxford Companion to Spanish Literature* (Oxford: Oxford University Press, 1978), 246–47, 258, 390–91.

20. It is important to Joseph M. Hone, an Irish reviewer, that Joyce's "struggle for freedom had to be fought before he left Ireland." Hone, "A Letter from Ireland," *London Mercury* 5 (January 1923): 306–8, reprint, in *James Joyce: The Critical Heritage*, ed. Robert H. Deming (New York: Barnes and Noble, 1970), 297–98. Similarly, Ernest Boyd, whose book *Ireland's Literary Renaissance* included Joyce in its revised edition, argues, "no Irish writer is more Irish than Joyce" and defends Joyce from "a prematurely cosmopolitan reputation," by which he means a reputation removed from the local context of Joyce's early life. For Boyd, it is important to prove "the separate existence of Anglo-Irish literature." Boyd, *Ireland's Literary Renaissance* (New York: Alfred A. Knopf, 1922), 404–5.

21. Joyce is wary of the strategies of cultural publicity that were affirmed in this period by African American intellectuals such as W. E. B. Du Bois and James Weldon Johnson, or that Boyd attributes to participants in the Irish Revival. Ross Posnock argues that Du Bois may have been wary of these strategies, too; Posnock contends that Du Bois embraced the distinctiveness of African American culture only as a "critical stage" on the way to a critique of authenticity. Ross Posnock, *Color and Culture: Black Writers and the Making of the Modern Intellectual* (Cambridge, Mass.: Harvard University Press, 1998), 91–107. Tracy Mishkin argues that intellectuals of both the Harlem and the Irish Renaissances tended to accept racial essence as a way to claim that African American or Irish culture provides an important and distinctive alternative to dominant American or English culture. Tracy Mishkin, *The Harlem and Irish Renaissances: Language, Identity, Representation* (Gainesville: University Press of Florida, 1998), 73.

22. James Joyce, "Ireland, Island of Saints and Sages" (1907), in *The Critical Writings of James Joyce*, ed. Ellsworth Mason and Richard Ellmann (New York: The Viking Press, 1959), 171.

23. James Joyce, "Home Rule Comes of Age" (1907), in *The Critical Writings of James Joyce*, ed. Ellsworth Mason and Richard Ellmann (New York: The Viking Press, 1959), 194–95.

24. James Joyce, "The Day of Rabblement" (1901), in *The Critical Writings of James Joyce*, ed. Ellsworth Mason and Richard Ellmann (New York: The Viking Press, 1959), 70.

25. See, for example, Joyce's claim that Ireland is not helped by "an appeal to the past" in Joyce, "Ireland, Island of Saints and Sages," 173–74.

26. "The Dead" is something of an exception to this rule. See Cheng, "'Terrible Queer Creatures,'" 25–26; Bruce Robbins, "The Newspapers Were Right: Cosmopolitanism, Forgetting, and 'The Dead'" *Interventions* 5, no. 1 (2003): 101–12.

27. See Duffy's discussion of Bloom's *flânerie* in *The Subaltern* Ulysses, 65.

28. James Joyce, "Two Gallants" in *Dubliners* (1914; reprint, New York: Penguin, 1993), 43–55.

29. Mark Manganaro, *Culture, 1922: The Emergence of a Concept* (Princeton, N.J.: Princeton University Press, 2002), p.121.

30. Since the Enlightenment, Luisa Passerini argues, French and English writers have assumed that courtly love is a cornerstone of modern European tradition, dating from Provençal love poetry and derived from contacts with the Celtic nations, Germans, Scandinavians, and Scythians (Russians); some writers have attributed elements of the courtly tradition to contacts with Moorish culture as well, thus undermining the claim that courtly love is "purely" European (*Europe in Love*, 2–3).

31. Joyce's story serves to undermine the ethical claims of British sovereignty by associating its conditions with a sordid narrative of Irish poverty. While I agree with Vincent Cheng that the British coin "robs [the characters] . . . of their own sovereignty" (*Joyce, Race, and Empire*, 116), I argue that Joyce's story also attempts to displace any sense that sovereignty can be entirely one's "own."

32. Joyce to Richards, 5 May 1906, in *Selected Letters*, 82.

33. Jonathan Culler, "The Call of the Phoneme," in *On Puns: The Foundation of Letters*, ed. Jonathan Culler (Oxford: Basil Blackwell, 1998), 4.

34. Theodor W. Adorno, "Is Art Lighthearted?" in *Notes to Literature*, vol. 2, ed. Rolf Tiedemann, trans. Shierry Weber Nicholsen (New York: Columbia University Press, 1992), 248.

35. Adorno, *Minima Moralia*, 101; and Theodor W. Adorno, *Aesthetic Theory*, ed. and trans. Robert Hullot-Kentor (Minneapolis: University of Minnesota Press, 1997), 312.

36. Joseph Litvak, *Strange Gourmets: Sophistication, Theory, and the Novel* (Durham, N.C.: Duke University Press, 1997), 3–4.

37. Adorno, *Aesthetic Theory*, 312.

38. Theodor W. Adorno, "Resignation," in *Critical Models: Interventions and*

Catchwords, trans. Henry W. Pickford (New York: Columbia University Press, 1998), 292.

39. Stephen thus participates in a kind of double heresy: refusing to accept the general principle that heretics write bad poetry and refusing to accept the congruence between moral and aesthetic badness.

40. See *OED*, 2nd edition, s.v. "funnel" and "tundish."

41. The dean tells Stephen, "you have certainly hit the nail on the head" (159); he is incapable of distinguishing between words spoken in sincerity and words spoken in irony, such as Stephen's use of the word "detain" (161).

42. See discussion of Stephen's allusion to Coleridge in Don Gifford, *Joyce Annotated* (Berkeley: University of California Press, 1982), 237.

43. James Joyce, *Ulysses* (1922; reprint, New York: Vintage, 1986). Joyce announces that "Father Conmee liked cheerful decorum" on the third page of the chapter (182), but even in the first paragraph Conmee thinks to himself, punning on the name of a man whose death has left his family destitute (Dignam), "*Vere dignum et instum est*": "It is indeed fitting and right" (180). This is the opening phrase of the Eucharist, but it implies, also, Conmee's abstract complacency in the face of misery. See Don Gifford, *Ulysses Annotated: Notes for Joyce's Ulysses*, 2nd ed. (Berkeley: University of California Press, 1988), 261. Consider this phrase alongside Wilfred Owen's poem about World War I, "Dulce et Decorum Est" (1918), which attacks the notion that it is fine and honorable to die for one's country by showing the physical suffering whose invisibility the rhetoric of decorum helps to maintain.

44. For example, one has to compare all of the invalids in the chapter, literal and figurative, to Blazes Boylan's claim that the basket of "shamefaced peaches" he is buying for Molly is "for an invalid" (187). The chapter gives as much attention to Boylan in his coarseness as it does to others in their suffering, if only to make the reader do the same and to make the reader notice that the salesgirl seems to have more sympathy for Boylan's fake invalid than most characters have for the invalids with whom they actually come in contact.

45. Stephen's sympathy for Dilly, his sister, makes him careful to conceal his true opinions; Molly's sympathy for the one-legged sailor leads her to reach out a hand and throw him a coin; in another scene, Boylan makes himself seem sympathetic in order to attract the interest of a salesgirl. These are imperfect encounters, but they are not based on an established, invoked correctness established in advance.

46. See, for example, Duffy's chapter on "Cyclops" in *The Subaltern* Ulysses, 93–129; Cheng's discussion in "Joyce, Race, and Empire," 191–224; and Neil Levi's in "'See that Straw? That's a Straw': Anti-Semitism and Narrative Form in *Ulysses*," *Modernism/Modernity* 9, no. 3 (September 2002): 375–88.

47. Gibson has argued that the rhetoric of the citizen and the nameless narrator, in its vulgarity, is in fact preferable to the decorous, flattened rhetoric of the impersonal, mythologized parodies, which Gibson associates with Anglo-Irish revivalism (*Joyce's Revenge*, 118–26). It seems right to me, as Gibson argues, that Joyce finds the false courtesy of Anglo-Irish nationalism far more insidious than the explicit and vulgar hostility of the Sinn Feiner (107). Duffy has observed that Bloom, like

the citizen, speaks in platitudes, which means that his perspectives are sometimes limited by the habits of his language (*The Subaltern Ulysses*, 112).

48. Lauren Berlant, *The Queen of America Goes to Washington City* (Durham: Duke University Press, 1997), 12.

49. Levi, "'See that Straw?'" 380–83.

50. For recent examples, see Cheng, *Joyce, Race, Empire*, 211–12; Duffy, *The Subaltern Ulysses*, 126–27; Gibson is an exception to this rule, in his striking focus on the Citizen as "a liberatingly comic relief" from the dour rhetoric of Anglo-Irish Revivalism (*Joyce's Revenge*, 124–26).

51. Paul Gilroy, *The Black Atlantic: Modernity and Double Consciousness* (Cambridge, Mass.: Harvard University Press, 1993), xi.

3. WOOLF'S EVASION

1. Bruce Robbins, "The Village of the Liberal Managerial Class," in *Cosmopolitan Geographies: New Locations in Literature and Culture*, ed. Vinay Dharwadker (New York: Routledge, 2001), 16.

2. Judith Butler, "Explanation and Exoneration, or What We Can Hear," *Social Text* 72 (Fall 2002): 180.

3. Fred Moten, "The New International of Decent Feelings," *Social Text* 72 (Fall 2002): 189.

4. Louis Althusser, "The International of Decent Feelings" (1946), in *The Spectre of Hegel: Early Writings*, trans. G. M. Goshgarian (London: Verso, 1997), 30.

5. See discussion of "planetary humanism" in the introduction to this book.

6. Jacques Lezra, "Unrelated Passions," *differences: A journal of Feminist Cultural Studies* 14, no. 1 (2003): 83–84.

7. Edward Said, "Heroism and Humanism," *Al-Ahram Weekly On-line*, no. 463 (6–12 January 2000), http://weekly.ahram.org.eg/2000/463/op10.htm.

8. I am grateful to Amanda Claybaugh for leading me to think about the semivisibility of servants in *Mrs. Dalloway*.

9. M. C. Bradbrook, "Notes on the Style of Mrs. Woolf," *Scrutiny* 1, no. 1 (1932): 33–38; Q. D. Leavis, "Caterpillars of the Commonwealth Unite!" *Scrutiny* 7, no. 1 (1938): 203–14.

10. Woolf imagines a "Society of Outsiders" in *Three Guineas* (1938), in *A Room of One's Own and Three Guineas*, ed. Michèle Barrett (London: Penguin, 2000), 232–45.

11. Others have noticed that Woolf was not an outsider alone: she was married to Leonard Woolf, who was Jewish and a strong advocate of antiwar efforts. See Natania Rosenfeld, *Outsiders Together: Virginia and Leonard Woolf* (Princeton, N.J.: Princeton University Press, 2000); and Christine Froula's discussion of Woolf's "outsider patriotism" in *Virginia Woolf and the Bloomsbury Avant-Garde: War, Civilization, Modernity* (New York: Columbia University Press, 2004), 270.

12. Late into the twentieth century, scholars continued to argue that Woolf's fiction is neither cosmopolitan nor modernist because it privileges England and the minutiae of upper-class life. For assertions and refutations of this argument, see

Terry Eagleton, *Exiles and Émigrés* (New York: Schocken, 1970), 17; Paul Fussell, *The Great War and Modern Memory* (London: Oxford University Press, 1975), 23; Hugh Kenner, "The Making of the Modernist Canon," *Chicago Review* 34, no. 2 (Spring 1984): 57; Susan Stanford Friedman, "Geopolitical Literary: Internationalizing Feminism at 'Home'—the Case of Virginia Woolf," in *Mappings: Feminism and the Cultural Geographies of Encounter* (Princeton, N.J.: Princeton University Press, 1998), 118; Brenda R. Silver, *Virginia Woolf Icon* (Chicago: University of Chicago Press, 1999), 35–76; and Froula, *Virginia Woolf and the Bloomsbury Avant-Garde.*

13. For example, see Rachel Bowlby, *Feminist Destinations and Further Essays on Virginia Woolf* (Edinburgh: Edinburgh University Press, 1997), 14–15; Michèle Barrett, "Virginia Woolf: Subjectivity and Politics," in *Imagination in Theory: Essays on Writing and Culture* (Cambridge: Polity Press, 1999), 35–67; William R. Handley, "War and the Politics of Narration in *Jacob's Room*," in *Virginia Woolf and War: Fiction, Reality, and Myth* (Syracuse, N.Y.: Syracuse University Press, 1991), 110–33; and Michele Pridmore-Brown, "1939–40: Of Virginia Woolf, Gramophones, and Fascism," *PMLA* 113, no. 3 (May 1998): 408–21.

14. Melba Cuddy-Keane, *Virginia Woolf, the Intellectual, and the Public Sphere* (Cambridge: Cambridge University Press, 2003), 118. Jessica Berman, *Modernist Fiction, Cosmopolitanism, and the Politics of Community* (Cambridge: Cambridge University Press, 2001), has proposed that *Orlando* and *The Waves*, "by constructing new narrative models of cosmopolitan community . . . intervene directly in the political life of Britain" (117).

15. R. D. Charques, "The Bourgeois Novel" (1933), in *Virginia Woolf: The Critical Heritage*, ed. Robin Majumdar and Allen McLaurin (London: Routledge, 1997), 344; Wyndham Lewis, *Men Without Art* (1934; reprint, Santa Rosa: Black Sparrow Press, 1987), 11.

16. While Leavis's review is focused on *Three Guineas* (1938), in which Woolf explicitly and contentiously aligns British tyranny at home with German tyranny abroad, Leavis's disdain is similar to the criticism that other critics directed at Woolf's earlier works of fiction and nonfiction.

17. Michèle Barrett presents these examples, taken from Fussell, *The Great War and Modern Memory*, in "The Great War and Post-Modern Memory," *New Formations* 41 (August 2000): 139.

18. E. M. Forster, "Visions" (1919), in *Virginia Woolf: The Critical Heritage*, ed. Robin Majumdar and Allen McLaurin (London: Routledge, 1997), 69.

19. Theodor W. Adorno, "The Essay as Form," in *Notes to Literature*, vol. 1, ed. Rolf Tiedemann, trans. Shierry Weber Nicholsen (New York: Columbia University Press, 1991), 4.

20. Leonard Woolf and Virginia Woolf, *Two Stories* (London: Hogarth Press, 1917).

21. Leonard Woolf, *Beginning Again: An Autobiography of the Years 1911 to 1918* (London: Hogarth Press, 1972), 241–42.

22. The Hogarth Press published a slightly revised version of "The Mark on the Wall" in 1919, under its own cover; the story was further revised for *Monday or Tuesday* in 1921.

23. Leonard's story precedes Virginia's in this publication. For a more extensive account of the relationship between Virginia's and Leonard's stories, see Rosenfeld, *Outsiders Together*.

24. David Cesarani, "An Embattled Minority: The Jews in Britain During the First World War," in *The Politics of Marginality: Race, the Radical Right, and Minorities in Twentieth-Century Britain*, ed. Tony Kushner and Kenneth Lunn (London: Frank Cass, 1990), 61–81.

25. Leonard Woolf, "Three Jews" in Woolf and Woolf, *Two Stories*, 6–8.

26. Virginia Woolf, "The Mark on the Wall," in *The Complete Shorter Fiction of Virginia Woolf*, 2nd ed., ed. Susan Dick (New York: Harcourt Brace, 1989), 89.

27. Also writing in 1917, Victor Shklovsky warns that habitual thought "devours works, clothes, furniture, one's wife, and the fear of war." Like Woolf, Shklovsky brings together the perception of everyday, domestic objects and the perception of war, arguing that stereotypes and metonymic thinking impede the experience both of furniture and of fear. Victor Shklovsky, "Art as Technique" (1917), in *Russian Formalist Criticism: Four Essays*, ed. and trans. Lee T. Lemon and Marion J. Reis (Lincoln: University of Nebraska Press, 1965), 12. Unlike Shklovsky, who presents his case for "defamiliarization" as a universal problem, Woolf uses evasion to respond to the specific conditions of British triumphalism.

28. *Virginia Woolf's Mrs. Dalloway*, dir. Marleen Gorris, videotape, Fox Lorber Films, 1997; Alex Zwerdling, *Virginia Woolf and the Real World* (Berkeley: University of California Press, 1986).

29. Virginia Woolf, *Mrs. Dalloway* (1925; reprint, New York: Harcourt, 1981), 3.

30. The film shows another scene from the past that the novel, significantly, omits: the scene of Clarissa's engagement to Richard, which in the film involves a kiss between them.

31. Theodor W. Adorno, "Parataxis: On Hölderlin's Late Poetry," in *Notes to Literature*, vol. 2, ed. Rolf Tiedemann, trans. Shierry Weber Nicholsen (New York: Columbia University Press, 1992), 131.

32. Barrett, "Virginia Woolf Meets Michel Foucault" in *Imagination in Theory*, 95.

33. Fussell, *The Great War and Modern Memory*, argues that after the First World War, it was no longer possible to use heroic language in everyday communication: before the war, "everyone knew what Glory was, and what Honor meant," Fussell explains (21). Although *Mrs. Dalloway* offers a sharp example of this phenomenon, Fussell presents Woolf as one of the modernist writers "not involved with the war" (314–15).

34. For Septimus, see Woolf, *Mrs. Dalloway*, 21, 25, 69; see Clarissa's "excitement" and "exquisite moment" on 34; and Peter's description of the "sharp, acute, uncomfortable grain" on 154, and his "excitement" in the final sentence of the novel, 194.

35. Pat Barker makes the conditions of stuttering and muteness the subject of *Regeneration*, a novel that takes as its principal topic the relationship between wartime doctors and returning soldiers. Pat Barker, *Regeneration* (London: Viking, 1991).

36. Gilles Deleuze, "A Conversation: What Is It? What Is It For?" in *Dialogues*, by Gilles Deleuze and Claire Parnet, trans. Hugh Tomlinson and Barbara Hammerjam (New York: Columbia University Press, 1987), 4.

37. Virginia Woolf, "Modern Fiction" (1925), in *The Common Reader*, ed. Andrew McNeillie (New York: Harcourt Brace, 1984), 150.

38. At the end of her career, Woolf thought she might create a new form of the novel, the "Novel-Essay," which would have combined the materials she came to publish separately as *Three Guineas* and *The Years*. See Michèle Barrett, introduction to Woolf, *A Room of One's Own and Three Guineas*, xxv.

39. Virginia Woolf, "Thoughts on Peace in an Air Raid," in *The Death of the Moth and Other Essays* (New York: Harcourt Brace, 1942), 244–47; Virginia Woolf, "The Artist and Politics," in *The Moment and Other Essays* (New York: Harcourt Brace and Jovanovich, 1948), 228.

40. "Camouflage" entered English usage during the First World War, when the technique of mimicry, drawn from the natural world of imitation, was widely adopted by military strategists to disguise armaments and supplies against enemy surveillance and attack. Camouflage was directed at aircraft photography, which could identify trucks or guns in the countryside far below because the natural environment, in its disorder, is easily distinguished from the artificial, man-made order of military equipment; the trick of camouflage is to break up the lines and boundaries between nature and art by making art as disordered as nature. The *Oxford English Dictionary*'s first citation for "camouflage" comes from 1917, when the term was still new enough for the *Daily Mail* to explain, "The act of hiding anything from your enemy is termed 'camouflage.'" See Roy M. Stanley II, *To Fool a Glass Eye* (Shrewsbury: Airlife Publishing, 1998); Tim Newark and Quentin Newark, *Brassey's Book of Camouflage* (London: Brassey's, 1996). Fussell observes that, at the start of the First World War, "camouflage" was a "new stylish foreign word" that people were embarrassed to pronounce (*The Great War and Modern Memory*, 29).

41. Camouflage is effective in war and in rhetoric because it transforms the fact of multiple, unrelated, perhaps hostile objects into the appearance of homogeneity and accordance. It aspires to impalpability: it seeks to obviate concealment and comparison, to neutralize the disruptive contrast between, say, "the hues of autumn leaves" and the "guns" used for shooting down German pilots, or between the vivid illusion of leaves and the "strips of green and brown stuff" whose lifeless reality goes unnoticed (Woolf, "Thoughts on Peace," 245–46).

42. Barrett, *Imagination in Theory*, 67.

43. As Woolf puts it in "The Artist and Politics," the artist is compelled by two, related causes: "The first is his own survival; the other is the survival of his art" (228). It is important to Woolf that the fight against war by artists should not ignore or aid the wartime fight against art. Woolf refuses priority to either of these causes by attaching one activity to the other: the compulsion to create art that conforms to political interests is, Woolf argues, always a symptom of aggression, and it is one of the social dangers against which artists must fight.

44. Erich Auerbach, *Mimesis: The Representation of Reality in Western Literature*, trans. Willard R. Trask (Princeton, N.J.: Princeton University Press, 1953), 546.

45. Georg Lukács, "Narrate or Describe?" (1936), in *Writer and Critic and Other Essays*, trans. Arthur D. Kahn (New York: Grosset & Dunlap, 1970), 144. Although Lukács does not discuss Woolf explicitly, he singles out for particular criticism any author who "writes from the point of view of his characters" (133).

46. M. M. Bakhtin, "Epic and Novel" (1941), in *The Dialogic Imagination*, ed. Michael Holquist, trans. Caryl Emerson and Michael Holquist (Austin: University of Texas Press, 1981), 13.

47. Theodor W. Adorno, *Minima Moralia: Reflections from a Damaged Life*, trans. E. F. N. Jephcott (London: Verso, 1978), 86.

48. Adorno makes the first comment on many occasions in his work, and takes it back or revises it at least twice: once in *Negative Dialectics*, trans. E. B. Ashton (New York: Continuum, 1983), 362; and once in the late essay "Is Art Lighthearted?" in *Notes to Literature*, vol. 2, 251. For an account of the development of Adorno's thinking on this topic, see Lyn Hejinian, "Barbarism," in *The Language of Inquiry* (Berkeley and Los Angeles: University of California Press, 2000), 325.

49. Adorno, *Minima Moralia*, 18.

50. Walter Benjamin, *Illuminations*, trans. Harry Zohn (New York: Schocken, 1968), 256.

51. Virginia Woolf, *The Years* (1938), ed. Hermione Lee (Oxford: Oxford University Press, 1992), 319. My thanks to Michèle Barrett for alerting me to this reference.

52. See editor's note in Virginia Woolf, *The Years*, 477–78; and Rowland Ryder, *Edith Cavell* (London: Hamish Hamilton, 1975), 237.

4. ISHIGURO'S TREASON

1. Kazuo Ishiguro, *An Artist of the Floating World* (1986; New York: Vintage, 1989); Kazuo Ishiguro, *The Remains of the Day* (1989; New York: Vintage, 1990). Future references to these texts will be designated, respectively, by the abbreviations *A* and *R*. Ishiguro's first novel, *A Pale View of Hills* (1982), which does seem to take place in or around the year of its publication, also involves memories of the 1950s and the interwar era. Kazuo Ishiguro, *A Pale View of Hills* (1982; New York: Vintage, 1990). Future references to this text will be designated by the abbreviation *P*.

2. Marcel Proust, *In Search of Lost Time*, vol. 6 (1927), trans. Andreas Mayor and Terence Kilmartin, rev. D. J. Enright (New York: The Modern Library: 1993), 290–91. For this idea of retrospective "recognition," see Lee Edelman, *Homographesis* (New York: Routledge, 1994), 19–21; Eve Kosofsky Sedgwick, *Epistemology of the Closet* (Berkeley: The University of California Press, 1990), 223.

3. Maud Ellmann, "'The Intimate Difference': Power and Representation in *The Ambassadors*," in Henry James, *The Ambassadors* (1903), ed. S. P. Rosenbaum, 2nd ed. (New York.: W. W. Norton, 1994), 508–9.

4. Henry James, preface to *The Golden Bowl* (1909), in *The Golden Bowl* (Oxford: Oxford University Press, 1983), lviii.

5. I mean here by "national allegory" both Fredric Jameson's sense of "private individual destiny" standing as metaphor for "public third-world culture and society" and individual or narrative self-presentation standing as national characteristic. Fredric Jameson, "Third-World Literature in the Era of Multinational Capitalism," *Social Text* 15 (Fall 1986): 69 and passim; Aijaz Ahmad, "Jameson's Rhetoric of Otherness and the 'National Allegory,'" *Social Text* 17 (Fall 1987): 12.

6. Ishiguro's effort resonates, in strategy and in practice, with Roland Barthes's attempt to conceive "what our language does not conceive": that is, to consider how language and other cultural systems create both limits and opportunities for knowledge. Barthes imagines "an aberrant grammar [that] would at least have the advantage of casting suspicion on the very ideology of our speech." Roland Barthes, *Empire of Signs*, trans. Richard Howard (New York: Hill and Wang, 1982), 7–8.

7. See my discussion of the Deleuzian stammer in chapter 3.

8. Gilles Deleuze, "A Conversation: What Is It? What Is It For?" in Gilles Deleuze and Claire Parnet, *Dialogues*, trans. Hugh Tomlinson and Barbara Hammerjam (New York: Columbia University Press, 1987), 5.

9. Theodor W. Adorno, "Words from Abroad," in *Notes to Literature*, vol. 2, ed. Rolf Tiedemann, trans. Shierry Weber Nichosen (New York: Columbia University Press, 1991), 185.

10. Homi K. Bhabha, *The Location of Culture* (London: Routledge, 1994), 224–28.

11. Bruce King, "The New Internationalism: Shiva Naipaul, Salman Rushdie, Buchi Emecheta, Timothy Mo, and Kazuo Ishiguro," in *The British and Irish Novel Since 1960*, ed. James Acheson (New York: St. Martin's Press, 1991), 207. Also, see Stanley Kauffmann, "The Floating World," *New Republic*, 6 November 1995, 43.

12. Valerie Purton, "The Reader in a Floating World: The Novels of Kazuo Ishiguro," in *The Literature of Place*, ed. Norman Page and Peter Preston (London: Macmillan, 1993), 170–71. This is not unlike Pico Iyer's remark that Ishiguro is "as Japanese as his name, and as English as the flawless prose he writes." Notice the parallel here between the distinct and self-evident nationality implied by a name and that offered by the perfection of a literary style. Pico Iyer, "Waiting Upon History," *Partisan Review* 58 (Summer 1991): 586.

13. Anne Chisholm, "Lost Worlds of Pleasure," *Times Literary Supplement*, 14 February 1986, 162.

14. Bhabha, *The Location of Culture*, 112; emphasis in the original.

15. Rey Chow, *Writing Diaspora: Tactics of Intervention in Contemporary Cultural Studies* (Bloomington: Indiana University Press, 1993), 33.

16. Chow, *Writing Diaspora*, 49; emphasis in the original.

17. Chow, *Writing Diaspora*, 30. Bhabha similarly argues that replacing bad images with good ones transforms an "'other' culture" into a "docile body of difference," forced to be "a good object of knowledge" (*The Location of Culture*, 31).

18. Slavoj Žižek, discussed in Chow, *Writing Diaspora*, 52–53. See Slavoj Žižek, "How the Non-Duped Err," *Qui Parle* 4, no. 1 (Fall 1990): 1–20.

19. Tom Wilhelmus, "Between Cultures," *The Hudson Review* 49, no. 2 (Summer 1996): 321.

20. Gabriele Annan, "On the High Wire," *The New York Review of Books*, 7 December 1989, 3.

21. Annan, "On the High Wire," 3–4.

22. James Clifford, *The Predicament of Culture* (Cambridge, Mass.: Harvard University Press, 1988), 95.

23. Kazuo Ishiguro, "A Family Supper," *Esquire* (March 1990): 207–11.

24. Alan Wolfe argues persuasively that "to mention suicide and Japan in the same sentence is to bring to bear a set of stereotypes that continue to shape Western perceptions of non-Western cultures": Alan Wolfe, *Suicidal Narrative in Modern Japan* (Princeton, N.J.: Princeton University Press, 1990), xiii.

25. The relationship between "the tradition of war-related or anachronistic suicides" and "appeals to a waning sense of national self-affirmation" is discussed at length in Wolfe, *Suicidal Narrative*, xv and passim.

26. Two of the twentieth-century's best-known Japanese novelists, Yukio Mishima and the Nobel laureate Yasunari Kawabata, committed suicide. Mishima and Kawabata often wrote about the effect of "foreign" culture on "Japanese" traditions.

27. Roland Barthes, *Mythologies*, trans. Annette Lavers (New York: Hill and Wang, 1972), 119.

28. Barthes, *Mythologies*, 109; emphasis in original.

29. Kathryn Morton, "After the War Was Lost," *New York Times Book Review*, 8 June 1986, 19; Hermione Lee, "Quiet Desolation," *New Republic*, 22 January 1990, 37; Louis Menand, "Anxious in Dreamland," *New York Times Book Review*, 15 October 1995, 7. Roland Barthes attributes the "reality effect" to those narrative details whose sole function is the promise of referentiality. See Roland Barthes, *The Rustle of Language*, trans. Richard Howard (Berkeley: University of California Press, 1989), 148.

30. In *The Artist of the Floating World*, there is a similar alliance between the art of painting that Ono has been taught and the art of the novel that his voice conveys.

31. Salman Rushdie, *Imaginary Homelands: Essays and Criticism, 1981–1991* (New York: Penguin, 1991), 67.

32. Chantal Zabus, "Language, Orality, and Literature," in *New National and Post-Colonial Literatures*, ed. Bruce King (Oxford: Oxford University Press, 1996), 34.

33. Kazuo Ishiguro and Oe Kenzaburo, "The Novelist in Today's World: A Conversation," *Boundary* 2 18, no. 3 (Fall 1991): 115.

34. If one needed any more evidence that Ichiro's "mistranslations" signify America by overgeneralized metonymy, one might note that an English reviewer misidentifies "Hi yo Silver" as the voice of Roy Rogers, a difference that in no way reduces the "Japaneseness" of the "great Samurai heroes" to which he is compared (Chisholm, "Lost Worlds," 162).

35. See Wayne C. Booth, *The Rhetoric of Fiction* (1961; Chicago: The University of Chicago Press, 1983), 158–59; Seymour Chatman, *Story and Discourse* (Ithaca, N.Y.: Cornell University Press, 1978), 148–49; Gerald Prince, *Dictionary of Narratology* (Lincoln: University of Nebraska Press, 1987), 101; and, for a more recent account of "unreliable narration" in the light of poststructuralist models of subjectivity,

see Kathleen Wall, "*The Remains of the Day* and Its Challenges to Theories of Unreliable Narration," *The Journal of Narrative Technique* 24, no. 1 (Winter 1994): 18–42.

36. Metaphorically, the "primal scene" is a traumatic event that is always out of reach: either because it is understood, if it is ever really understood, only at a later time or because it is fantasized in retrospect, patched together from later echoes. Sigmund Freud, "The Paths to the Formation of Symptoms" (1917), in *Introductory Lectures on Psycho-Analysis (Part III)*, in *The Standard Edition of the Complete Psychological Works of Sigmund Freud*, vol. 16, ed. James Strachey (London: The Hogarth Press and the Institute of Psycho-Analysis, 1968), 369–70; Marjorie Garber, *Vested Interests: Cross-Dressing and Cultural Anxiety* (New York: Routledge, 1992), 388.

37. The film that Ono and Ichiro attend is recognizable as the Japanese original of *Godzilla*, which was first released in 1954. In the film, the monster's destructiveness evokes the destructiveness of the atom bombs, though Godzilla destroys Tokyo rather than Hiroshima or Nagasaki. Whether or not Ichiro and Ono watch *Godzilla*—the title is never given and Ono remembers seeing the film in 1948, six years before the film was actually released—what they see is a disturbing reminder of the past, both because the film shows violence against Japan and because it encourages its viewers to take pleasure in the spectacle.

38. For Ishiguro's extended meditation on failed consolation, see his fourth novel, *The Unconsoled* (1995; New York: Vintage, 1996).

5. RUSHDIE'S MIX-UP

1. Salman Rushdie, *The Satanic Verses* (Dover, Del.: Consortium, 1992), 343. Homi K. Bhabha, "DissemiNation" (1990), in *The Location of Culture* (London and New York: Routledge, 1994), 167.

2. Ian Baucom, *Out of Place: Englishness, Empire, and the Locations of Identity* (Princeton, N.J.: Princeton University Press, 1999), 3.

3. For example, see Salman Rushdie, " 'Commonwealth Literature' Does Not Exist," in *Imaginary Homelands: Essays and Criticism, 1981–1991* (London: Penguin, 1991), 67. For the claim that Rushdie and other "cosmopolitan" writers are indiscriminate in their celebration of hybridity, see Timothy Brennan, "Cosmopolitans and Celebrities," *Race and Class* 31, no. 1 (1989): 1–19.

4. Timothy Brennan has called the world of the cosmopolitan novelist "a convenient no-place," and Aijaz Ahmad condemns "postmodern" international writers for validating "the pleasures of . . . unbelonging." Timothy Brennan, *At Home in the World: Cosmopolitanism Now* (Cambridge, Mass.: Harvard University Press, 1997), 306; Aijaz Ahmad, *In Theory* (London: Verso, 1992), 157–58.

5. Brennan, *At Home in the World*, 306.

6. See Timothy Brennan, *Salman Rushdie and the Third World: Myths of the Nation* (London: Macmillan, 1989), xiii. For critique of Brennan's charges against cosmopolitan writers, see Rosemary Marangoly George, "The Cosmopolitan Club," *Novel* 25, no. 1 (Fall 1991): 103–5.

7. Adam Phillips, *On Flirtation* (Cambridge, Mass.: Harvard University Press, 1994), xxii–xiii.

8. Suspicious of "apostolic" drama, Bruce Robbins calls for "an internationalist ethics of the everyday, one that will not tell us solely what to die or kill for but also how action at a distance can be part of how we live." Bruce Robbins, *Feeling Global: Internationalism in Distress* (New York: New York University Press, 1999), 23.

9. Michel de Certeau, *The Practice of Everyday Life*, trans. Steven Rendell (Berkeley: University of California Press, 1984), xii–xv. First published in French in 1974.

10. Gerald Mazorati, "Salman Rushdie: Fiction's Embattled Infidel," *New York Times*, 29 January 1989.

11. Brennan, *Salman Rushdie*, 149.

12. See Lisa Appignanesi and Sarah Maitland, eds., *The Rushdie File* (Syracuse, N.Y.: Syracuse University Press, 1990); and Malise Ruthven, *A Satanic Affair: Salman Rushdie and the Wrath of Islam* (London: The Hogarth Press, 1990).

13. Salman Rushdie, "In Good Faith" (1990), in *Imaginary Homelands*, 394.

14. Rushdie describes this scenario in *Fury* (New York: Random House, 2001), 35–36. See my discussion at the end of this chapter.

15. Stuart Hall, "The New Ethnicities" (1988), in *Ethnicity*, ed. John Hutchinson and Anthony D. Smith (Oxford: Oxford University Press, 1996), 162.

16. One example of Sisodia's entanglement with English culture is his invocation of Charles Dodgson, also known as Lewis Carroll, the author of *Alice in Wonderland*. Dodgson, who stuttered throughout his life, called himself "the Dodo" because "Do, Do" were the first two syllables of his last name, as he pronounced it. Sisodia may give the name "Dodo" to the English, but the stutter allows Rushdie to suggest that "Dodo" fits Sisodia as well. For a discussion of Dodgson's stutter, see Hugh Haughton, introduction to *Alice's Adventures in Wonderland and Through the Looking Glass*, by Lewis Carroll, ed. Hugh Haughton (London: Penguin, 1998), xvi. There are many other references to Carroll's work in Rushdie's fiction, some of which I mention later in this chapter. In general, the image of a child falling through a looking glass into a mysterious, somewhat aggressive, somewhat fantastic world suits Rushdie's seriocomic image of immigrant experience.

17. Robert J. C. Young, *Colonial Desire: Hybridity in Theory, Culture, and Race* (London: Routledge, 1995), 3.

18. Salman Rushie, quoted in Mazorati, "Salman Rushdie: Fiction's Embattled Infidel," 100.

19. By 1991, critics were putting authenticity in quotation marks. Henry Louis Gates Jr., "'Authenticity,' or the Lesson of Little Tree," *New York Times Book Review*, 24 November 1991. For a discussion of the critical shift into and away from authenticity, see Nancy K. Miller, *Getting Personal: Feminist Occasions and Other Autobiographical Acts* (New York: Routledge, 1991).

20. Jeremy Waldron, "Minority Cultures and the Cosmopolitan Alternative," in *The Rights of Minority Cultures*, ed. Will Kymlicka (Oxford: Oxford University Press, 1995), 100–101. Waldron's essay was first published in the *Michigan Journal of Law Reform* in 1992.

21. See Salman Rushdie, "Imaginary Homelands" (1982) and " 'Commonwealth Literature' Does Not Exist," in *Imaginary Homelands*, 16–17 and 63–67. In " 'Commonwealth Literature,' " Rushdie asserts that he is reluctant to resign the category of "British writer," unmodified, to authors who are white or native to the British Isles, especially because he does not promote his own work as an authentic representation of India or Pakistan in miniature, "homogenous and unbroken" (67).

22. Salman Rushdie, "Imaginary Homelands," 20.

23. For a model of uncommitted cosmopolitanism, see Alex Zwerdling's account of T. S. Eliot's internationalism in Alex Zwerdling, *Improvised Europeans: American Literary Expatriates in London* (New York: Basic Books, 1998); for a model of cosmopolitanism as "worldwide allegiance," see Martha C. Nussbaum, "Patriotism and Cosmopolitanism," *Respondents, For Love of Country: Debating the Limits of Patriotism*, ed. Joshua Cohen, (Boston: Beacon Press, 1996), 4.

24. Salman Rushdie, "In Good Faith," 394.

25. For an argument in favor of this shift, see Michel Foucault, "So Is It Important to Think?" in *Power*, ed. James D. Faubion, in *The Essential Works of Michel Foucault, 1954–1984*, ed. Paul Rabinow, vol. 3 (New York: The New York Press, 2000), 457. For a discussion of this shift, see Henry Louis Gates Jr., " 'Authenticity.' "

26. See Homi K. Bhabha on the "self-critical joke" in "On Cultural Choice," in *The Turn to Ethics*, ed. Marjorie Garber, Beatrice Hanssen, and Rebecca L. Walkowitz (New Yorkn: Routledge, 2000), 196.

27. Judith Butler, *Excitable Speech* (New York: Routledge, 1997), 163.

28. Judith Butler, *Bodies That Matter: On the Discursive Limits of "Sex"* (New York: Routledge, 1993), 228.

29. James Thomson, "Ode: Rule, Britannia" (1740), in *The Norton Anthology of English Literature*, vol. 1, fifth ed., ed. M. H. Abrams (New York: Norton, 1986), 2474–75.

30. Bhabha, "How Newness Enters the World," in *The Location of Culture*, 225.

31. Salman Rushdie, "Good Advice Is Rarer Than Rubies," in *East, West* (New York: Random House, 1994), 3–16.

32. Two of the other proverbs in the story are also Miss Rehana's: "Good advice should find good money" and, "When Fate sends a gift, one receives good fortune" (6–7). Muhammad Ali introduces one proverb, but he does not understand its full meaning: "The oldest fools are bewitched by the youngest girls" (11).

33. These are the story's implicit truisms. The explicit truisms, voiced by Muhammad Ali, are "one's parents act in one's best interests"; "they found you a good and honest man who has kept his word and sent for you"; "now you have a lifetime to get to know him, and to love" (14).

34. Salman Rushdie, "The Courter," in *East, West*, 173–211.

35. Chess was first played in India; its modern rules are European but the pieces are Indian and Persian in origin. Richard Eales, *Chess: The History of the Game* (London: Batsford, 1985).

36. "You see it's like a portmanteau," Humpty Dumpty explains to Alice: "there are two meanings packed into one word." Lewis Carroll, *Though the Looking Glass*, in

Alice in Wonderland, 2nd ed., ed. Donald J. Gray (New York: Norton, 1992), 164. Gray defines a portmanteau, in the literal sense, as "a traveling bag that opens, like a book, into two equal compartments (164 n. 1).

37. Haughton, introduction, xvi.

38. Derek Attridge, "Unpacking the Portmanteau, or Who's Afraid of *Finnegans Wake?*" in *On Puns: The Foundation of Letters*, ed. Jonathan Culler (London: Blackwell, 1998), 145.

39. The narrator and his siblings call their ayah "Aya" or "Jumble-Aya," dropping the "h" in order to make her job into an intimate name and into a game, the palindrome and the pun ("jambalaya" is a mixture of ingredients, in the mixture of languages called Creole) personalizing for the children what is otherwise a category of person.

40. Amitava Kumar makes this point persuasively in his discussion of antinationalist and capitalist forms of hybridity. Amitava Kumar, *Bombay-London–New York* (New York: Routledge, 2002), 54–55.

6. SEBALD'S VERTIGO

1. Susan Sontag, "A Mind in Mourning," (2000) in *Where the Stress Falls* (New York: Farrar, Straus and Giroux, 2001), 41–48.

2. W. G. Sebald, *The Emigrants*, trans. Michael Hulse (New York: New Directions, 1996); first published in German in 1992. Future references to this novel will be designated by the abbreviation *E*. W. G. Sebald, *The Rings of Saturn*, trans. Michael Hulse (New York: New Directions, 1998); first published in German in 1995. Future references to this novel will be designated by the abbreviation *R*.

3. W. G. Sebald, *Vertigo*, trans. Michael Hulse (New York: New Directions, 1999); first published in German in 1990. Future references to this novel will be designated by the abbreviation *V*.

4. Peter Novick has attributed "the centering of the Holocaust in the minds of American Jews" at the end of the twentieth century to the desire for a political vision that does without "moral ambiguities." Peter Novick, "The Holocaust in American Life," in *The Holocaust: Theoretical Readings*, ed. Neil Levi and Michael Rothberg (New Brunswick, N.J.: Rutgers University Press, 2003), 478, 476.

5. Susan Sontag, *Regarding the Pain of Others* (New York: Picador, 2003), 88, emphasis in original.

6. Susan Sontag, "Against Interpretation," in *Against Interpretation and Other Essays* (New York: Delta, 1966), 3–14, esp. 13; Sontag, *AIDS and Its Metaphors* (New York: Farrar, Straus and Giroux, 1989), 14. On Sontag's politics of metaphor, see D. A. Miller, "Sontag's Urbanity," in *The Lesbian and Gay Studies Reader*, ed. Henry Abelove, Michèle Aina Barale, and David M. Halperin (New York: Routledge, 1993), 212–20.

7. Andreas Huyssen and to some extent Amir Eshel have suggested that Sebald's narratives combine many instances of violence and genocide (the Holocaust, British imperialism in Ireland, Belgian imperialism in the Congo, Napoleon's

march through Europe, etc.) into one unerring, uncompromising "'paradigm' of organizing, aggressive rationality" (Eshel), in which there is no resistance, no human agency, and none of the idiosyncrasy or accident that a more ironic style of analysis would display. Simon Ward argues, in response to Huyssen, that this irony is present in Sebald's visible fragmentation of his own narratives and in his dialectical movement between details and high vantage points. Andreas Huyssen, "Rewritings and New Beginnings: W. G. Sebald and the Literature of the Air War," in *Present Pasts: Urban Palimpsests and the Politics of Memory* (Stanford, Calif.: Stanford University Press, 2003), 138–57; Amir Eshel, "Against the Power of Time: The Poetics of Suspension in W. G. Sebald's *Austerlitz*," *New German Critique* 88 (Winter 2003): 71–96, esp. 88–89; Simon Ward, "Ruins and Poetics in the Works of W. G. Sebald," in *W. G. Sebald: A Critical Companion*, ed. J. J. Long and Anne Whitehead (Seattle: University of Washington Press, 2004), 66–67.

8. Alan Milchman and Alan Rosenberg argue that "the historicization of the Holocaust [risks] becoming an occasion for its relativization, and normalization," in "Two Kinds of Uniqueness: The Universalization of the Holocaust" in *The Holocaust: Theoretical Readings*, ed. Neil Levi and Michael Rothberg (New Brunswick, N.J.: Rutgers University Press, 2003), 444.

9. Neil Levi and Michael Rothberg, "Uniqueness, Comparison, and the Politics of Memory: Introduction," in *The Holocaust: Theoretical Readings*, ed. Neil Levi and Michael Rothberg (New Brunswick, N.J.: Rutgers University Press, 2003), 441.

10. And Sebald insists that the Allied air war, however much destruction it caused in German cities, was "provoked" by German atrocities. W. G. Sebald, "Air War and Literature," in *On the Natural History of Destruction*, trans. Anthea Bell (New York: Random House, 2003), 103. Future references to this essay will be designated by the abbreviation "AW."

11. Roland Barthes, *Mythologies*, trans. Annette Lavers (New York: Hill and Wang, 1972).

12. W. G. Sebald, "Between History and Natural History: On the Literary Description of Total Destruction," in *Campo Santo* (New York: Random House, 2005), 77. Future references to this essay will be designated by the abbreviation "BH." In "Rewritings and New Beginnings," Andreas Huyssen argues convincingly that "Air War and Literature" is a reworking of "Between History and Natural History" (148).

13. Eva Hoffman, *After Such Knowledge: Memory, History, and the Legacy of the Holocaust* (New York: Public Affairs, 2004), 12.

14. In an excellent analysis of *Eichmann in Jerusalem*, Kim Rostan presents a theory of "speculative witnessing," which, she argues, allowed Hannah Arendt to supplement Eichmann's testimony with the scenes he refused to remember. Rostan's essay has helped me to think about the significance of speculation in Sebald's work. Kim Rostan, "Arendt's Speculative Witnessing," work in progress.

15. In *Austerlitz*, Sebald's last novel, a character recalling the occupation of Prague by the Nazis admits that she was "particularly upset"—really, upset for the first time—by "the instant change to driving on the right." W. G. Sebald, *Austerlitz*, trans. Anthea Bell (New York: Random House, 2001), 171. Future references to

this text will be designated by the abbreviation *A*. In *Vertigo*, the narrator reports that when his wife's grandmother died, what he thought about most was "the blue half-empty pack of Bad Ischl salt under the sink in her council flat in Lorez Mandl Gasse and which she would never now be able to use up" (*V* 46); in *The Emigrants*, Max Ferber, whose mother perished in a concentration camp while he was sent to England as a child, wishes that he had never unpacked the suitcase she had packed for him (*E* 188). The final example of the budgerigars is from *R* 176–77.

16. Georg Lukács, "Narrate or Describe?" (1936), in *Writer and Critic and Other Essays*, trans. Arthur D. Kahn (New York: Grosset & Dunlap, 1971), 110–48.

17. Amitava Kumar, *Passport Photos* (Berkeley and Los Angeles: University of California Press, 2000), ix.

18. Amitava Kumar, ed., *Away: The Indian Writer as Expatriate* (New York: Routledge, 2004), xix.

19. In one story that Kumar includes in his anthology, a young man comes to know London by learning the *A to Z* (the London street map) by heart. This is an extract from Amitav Ghosh's novel, *Shadow Lines* (London: Bloomsbury, 1988). In Kumar's anthology, the extract is entitled "A to Z Street Atlas."

20. Among the many discussions of Sebald's debt to Walter Benjamin are Eshel, "Against the Power of Time," 83; Andreas Huyssen, "Grey Zones of Remembrance," in *A New History of German Literature*, ed. David E. Wellbery (Cambridge, Mass.: Belknap Press of Harvard University Press, 2004), 971; Martin Swales, "Theoretical Reflections on the Work of W. G. Sebald," in *W. G. Sebald: A Critical Companion*, ed. J. J. Long and Anne Whitehead (Seattle: University of Washington Press, 2004), 28; Massimo Leone, "Textual Wanderings: A Vertiginous Reading of W. G. Sebald," in *W. G. Sebald: A Critical Companion*, ed. J. J. Long and Anne Whitehead (Seattle: University of Washington Press, 2004), 98; and Sebald, "AW" 67–68.

21. See Benjamin's famous dictum: "There is no document of civilization which is not at the same time a document of barbarism." Walter Benjamin, *Illuminations*, trans. Harry Zohn (New York: Schocken, 1968), 256.

22. Leone, "Textual Wanderings," 97–98; Benjamin, *Illuminations*, 263.

23. See my discussion of Horkheimer and the tradition of critical theory in the introduction to this book.

24. Eshel, "Against the Power of Time," 92.

25. He shares this project with Étienne Balibar, who wants citizenship to be seen as "a civil process" rather than a "legal status." See Étienne Balibar, *We, the People of Europe? Reflections on Transnational Citizenship* (Princeton, N.J.: Princeton University Press, 2003), 132.

26. By writable, I mean that Sebald allows the stories of famous people to be interpreted rather than invoked as if they mean something by themselves. See Roland Barthes, *S/Z*, trans. Richard Miller (Oxford: Blackwell, 1992), 15–16.

27. Sebald's last novel focuses on a noncelebrity who wants to undo the anonymity that a change of name has imposed. The novel records the narrator's intermittent but intense friendship with Jacques Austerlitz, who until his adolescence was called Dafydd Elias by the Welsh couple that raised him. Austerlitz, it turns out,

was part of a *kindertransport*, which brought him to Britain, at age four, from Nazi-occupied Prague. On arrival, he was given not an English but a Welsh name, which erased his attachment to a Jewish-Czech family in cosmopolitan Prague and replaced it with an attachment to a Calvinist family in provincial Wales. The novel describes Austerlitz's efforts to perceive and to analyze the process of erasure and replacement, both in his own history and in the recent history of Europe.

28. Sebald, *A* 151; W. G. Sebald, *After Nature*, trans. Michael Hamburger (New York: Random House, 2002), 89.

29. Brian McHale, *Postmodernist Fiction* (New York: Methuen, 1987), xiii; Tyrus Miller, *Late Modernism: Politics, Fiction, and the Arts Between the World Wars* (Berkeley: University of California Press, 1999), 7–13; Joseph Margolis, *What, After All, Is a Work of Art? Lectures in the Philosophy of Art* (University Park: Pennsylvania State University Press, 1999), 5.

30. Swales, "Theoretical Reflections," 25.

31. Eshel, "Against the Power of Time," 75, 89. Huyssen, "Gray Zones," 972.

32. Gillian Tindall has proposed that Sebald's novels seem to have been "thought in English" before being written in German, and Arthur Williams asserts that even if the novels are thought and written in German, they "arrive at a presentation of German issues in a framework which is anything but German." Gillian Tindall, "The Fortress of the Heart," *The Times Literary Supplement*, 19 October 2001, 21; Arthur Williams, "W. G. Sebald: A Holistic Approach to Borders, Texts, and Perspectives," in *German-Language Literature Today: International and Popular?* ed. Arthur Williams, Stuart Parks, and Julian Preece (Oxford: Peter Lang, 2000), 99. Williams thinks of Sebald not as English or German but as "European."

33. Caryl Phillips, "Extravagant Strangers," in *A New World Order* (New York: Vintage, 2001), 292.

34. Dipesh Chakrabarty, quoted in Antoinette Burton, "Introduction: On the Inadaquacy and Indespenability of the Nation," in *After the Imperial Turn: Thinking With and Through the Nation*, ed. Antoinette Burton (Durham: Duke University Press, 2003), 2.

35. Burton, "Introduction," 1.

36. Peter Hulme, quoted in Burton, "Introduction," 3.

37. For a description and helpful analysis of this conventional usage, see Elaine K. Ginsberg, "The Politics of Passing," in *Passing and the Fictions of Identity*, ed. Elaine K. Ginsberg (Durham: Duke University Press, 1996), 1–18.

38. W. G. Sebald, *Die Ringes Des Saturn: Eine Englische Wallfahrt* (Frankfurt: Eichborn Verlag, 1995), 5.

39. The English edition of the novel, which foregoes the first epigraph and translates the German quotation (a definition of the novel's title phrase) into English, offers this effect somewhat less powerfully. In the English edition, Sebald discards Milton's remark, "Good and evil we know in the field of this world grow up together almost inseparably." In the German edition, this quotation is mistakenly attributed to *Paradise Lost.*

40. In English: "those unhappy souls . . . who look uncomprehendingly upon the horror

of the struggle, the joy of victory, the profound hopelessness of the vanquished": Conrad to Marguerite Poradowska, 23 March 1890, in *The Collected Works of Joseph Conrad*, vol. 1 (1861–1897), ed. Frederick R. Karl and Laurence Davies (Cambridge: Cambridge University Press, 1983), 43.

41. Silk appears in the chapter on Conrad and Casement as the material of an armchair in which the narrator falls asleep, as the material of a dress (worn by Conrad's mother "as a token of mourning for her people suffering the humiliation of foreign rule"), as a poetic figure (the soot ash of burning manuscripts is "like a scrap of black silk"), and possibly as the substance of a hangman's rope (Casement's) (*R* 103, 106, 108, 134). In the German edition, the novel is called *The Rings of Saturn: An English Pilgrimage*. There is no subtitle in the English edition.

42. Ian Watt, *Conrad in the Nineteenth Century* (Berkeley: University of California Press, 1979), 88.

43. Pericles Lewis, *Modernism, Nationalism, and the Novel* (Cambridge: Cambridge University Press, 2000), 101.

44. Colm Tóibín, "The Tragedy of Roger Casement," *New York Review of Books*, 27 May 2004, 53–57.

45. Cynthia Enloe, *Bananas, Beaches, and Bases* (Berkeley: University of California Press, 1990), 196–97. Marking the difference between 1916 and 1995, Sebald argues that Casement's homosexuality, far from compromising his defense of Ireland, schooled him in the observation of marginal experiences: "it was precisely Casement's homosexuality that sensitized him to the continuing oppression, exploitation, enslavement and destruction, across the borders of social class and race, of those who were furthest from the centers of power" (*R* 134).

46. Leone, "Textual Wanderings," 92.

47. Michael Rothberg, "W. E. B. Du Bois in Warsaw: Holocaust Memory and the Color Line, 1949–1952," *The Yale Journal of Criticism* 14, no. 1 (2001): 176.

48. Peter Craven, "W. G. Sebald: Anatomy of Faction," *Heat* 13 (1999): 220.

Adorno, Theodor W. *Aesthetic Theory*. Ed. and trans. Robert Hullot-Kentor. Minneapolis: University of Minnesota Press, 1997.

——. *Critical Models: Interventions and Catchwords*. Trans. Henry W. Pickford. New York: Columbia University Press, 1998.

——. *Minima Moralia: Reflections from a Damaged Life*. Trans. E. F. N. Jephcott. London: Verso, 1978.

——. *Negative Dialectics*. Trans. E. B. Ashton. New York: Continuum, 1983.

——. *Notes to Literature*. Vol. 1. Ed. Rolf Tiedemann. Trans. Shierry Weber Nicholsen. New York: Columbia University Press, 1991.

——. *Notes to Literature*. Vol. 2. Ed. Rolf Tiedemann. Trans. Shierry Weber Nicholsen. New York: Columbia University Press, 1992.

Ahmad, Aijaz. *In Theory*. London: Verso, 1992.

——. "Jameson's Rhetoric of Otherness and the 'National Allegory.'" *Social Text* 17 (Fall 1987): 3–25.

Althusser, Louis. "The International of Decent Feelings." 1946. In *The Spectre of Hegel: Early Writings*, trans. G. M. Goshgarian, 21–35. London: Verso, 1997.

Anderson, Amanda. "Argument and Ethos." In *Polemic: Critical or Uncritical*, ed. Jane Gallop, 103–34. New York: Routledge, 2004.

——. "Cosmopolitanism, Universalism, and the Divided Legacies of Modernity." *Cosmopolitics: Thinking and Feeling Beyond the Nation*, ed. Pheng Cheah and Bruce Robbins, 265–89. Minneapolis: University of Minnesota Press, 1998.

——. *The Powers of Distance: Cosmopolitanism and the Cultivation of Detachment*. Princeton, N.J.: Princeton University Press, 2001.

Anderson, Benedict. *Imagined Communities*. 1983. Reprint, London: Verso, 1991.

Annan, Gabriele. "On the High Wire." *The New York Review of Books*, 7 December 1989, 3–4.

Anonymous. Unsigned review of *The Secret Agent*, by Joseph Conrad. *Times Literary Supplement*, 20 September 1907, 285. Reprint, in *Conrad: The Critical Heritage*, ed. Norman Sherry, 185. Cambridge: Cambridge University Press, 1983.

Appadurai, Arjun. *Modernity at Large: Cultural Dimensions of Globalization.* Minneapolis: University of Minnesota Press, 1996.

Appiah, Kwame Anthony. "Cosmopolitan Patriots." *Critical Inquiry* 23, no. 3 (Spring 1997): 617–39.

Appignanesi, Lisa, and Sarah Maitland, eds. *The Rushdie File.* Syracuse, N.Y.: Syracuse University Press, 1990.

Attridge, Derek. "Unpacking the Portmanteau, or Who's Afraid of *Finnegan's Wake*?" In *On Puns: The Foundation of Letters*, ed. Jonathan Culler, 140–55. London: Blackwell, 1998.

Attridge, Derek, and Marjorie Howes, eds. *Semicolonial Joyce.* Cambridge: Cambridge University Press, 2000.

Auerbach, Erich. *Mimesis: The Representation of Reality in Western Literature.* Trans. Willard R. Trask. Princeton, N.J.: Princeton University Press, 1953.

Bakhtin, M.M. *The Dialogic Imagination: Four Essays.* Ed. Michael Holquist. Trans. Caryl Emerson and Michael Holquist. Austin: The University of Texas Press, 1981.

Balibar, Etienne. "The Nation Form: History and Ideology." In *Race, Nation, Class*, ed. Etienne Balibar and Immanuel Wallerstein, trans. Chris Turner, 86–106. London: Verso, 1991.

——. *We, the People of Europe? Reflections on Transnational Citizenship.* Princeton, N.J.: Princeton University Press, 2003.

Ball, John Clement. *Imagining London: Postcolonial Fiction and the Transnational Metropolis.* Toronto: University of Toronto Press, 2004.

Barish, Jonas. *The Anti-Theatrical Prejudice.* Berkeley: University of California Press, 1981.

Barker, Pat. *Regeneration.* London: Viking, 1991.

Barrett, Michèle. "The Great War and Post-Modern Memory." *New Formations* 41 (August 2000): 148–57.

——. *Imagination in Theory: Essays on Writing and Culture.* Cambridge: Polity Press, 1999.

Barthes, Roland. *Empire of Signs.* Trans. Richard Howard. New York: Hill and Wang, 1982.

——. *Mythologies.* Trans. Annette Lavers. New York: Hill and Wang, 1972.

——. *The Rustle of Language.* Trans. Richard Howard. Berkeley: University of California Press, 1989.

——. *S/Z.* Trans. Richard Miller. Oxford: Blackwell, 1992.

Bate, Jonathan. General preface to *The Oxford English Literary History*, in *The Internationalization of English Literature*, vol. 13, ed. Bruce King, viii–x. In *The Oxford Literary History.* Oxford: Oxford University Press, 2003.

Baucom, Ian. *Out of Place: Englishness, Empire, and the Locations of Identity.* Princeton, N.J.: Princeton University Press, 1999.

Benjamin, Walter. *Illuminations.* Trans. Harry Zohn. New York: Schocken, 1968.

Berlant, Lauren. *The Anatomy of National Fantasy: Hawthorne, Utopia, and Everyday Life*. Chicago: University of Chicago Press, 1991.

———. *The Queen of America Goes to Washington City*. Durham, N.C.: Duke University Press, 1997.

Berman, Jessica. *Modernist Fiction, Cosmopolitanism, and the Politics of Community*. Cambridge: Cambridge University Press, 2001.

Bhabha, Homi, K. "Editor's Introduction: Minority Maneuvers and Unsettled Negotiations." *Critical Inquiry* 23, no. 3 (Spring 1997): 431–59.

———. *The Location of Culture*. London: Routledge, 1994.

———. "On Cultural Choice." In *The Turn to Ethics*, ed. Marjorie Garber, Beatrice Hanssen, and Rebecca L. Walkowitz, 181–200. New York: Routledge, 2000.

Bloch, Ernst, et al. *Aesthetics and Politics*. London: Verso, 1980.

Booth, Wayne C. *The Rhetoric of Fiction*. 1961. Chicago: University of Chicago Press, 1983.

Bowlby, Rachel. *Feminist Destinations and Further Essays on Virginia Woolf*. Edinburgh: Edinburgh University Press, 1997.

Boyd, Ernest. *Ireland's Literary Renaissance*. New York: Alfred A. Knopf, 1922.

Bradbrook, M. C. "Notes on the Style of Mrs. Woolf." *Scrutiny* 1, no. 1 (1932): 33–38.

Brantlinger, Patrick. "*Heart of Darkness*: Anti-Imperialism, Racism, or Impressionism?" In *Case Studies in Contemporary Criticism: Heart of Darkness*, ed. Ross C. Murfin, 277–98. Boston: Bedford, 1996.

Brennan, Timothy. *At Home in the World: Cosmopolitanism Now*. Cambridge, Mass.: Harvard University Press, 1997.

———. "Cosmopolitans and Celebrities." *Race and Class* 31, no. 1 (1989): 1–19.

———. *Salman Rushdie and the Third World: Myths of the Nation*. London: Macmillan, 1989.

Burton, Antoinette. "Introduction: On the Inadequacy and Indispensability of the Nation." In *After the Imperial Turn: Thinking With and Through the Nation*, ed. Antoinette Burton, 1–26. Durham, N.C.: Duke University Press, 1999.

———. "The Postcolonial Careers of Santha Rama Rau." Work in progress.

Butler, Judith. *Bodies That Matter: On the Discursive Limits of "Sex."* New York: Routledge, 1993.

———. *Excitable Speech*. New York: Routledge, 1997.

———. "Explanation and Exoneration, or What We Can Hear." *Social Text* 72 (Fall 2002): 177–88.

Carroll, Lewis. *Alice in Wonderland*. 2nd ed. Ed. Donald J. Gray. New York; London: Norton, 1992.

Cesarani, David. "An Embattled Minority: The Jews in Britain During the First World War." In *The Politics of Marginality: Race, the Radical Right, and Minorities in Twentieth-Century Britain*, ed. Tony Kushner and Kenneth Lunn, 61–81. London: Frank Cass, 1990.

Chakrabarty, Dipesh. *Provincializing Europe: Postcolonial Thought and Historical Difference*. Princeton, N.J.: Princeton University Press, 2000.

Chatman, Seymour. *Story and Discourse*. Ithaca, N.Y.: Cornell University Press, 1978.

Chaudhuri, Amit. "In the Waiting-Room of History." *London Review of Books*, 24 June 2004, 3–5.

Cheng, Vincent J. *Jocye, Race, and Empire*. Cambridge: Cambridge University Press, 1995.

——. "'Terrible Queer Creatures': Joyce, Cosmopolitanism, and the Inauthentic Irishman." In *James Joyce and the Fabrication of Irish Identity*, ed. Michael Patrick Gillespie, 11–38. Amsterdam: Rodolfi, 2001.

Chisholm, Anne. "Lost Worlds of Pleasure." *Times Literary Supplement*, 14 February 1986, 162.

Chrisman, Laura. "Imperial Space, Imperial Place: Theories of Empire and Culture in Fredric Jameson, Edward Said, and Gayatri Spivak." *New Formations* 34 (Summer 1998): 53–69.

Chow, Rey. *Writing Diaspora: Tactics of Intervention in Contemporary Cultural Studies*. Bloomington: Indiana University Press, 1993.

Clifford, James. "Mixed Feelings." In *Cosmopolitics: Thinking and Feeling Beyond the Nation*, ed. Pheng Cheah and Bruce Robbins, 362–70. Minneapolis: University of Minnesota Press, 1998.

——. *The Predicament of Culture: Twentieth-Century Ethnography, Literature, and Art*. Cambridge, Mass.: Harvard University Press, 1998.

——. *Routes*. Cambridge, Mass.: Harvard University Press, 1997.

Cohen, Deborah. "Who Was Who? Race and Jews in Turn-of-the-Century Britain." *Journal of British Studies* 41 (October 2002): 460–83.

Cole, Sarah. *Modernism, Male Friendship, and the First World War*. Cambridge: Cambridge University Press, 2003.

Collini, Stefan. "On Variousness; and on Persuasion." *New Left Review* 27 (May/June 2004): 65–97.

Conrad, Joseph. "Author's Note." In *A Personal Record* (1912). Reprint, in *The Mirror of the Sea; and A Personal Record*, iii–x. London: J. M. Dent, 1968.

——. *The Collected Works of Joseph Conrad*. Ed. Frederick R. Karl and Laurence Davies. Cambridge: Cambridge University Press, 1983.

——. *Heart of Darkness*. 1899. In *"Heart of Darkness" and Other Tales*, ed. Cedric Watts, 133–252. Oxford: Oxford University Press, 1990.

——. Letter to Hugh-Durand Davray. January 1908. In *The Collected Letters of Joseph Conrad*, ed. Frederick R. Karl and Laurence Davies, 4:28–29. Cambridge: Cambridge University Press, 1983.

——. *Lord Jim*. 1900. New York: Norton, 1968.

——. *Nostromo*. 1904. London: Penguin, 1983.

——. *The Nigger of the "Narcissus."* 1898. New York: Norton, 1979.

——. *The Secret Agent*. 1907. Ed. Martin Seymour-Smith. London: Penguin, 1990.

Coppa, Francesca. "'I Seem to Recognize a Device That Has Done Duty in Bygone Plays': Oscar Wilde and the Theatre of Epigram." In *Reading Wilde, Querying Spaces: An Exhibition Commemorating the One Hundredth Anniversary of the Trials of Oscar Wilde*, 11–19. New York: Fales Library, New York University, 1995.

"Cosmopolitan Art—a Friendly Dispute Between Selwyn Image and Lewis F. Day." *The Art Journal* 18 (December 1902): 374–75.

Craven, Peter. "W. G. Sebald: Anatomy of Faction." *Heat* 13 (1999): 212–24.

Cuddy-Keane, Melba. "Modernism, Geopolitics, Globalization." *Modernism/Modernity* 10, no. 3 (2003): 539–58.

——. *Virginia Woolf, the Intellectual, and the Public Sphere.* Cambridge: Cambridge University Press, 2003.

Culler, Jonathan. "The Call of the Phoneme." In *On Puns: The Foundation of Letters*, ed. Jonathan Culler, 1–16. Oxford: Basil Blackwell, 1998.

Dames, Nicholas. "Brushes with Fame: Thackeray and the Work of Celebrity." *Nineteenth Century Literature* 56, no. 1 (2001): 23–51.

Damrosch, David. Preface to *The Longman Anthology of British Literature*, vol. 2, xxxiii–xxxvii. New York: Longman, 1999.

——. *What Is World Literature?* Princeton, N.J.: Princeton University Press, 2003.

de Certeau, Michel. *The Practice of Everyday Life.* Trans. Steven Rendell. Berkeley: University of California Press, 1984. First published in French, 1974.

Deleuze, Gilles. "A Conversation: What Is It? What Is It For?" In *Dialogues*, by Gilles Deleuze and Claire Parnet, trans. Hugh Tomlinson and Barbara Hammerjam, 1–35. New York: Columbia University Press, 1987.

Dever, Carolyn. *Skeptical Feminism: Activist Theory, Activist Practice.* Minneapolis: University of Minnesota Press, 2003.

Dharwadker, Vinay. Introduction to *Cosmopolitan Geographies: New Locations in Literature and Culture*, ed. Vinay Dharwadker, 1–14. New York: Routledge, 2001.

Donald, James. *Imagining the Modern City.* Minneapolis: University of Minnesota Press, 1999.

Du Bois, W. E. B. *The Souls of Black Folk.* 1903. New York: Penguin, 1989.

Duffy, Enda. *The Subaltern Ulysses.* Minneapolis: University of Minnesota Press, 1994.

Eagleton, Terry. *Exiles and Émigrés.* New York: Schocken, 1970.

Eales, Richard. *Chess: The History of the Game.* London: Batsford, 1985.

Edelman, Lee. *Homographesis.* New York: Routledge, 1994.

Ellmann, Maud. "'The Intimate Difference': Power and Representation in *The Ambassadors.*" In Henry James, *The Ambassadors* (1903), 2nd ed., ed. S. P. Rosenbaum, 501–13. New York: W. W. Norton, 1994.

Ellmann, Richard. "Introduction: The Critic as Artist as Wilde." In *The Artist as Critic: Critical Writings of Oscar Wilde*, ed. Richard Ellmann, ix–xviii. New York: Random House, 1969.

——. *James Joyce.* New York: Oxford University Press, 1959.

Engstrom, Alfred Garvin, and Clive Scott. "Decadence." In *The New Princeton Encyclopedia of Poetry and Poetics*, ed. Alex Preminger and T. V. F. Brogan. Princeton, N.J.: Princeton University Press, 1993.

Enloe, Cynthia. *Bananas, Beaches, and Bases.* Berkeley: University of California Press, 1990.

Eshel, Amir. "Against the Power of Time: The Poetics of Suspension in W. G. Sebald's *Austerlitz.*" *New German Critique* 88 (Winter 2003): 71–96.

Esty, Jed. *A Shrinking Island: Modernism and National Culture in England.* Princeton, N.J.: Princeton University Press, 2004.

Fanon, Frantz. *Black Skin, White Masks*. Trans. Charles Lam Markmann. New York: Grove, 1967.

Feldman, Jessica R. *Gender on the Divide: The Dandy in Modernist Literature*. Ithaca, N.Y.: Cornell University Press, 1993.

Felski, Rita. *The Gender of Modernity*. Cambridge, Mass.: Harvard University Press, 1995.

Fillen-Yeh, Susan, ed. *Dandies: Fashion and Finesse in Art and Culture*. New York: New York University Press, 2001.

Foucault, Michel. "So It Is Important to Think?" In *Power*, ed. James D. Faubion, in *The Essential Works of Michel Foucault, 1954–1984*, ed. Paul Rabinow, vol. 3, 454–58. New York: The New York Press, 2000.

——. "What Is Enlightenment?" In *The Foucault Reader*, ed. Paul Rabinow, trans. Catherine Porter, 32–51. New York: Pantheon, 1984.

Freud, Sigmund. "The Paths to the Formation of Symptoms." 1917. In *Introductory Lectures on Psycho-Analysis (Part III)*. In *The Standard Edition of the Complete Psychological Works of Sigmund Freud*, vol. 16, ed. James Strachey. London: The Hogarth Press and the Institute of Psycho-Analysis, 1968.

Fried, Michael. *Realism, Writing, Disfiguration: On Thomas Eakins and Stephen Crane*. Chicago: University of Chicago Press, 1987.

Friedman, Susan Stanford. "Definitional Excursions: The Meanings of Modern/ Modernity/ Modernism." *Modernism/Modernity* 8, no. 3 (September 2001): 493–513.

——. "Geopolitical Literacy: Internationalizing Feminism at 'Home'—the Case of Virginia Woolf." In *Mappings: Feminism and the Cultural Geographies of Encounter*, 107–31. Princeton, N.J.: Princeton University Press, 1998.

Froula, Christine. *Virginia Woolf and the Bloomsbury Avant-Garde: War, Civilization, Modernity*. New York: Columbia University Press, 2005.

Fussell, Paul. *The Great War and Modern Memory*. London: Oxford University Press, 1975.

Gainer, Bernard. *The Alien Invasion: The Origins of the Aliens Act of 1905*. London: Heinemann, 1972.

Gallop, Jane. *Anecdotal Theory*. Durham, N.C.: Duke University Press, 2002.

Gaonkar, Dilip Parameshwar, ed. *Alternative Modernities*. Durham, N.C.: Duke University Press, 2001.

Garber, Marjorie. *Vested Interests: Cross-Dressing and Cultural Anxiety*. New York: Routledge, 1992.

Garnett, Edward. Unsigned review of *The Secret Agent*, by Joseph Conrad. *Nation*, 28 September 1907. Reprint, in *Conrad: The Critical Heritage*, ed. Norman Sherry, 191–93. London: Routledge & Kegan Paul, 1973.

Gates, Henry Louis, Jr. "'Authenticity,' or the Lesson of Little Tree." *The New York Times Book Review*, 24 November 1991.

George, Rosemary Marangoly. "The Cosmopolitan Club." *Novel* 25, no. 1 (Fall 1991): 103–5.

Ghosh, Amitav. *The Shadow Lines*. London: Bloomsbury, 1988.

Ghosh, Bishnupriya. *When Borne Across: Literary Cosmopolitics in the Contemporary Indian Novel*. New Brunswick, N.J.: Rutgers University Press, 2004.

Gibson, Andrew. *Joyce's Revenge: History, Politics, and Aesthetics in* Ulysses. Oxford: Oxford University Press, 2002.

Gifford, Don. *Joyce Annotated*. Berkeley: University of California Press, 1982.

——. Ulysses *Annotated: Notes for Joyce's* Ulysses. 2nd ed. Berkeley: University of California Press, 1988.

Gikandi, Simon. *Maps of Englishness: Writing Identity in the Culture of Colonialism*. New York: Columbia University Press, 1996.

Gillon, Adam. "Joseph Conrad: Polish Cosmopolitan." In *Joseph Conrad: Theory and World Fiction*, ed. Wolodymyr T. Zyla and Wendell M. Aycock, 41–69. Lubbock: Texas Tech University Press, 1974.

Gilroy, Paul. *The Black Atlantic: Modernity and Double Consciousness*. Cambridge, Mass.: Harvard University Press, 1993.

——. *After Empire: Melancholia or Convivial Culture?* London: Routledge, 2004.

——. *Against Race: Imagining Political Culture Beyond the Color Line*. Cambridge, Mass.: Harvard University Press, 2000.

Ginsberg, Elaine K. "The Politics of Passing." In *Passing and the Fictions of Identity*, ed. Elaine K. Ginsberg, 1–18. Durham: Duke University Press, 1996.

Hall, Stuart. "The New Ethnicities." 1988. In *Ethnicity*, ed. John Hutchinson and Anthony D. Smith, 161–64. Oxford: Oxford University Press, 1996.

——. "What Is This 'Black' in Black Popular Culture?" In *Black Popular Culture*, ed. Michele Wallace and Gina Dent, 121–33. Seattle: Bay Press, 1992.

Handley, William R. "War and the Politics of Narration in *Jacob's Room*." In *Virginia Woolf and War: Fiction, Reality, and Myth*, 110–33. Syracuse, N.Y.: Syracuse University Press, 1991.

Hanson, Ellis. *Decadence and Catholicism*. Cambridge, Mass.: Harvard University Press, 1997.

Harpham, Geoffrey Galt. "Abroad Only by a Fiction: Creation, Irony, and Necessity in Conrad's *The Secret Agent*." *Representations* 37 (Winter 1992): 79–103.

——. *One of Us: The Mastery of Joseph Conrad*. Chicago: The University of Chicago Press, 1996.

Haughton, Hugh. Introduction to *Alice's Adventures in Wonderland and Through the Looking Glass*, by Lewis Carroll, ed. Hugh Haughton, ix–ixv. London: Penguin, 1998.

Hejinian, Lyn. "Barbarism." In *The Language of Inquiry*, 318–36. Berkeley and Los Angeles: University of California Press, 2000.

Hervouet, Yves. *The French Face of Joseph Conrad*. Cambridge: Cambridge University Press, 1990.

Hoffman, Eva. *After Such Knowledge: Memory, History, and the Legacy of the Holocaust*. New York: Public Affairs, 2004.

Hone, Joseph M. "A Letter from Ireland." *London Mercury* 5 (January 1923): 306–8. Reprint, in *James Joyce: The Critical Heritage*, ed. Robert H. Deming, 297–8. New York: Barnes and Noble, 1970.

Horkheimer, Max. "Traditional and Critical Theory." In *Critical Theory: Selected Essays*, trans. Matthew J. O'connell et al., 188–243. New York: Herder and Herder, 1972.

Huyssen, Andreas. "Grey Zones of Remembrance." In *A New History of German*

Literature, ed. David E. Wellbery,   970–75. Cambridge, Mass.: Belknap Press of Harvard University Press, 2004.

——. "Rewritings and New Beginnings: W. G. Sebald and the Literature of the Air War." In *Present Pasts: Urban Palimpsests and the Politics of Memory*, 138–57. Stanford, Calif.: Stanford University Press, 2003.

Hynes, Samuel. *A War Imagined: The First World War and English Culture*. London: The Bodley Head, 1990.

Ishiguro, Kazuo. *An Artist of the Floating World*. 1986. New York: Vintage, 1989.

——. "A Family Supper." *Esquire* (March 1990): 207–11.

——. *A Pale View of Hills*. 1982. New York: Vintage, 1990.

——. *The Remains of the Day*. 1989. New York; London: Vintage, 1990.

——. *The Unconsoled*. 1995. New York: Vintage, 1996.

Ishiguro, Kazuo, and Oe Kenzaburo. "The Novelist in Today's World: A Conversation." *Boundary 2* 18, no. 3 (Fall 1991): 109–22.

Israel, Nico. *Outlandish: Writing Between Exile and Diaspora*. Stanford, Calif.: Stanford University Press, 2000.

Iyer, Pico. "Waiting Upon History." *Partisan Review* 58 (Summer 1991): 585–89.

Jack, Ian. "Introduction." *Granta* 81 (Spring 2003): 9–14.

James, Henry. Preface to *The Golden Bowl*. 1909. Oxford: Oxford University Press, 1983.

Jameson, Fredric. "Romance and Reification: Plot Construction and Ideological Closure in Joseph Conrad." In *The Political Unconscious: Narrative as a Socially Symbolic Act*, 206–80. Ithaca, N.Y.: Cornell University Press, 1981.

——. "Modernism and Imperialism." In *Nationalism, Colonialism, and Literature*, ed. Terry Eagleton, Fredric Jameson, and Edward W. Said, 43–68. Minneapolis: University of Minnesota Press, 1990.

——. "Third-World Literature in the Era of Multinational Capitalism." *Social Text* 15 (Fall 1986): 65–88.

Johnson, Bruce. "Conrad's Impressionism and Watt's 'Delayed Decoding.'" In *Conrad Revisited: Essays for the Eighties*, ed. Ross C. Murfin, 51–70. Tuscaloosa: University of Alabama Press, 1985.

Joyce, James. *The Critical Writings of James Joyce*, ed. Ellsworth Mason and Richard Ellman. New York: The Viking Press, 1959.

——. *Dubliners*. 1914. Reprint, New York: Penguin, 1993.

——. *The Portrait of the Artist as a Young Man*. 1916. Reprint, New York: Penguin, 1999.

——. *Selected Letters of James Joyce*. Ed. Richard Ellmann. New York: Viking Press, 1979.

——. *Ulysses*. 1922. New York: Vintage, 1986.

Kant, Immanuel. "An Answer To The Question: 'What Is Enlightenment?'" In *Kant: Political Writings*, 2nd ed., ed. Hans Reiss, trans. H. B. Nisbet, 54–60. Cambridge: Cambridge University Press, 1991.

——. "Idea For A Universal History With A Cosmopolitan Purpose." In *Kant: Political Writings*, 2nd ed., ed. Hans Reiss, trans. H. B. Nisbet, 41–53. Cambridge: Cambridge University Press, 1991.

——. "Perpetual Peace: A Philosophical Sketch." In *Kant: Political Writings*, 2nd edition, ed. Hans Reiss, trans. H. B. Nisbet, 93–130. Cambridge: Cambridge University Press, 1991.

Kaplan, Caren. *Questions of Travel: Postmodern Discourses of Displacement.* Durham, N.C.: Duke University Press, 1996.

Karl, Frederick R. *Joseph Conrad: The Three Lives.* New York: Farrar, Straus and Giroux, 1979.

Kauffmann, Stanley. "The Floating World." *New Republic,* 6 November 1995, 42–45.

Kenner, Hugh. "The Making of the Modernist Canon." *Chicago Review* 34, no. 2 (Spring 1984): 49–61.

Kerkering, John. *The Poetics of National and Racial Identity in Nineteenth-Century American Literature.* Cambridge: Cambridge Univeristy Press, 2003.

King, Bruce, ed. *The Internationalization of English Literature.* Vol. 13 of *The Oxford Literary History.* Oxford: Oxford University Press, 2004.

——. "The New Internationalism: Shiva Naipaul, Salman Rushdie, Buchi Emecheta, Timothy Mo, and Kazuo Ishiguro." In *The British and Irish Novel Since 1960,* ed. James Acheson, 192–211. New York: St. Martin's Press, 1991.

Kirschner, Paul. "Wilde's Shadow in Conrad's 'The Return.'" *Notes and Queries* 40 (December 1993): 495–96.

Kumar, Amitava, ed. *Away: The Indian Writer as Expatriate.* New York: Routledge, 2004.

——. *Bombay-London–New York.* New York: Routledge, 2002.

——. *Passport Photos.* Berkeley and Los Angeles: University of California Press, 2000.

Larbaud, Valéry. "James Joyce." *Nouvelle Revue Française* 18 (April 1922): 385–405. Reprint, in *James Joyce: The Critical Heritage,* ed. Robert H. Deming, 252–62. New York: Barnes and Noble, 1970.

Leavis, F. R. *The Great Tradition.* London: Chatto and Windus, 1960.

Leavis, Q. D. "Caterpillars of the Commonwealth Unite!" *Scrutiny* 7, no. 1 (1938): 203–14.

Lee, Benjamin. "Critical Internationalism." *Public Culture* 7, no. 3 (Spring 1995): 559–92.

Lee, Hermione. "Quiet Desolation." *New Republic,* 22 January 1990, 37.

Leone, Massimo. "Textual Wanderings: A Vertiginous Reading of W. G. Sebald." In *W. G. Sebald: A Critical Companion,* ed. J. J. Long and Anne Whitehead, 89–101. Seattle: University of Washington Press, 2004.

Levenson, Michael H. "Does *The Waste Land* Have A Politics?" *Modernism/Modernity* 6, no. 3. (September 1999): 1–13.

Levi, Neil. "'See that Straw? That's a Straw': Anti-Semitism and Narrative Form in *Ulysses.*" *Modernism/Modernity* 9, no. 3 (September 2002): 375–88.

Levi, Neil, and Michael Rothberg. "Uniqueness, Comparison, and the Politics of Memory: Introduction." In *The Holocaust: Theoretical Readings,* ed. Neil Levi and Michael Rothberg, 441–43. New Brunswick, N.J.: Rutgers University Press, 2003.

Levine, Caroline. *The Serious Pleasures of Suspense.* Charlottesville: University of Virginia Press, 2003.

Lewis, Pericles. *Modernism, Nationalism, and the Novel.* Cambridge: Cambridge University Press, 2000.

Lewis, Wyndham. *Blast* 1 (June 1914).

——. *Men Without Art.* 1934. Reprint, Santa Rosa: Black Sparrow Press, 1987.

Lezra, Jacques. "Unrelated Passions." *differences: A journal of Feminist Cultural Studies* 14, no. 1 (2003): 74–87.

Litvak, Joseph. *Strange Gourmets: Sophistication, Theory, and the Novel.* Durham, N.C.: Duke University Press, 1997.

Lloyd, David. *Anomalous States: Irish Writing and the Post-Colonial Moment.* Dublin: The Lilliput Review, 1993.

Love, Heather K. "Forced Exile: Walter Pater's Queer Modernism." In *Bad Modernisms*, ed. Douglas Mao and Rebecca L. Walkowitz, 19–43. Durham: Duke University Press, 2006.

Lukács, Georg. "Narrate or Describe?" 1936. In *Writer and Critic and Other Essays*, trans. Arthur D. Kahn, 110–48. New York: Grosset & Dunlap, 1971.

Lynd, Robert. Review. *Daily News*, 10 August 1908, 3. Reprint: In *Conrad: The Critical Heritage*, ed. Norman Sherry, 210–12. London: Routledge & Kegan Paul, 1973.

Lyotard, Jean-François. *The Postmodern Condition: A Report on Knowledge*, trans. Geoff Bennington and Brian Massumi. Minneapolis: University of Minnesota Press, 1984.

Mais, S. P. B. "An Irish Revel: And Some Flappers." *Daily Express*, 25 March 1922, 5. Reprint, in *Joyce: The Critical Heritage*, ed. Robert H. Deming, 1:191. New York: Barnes & Noble, 1970.

Majumdar, Robin, and Allen McLaurin. *Virginia Woolf: The Critical Heritage.* London; New York: Routledge, 1997.

Manganaro, Mark. *Culture, 1922: The Emergence of a Concept.* Princeton, N.J.: Princeton University Press, 2002.

Marcus, Sharon. "Anne Frank and Hannah Arendt, Universalism and Pathos." In *Cosmopolitan Geographies: New Locations Literature and Culture*, ed. Vinay Dhardwadker, 89–132. New York: Routledge, 2001.

Margolis, Joseph. *What, After All, Is a Work of Art? Lectures in the Philosophy of Art.* University Park: Pennsylvania State University Press, 1999.

Martin, Joseph. *The Shock of Trifles: Decadence in the Novels of Joseph Conrad.* Ph.D. diss., Purdue University, 1990.

Matz, Jesse. *Literary Impressionism and Modernist Aesthetics.* Cambridge: Cambridge University Press, 2001.

Mazorati, Gerald. "Salman Rushdie: Fiction's Embattled Infidel." *New York Times*, 29 January 1989.

McCrum, Robert. "The World of Books: Parochial, Smug, Ill-Informed. And That's Just the Critics." *The Observer*, 26 May 2002, 18.

McHale, Brian. *Postmodernist Fiction.* New York: Methuen, 1987.

Menand, Louis. "Anxious in Dreamland." *New York Times Book Review*, 15 October 1995, 7.

Meyers, Jeffrey. *Joseph Conrad.* New York: Charles Scribner, 1991.

Mignolo, Walter D. "The Many Faces of Cosmo-polis: Border Thinking and Critical Cosmopolitanism." In *Cosmopolitanism*, ed. Carol A. Breckenridge, Sheldon Pollock, Homi K. Bhabha, and Dipesh Chakrabarty, 157–88. Durham, N.C.: Duke University Press, 2002.

——. *Local Histories, Global Designs: Coloniality, Subaltern Knowledges, and Border Thinking.* Princeton, N.J.: Princeton University Press, 2000.

Milchman, Alan, and Alan Rosenberg. "Two Kinds of Uniqueness: The Universalization of the Holocaust." In *The Holocaust: Theoretical Readings,* ed. Neil Levi and Michael Rothberg, 444–50. New Brunswick, N.J.: Rutgers University Press, 2003.

Miller, D. A. "Sontag's Urbanity." In *The Lesbian and Gay Studies Reader,* ed. Henry Abelove, Michèle Aina Barale, and David M. Halperin, 212–20. New York: Routledge, 1993.

Miller, Monica L. "The Black Dandy as Bad Modernist." In *Bad Modernisms,* ed. Douglas Mao and Rebecca L. Walkowitz, 179–205. Durham: Duke University Press, 2006.

Miller, Nancy K. *Getting Personal: Feminist Occasions and Other Autobiographical Acts.* New York: Routledge, 1991.

Miller, Tyrus. *Late Modernism: Politics, Fiction, and the Arts Between the World Wars.* Berkeley: University of California Press, 1999.

Mishkin, Tracy. *The Harlem and Irish Renaissances: Language, Identity, Representation.* Gainesville: University Press of Florida, 1998.

Mitchell, Angus. *Casement.* London: Haus Publishing, 2003.

Morton, Kathryn. "After the War Was Lost." *New York Times Book Review,* 8 June 1986, 19.

Moten, Fred. "The New International of Decent Feelings." *Social Text* 72 (Fall 2002): 188–99.

Mouffe, Chantal. *The Democratic Paradox.* London: Verso, 2000.

——. "Which Ethics for Democracy." In *The Turn to Ethics,* ed. Marjorie Garber, Beatrice Hanssen, and Rebecca L. Walkowitz, 85–94. New York: Routledge, 2000.

Murry, John Middleton. "The Classical Revival." *The Adelphi* 3, no. 9 (February 1926): 585–95.

——. "Mr. Joyce's *Ulysses.*" (1922). Reprint, in *Defending Romanticism: Selected Criticism of Johh Middleton Murry,* ed. Malcolm Woodfield. Bristol, 117–20. The Bristol Press, 1989.

——. *The Problem of Style.* London: Oxford University Press, 1921.

Nava, Mica. "Cosmopolitan Modernity: Everyday Imaginaries and the Register of Difference." *Theory, Culture, and Society* 19, no. 1–2 (2002): 81–100.

Newark, Tim, and Quentin Newark. *Brassey's Book of Camouflage.* London: Brassey's, 1996.

Ngai, Sianne. *Ugly Feelings.* Cambridge, Mass.: Harvard University Press, 2005.

Novick, Peter. "The Holocaust in American Life." In *The Holocaust: Theoretical Readings,* ed. Neil Levi and Michael Rothberg, 474–79. New Brunswick, N.J.: Rutgers University Press, 2003.

Nussbaum, Martha C. "Patriotism and Cosmopolitanism?" In *Respondents, For Love of Country: Debating the Limits of Patriotism,* ed. Joshua Cohen, 2–20. Boston: Beacon Press, 1996.

Parker, David. "Diaspora, Dissidence, and the Dangers of Cosmopolitanism." *Asian Studies Review* 27, no. 2 (June 2003): 155–79.

Passerini, Luisa. *Europe in Love, Love in Europe: Imagination and Politics Between the Wars*. New York: New York University Press, 1999.

Pater, Walter. *The Renaissance*. New York: Modern Library, 1919.

Phillips, Adam. *On Flirtation*. Cambridge, Mass.: Harvard University Press, 1994.

Phillips, Caryl. "Extravagant Strangers." In *A New World Order*, 288–97. New York: Vintage, 2001.

Pollock, Sheldon, Homi K. Bhabha, Carol A. Breckenridge, and Dipesh Chakrabarty. "Cosmopolitanisms." In *Cosmopolitanism*, ed. Carol A. Breckenridge, Sheldon Pollock, Homi K. Bhabha, and Dipesh Chakrabarty, 1–14. Durham, N.C.: Duke University Press, 2002.

Posnock, Ross. *Color and Culture: Black Writers and the Making of the Modern Intellectual*. Cambridge, Mass.: Harvard University Press, 1998.

Pridmore-Brown, Michele. "1939–40: Of Virginia Woolf, Gramophones, and Fascism." *PMLA* 113, no. 3 (May 1998): 408–21.

Prince, Gerald. *Dictionary of Narratology*. Lincoln: University of Nebraska Press, 1987.

Proust, Marcel. *Contra Saint-Beuve*. In *Marcel Proust on Art and Literature, 1896–1919*, trans. Sylvia Townsend Warner. New York: Carroll & Graf, 1984.

——. *In Search of Lost Time*. 6 vols. 1913–27. Trans. Andreas Mayor and Terence Kilmartin. Rev. D. J. Enright. New York: The Modern Library: 1993.

Purton, Valerie. "The Reader in a Floating World: The Novels of Kazuo Ishiguro." In *The Literature of Place*, ed. Norman Page and Peter Preston, 170–79. London: Macmillan, 1993.

Radhakrishnan, R. *Theory in an Uneven World*. Oxford: Blackwell, 2003.

Reed, Christopher. *Bloomsbury Rooms: Modernism, Subculture, and Domesticity*. New Haven, Conn.: Yale University Press, 2004.

Reed, John R. *Decadent Style*. Athens: Ohio University Press, 1985.

Renan, Ernest. "What Is a Nation?" In *Becoming National: A Reader*, ed. Geoff Eley and Ronald Grigor Suny, 41–55. New York: Oxford University Press, 1996.

Richardson, Brian. "Remapping the Present: The Master Narrative of Modern Literary History and the Lost Forms of Twentieth-Century Fiction." *Twentieth Century Literature* 43, no. 3 (Autumn 1997): 291–309.

Robbins, Bruce. *Feeling Global: Internationalism in Distress*. New York: New York University Press, 1999.

——. "Introduction, Part 1: Actually Existing Cosmopolitanism." In *Cosmopolitics: Thinking and Feeling Beyond the Nation*, ed. Pheng Cheah and Bruce Robbins, 1–19. Minneapolis: University of Minnesota Press, 1998.

——. *Secular Vocations*. London: Verso, 1993.

——. "The Sweatshop Sublime." *PMLA* 117, no. 1 (January 2002): 84–97.

——. "The Village of the Liberal Managerial Class." In *Cosmopolitan Geographies: New Locations in Literature and Culture*, ed. Vinay Dharwadker, 15–32. New York: Routledge, 2001.

Rosenberg, Jordana. "The Bosom of the Bourgeoisie: Edgeworth's *Belinda*." *ELH* 70 (2003): 575–96.

Rosenfeld, Natania. *Outsiders Together: Virginia and Leonard Woolf.* Princeton, N.J.: Princeton University Press, 2000.

Rostan, Kim. "Arendt's Speculative Witnessing." Work in progress.

Rothberg, Michael. "W. E. B. Du Bois in Warsaw: Holocaust Memory and the Color Line, 1949–1952." *The Yale Journal of Criticism* 14, no. 1 (2001): 169–89.

Rushdie, Salman. *Fury.* New York: Random House, 2001.

——. "Good Advice Is Rarer Than Rubies." *East, West,* 3–16. New York: Random House, 1994.

——. *Imaginary Homelands: Essays and Criticism, 1981–1991.* New York: Penguin, 1991.

——. *The Satanic Verses.* Dover, Del.: Consortium, 1992.

Ruthven, Malise. *A Satanic Affair: Salman Rushdie and the Wrath of Islam.* London: The Hogarth Press, 1990.

Ryder, Rowland. *Edith Cavell.* London: Hamish Hamilton, 1975.

Said, Edward W. *Culture and Imperialism.* New York: Knopf, 1994.

——. "Heroism and Humanism." *Al-Ahram Weekly Online* 463 (6–12 January 2000). http://weekly.ahram.org.eg/2000/463/op10.htm.

——. *The World, the Text, and the Critic.* Cambridge, Mass.: Harvard University Press, 1983.

Sartre, Jean-Paul. *"What is Literature?" and Other Essays,* trans. Steven Ungar. Cambridge, Mass.: Harvard University Press, 1988.

Scheffler, Samuel. "Conceptions of Cosmopolitanism." *Utilitas* 11, no. 3 (November 1999): 255–76.

Scott, Joan W. "Experience." In *Feminists Theorize the Political,* ed. Judith Butler and Joan W. Scott, 51–71. New York: Routledge, 1990.

Sebald, W. G. *After Nature.* Trans. Michael Hamburger. New York: Random House, 2002.

——. *Austerlitz.* Trans. Anthea Bell. New York: Random House, 2001.

——. "Between History and Natural History: On the Literary Description of Total Destruction." In *Campo Santo,* trans. Anthea Bell, 65–96. New York: Random House, 2005.

——. *Die Ringes Des Saturn: Eine Englische Wallfahrt.* Frankfurt: Eichborn Verlag, 1995.

——. *The Emigrants.* Trans. Michael Hulse. New York: New Directions, 1996.

——. *On the Natural History of Destruction.* Trans. Anthea Bell. New York: Random House, 2003.

——. *The Rings of Saturn.* Trans. Michael Hulse. New York: New Directions, 1998.

——. *Vertigo.* Trans. Michael Hulse. New York: New Directions, 1999.

Sedgwick, Eve Kosofsky. *Epistemology of the Closet.* Berkeley: The University of California Press, 1990.

——. "Paranoid Reading and Reparative Reading; Or, You're So Paranoid, You Probably Think This Introduction Is About You." In *Novel-Gazing: Queer Reading In Fiction,* ed. Eve Kosofsky Sedgwick, 1–37. Durham, N.C.: Duke University Press, 1997.

Seidel, Michael. *Exile and the Narrative Imagination.* New Haven, Conn.: Yale University Press, 1986.

Sherry, Norman, ed. *Conrad: The Critical Heritage*. London: Routledge & Kean Paul, 1973.

Shklovsky, Victor. "Art as Technique." 1917. In *Russian Formalist Criticism: Four Essays*, ed. and trans. Lee T. Lemon and Marion J. Reis, 13–24. Lincoln: University of Nebraska Press, 1965.

Silver, Brenda R. *Virginia Woolf Icon*. Chicago: University of Chicago Press, 1999.

Sinfield, Alan. *The Wilde Century: Effeminacy, Oscar Wilde, and the Queer Moment*. New York: Columbia University Press, 1994.

Sontag, Susan. "Against Interpretation." In *Against Interpretation and Other Essays*, 3–14. New York: Delta, 1966.

——. *AIDS and Its Metaphors*. New York: Farrar, Straus and Giroux, 1989.

——. "A Mind in Mourning." 2000. In *Where the Stress Falls*, 41–48. New York: Farrar, Straus and Giroux, 2001.

——. *Regarding the Pain of Others*. New York: Picador, 2003.

Stanley, Roy M., II. *To Fool a Glass Eye*. Shrewsbury: Airlife Publishing, 1998.

Steiner, George. *Extra-Territorial: Papers on Literature and the Language Revolution*. New York: Atheneum, 1971.

Swales, Martin. "Theoretical Reflections on the Work of W. G. Sebald." In *W. G. Sebald: A Critical Companion*, ed. J. J. Long and Anne Whitehead, 23–28. Seattle: University of Washington Press, 2004.

Symons, Arthur. "Conrad." In *Dramatis Personae*. Indianapolis: Bobbs-Merrill, 1923.

Thomson, James. "Ode: Rule, Brittania." 1740. In *The Norton Anthology of English Literature*, vol. 1, 5th ed., ed. M. H. Abrams, 2474–75. New York: Norton, 1986.

Tindall, Gillian. "The Fortress of the Heart." *Times Literary Supplement*, 19 October 2001, 21.

Tóibín, Colm. "The Tragedy of Roger Casement." *New York Review of Books*, 27 May 2004, 53–57.

Turner, W. J. "Stravinsky in London and Paris." *The New Statesman*, 31 July 1920, 475.

Valente, Joseph. "James Joyce and the Cosmopolitan Sublime." In *Joyce and the Subject of History*, ed. Mark A. Wollaeger, Victor Luftig, and Robert Spoo, 59–80. Ann Arbor: University of Michigan Press, 1996.

Waldron, Jeremy. "Minority Cultures and the Cosmopolitan Alternative." *Michigan Journal of Law Reform* 25, no. 3–4 (1992): 751–93. Reprint, in *The Rights of Minority Cultures*, ed. Will Kymlicka, 341–49. Oxford: Oxford University Press, 1995.

Walkowitz, Judith R. "The 'Vision of Salome': Cosmopolitanism and Erotic Dancing in Central London, 1908–1918." *American Historical Review* 108, no. 2 (April 2003): 337–76.

Walkowitz, Rebecca L. "Cosmopolitan Ethics." In *The Turn to Ethics*, ed. Marjorie Garber, Beatrice Hanssen, and Rebecca L. Walkowitz, 221–30. New York: Routledge, 2000.

——. "Ishiguro's Floating Worlds." *ELH* 68, no. 4 (Winter 2001): 1037–64.

——. "Shakespeare in Harlem: *The Norton Anthology*, 'Propaganda,' Langston Hughes." *Modern Language Quarterly* 60, no. 4 (December 1999): 495–519.

Wall, Kathleen. "*The Remains of the Day* and Its Challenges to Theories of Unreliable Narration." *The Journal of Narrative Technique* 24, no. 1 (Winter 1994): 18–42.

Walpole, Hugh. *Joseph Conrad*. Rev. ed. London: Nisbet & Co., 1924.

Ward, Philip, ed. *The Oxford Companion to Spanish Literature*. Oxford: Oxford University Press, 1978.

Ward, Simon. "Ruins and Poetics in the Works of W. G. Sebald." In *W. G. Sebald: A Critical Companion*, ed. J. J. Long and Anne Whitehead, 58–71. Seattle: University of Washington Press, 2004.

Warner, Michael. "Uncritical Reading." In *Polemic: Critical or Uncritical*, ed. Jane Gallop, 13–38. New York: Routledge, 2004.

Watt, Ian. *Conrad in the Nineteenth Century*. Berkeley: University of California Press, 1979.

Wicke, Jennifer. "*Mrs. Dalloway* Goes to Market: Woolf, Keynes, and Modern Markets." *Novel* 28, vol. 1 (Fall 1994): 5–23.

Wilde, Oscar. "The Decay of Lying." 1889. In *The Artist as Critic: Critical Writings of Oscar Wilde*, ed. Richard Ellmann, 290–319. Chicago: University of Chicago Press, 1982.

——. *The Importance of Being Earnest*. 1895. In *The Importance of Being Earnest and Other Plays*, ed. Peter Raby, 247–307. Oxford: Oxford University Press, 1995.

——. Preface to *The Picture of Dorian Gray*. In *The Artist as Critic: Critical Writings of Oscar Wilde*, ed. Richard Ellmann, 235–36. Chicago: University of Chicago Press, 1982.

Wilhelmus, Tom. "Between Cultures." *The Hudson Review* 49, no. 2 (Summer 1996): 316–22.

Williams, Arthur. "W. G. Sebald: A Holistic Approach to Borders, Texts, and Perspectives." In *German-Language Literature Today: International and Popular?* ed. Arthur Williams, Stuart Parks, and Julian Preece, 99–118. Oxford: Peter Lang, 2000.

Williams, Raymond. *Culture and Society, 1780–1950*. New York: Harper & Row, 1958.

——. *Keywords: A Vocabulary of Culture and Society*. New York: Oxford University Press, 1983.

——. "Metropolitan Perceptions and the Emergence of Modernism." In *The Politics of Modernism: Against the New Conformists*, ed. Tony Pinkney, 37–48. London: Verso, 1989.

Wolfe, Alan. *Suicidal Narrative in Modern Japan*. Princeton, N.J.: Princeton University Press, 1990.

Wolff, Janet. "The Feminine in Modern Art: Benjamin, Simmel, and the Gender of Modernity." *Theory, Culture, and Society* 17 (2000): 33–53.

Woolf, Leonard. *Beginning Again: An Autobiography of the Years 1911 to 1918*. London: Hogarth Press, 1972.

Woolf, Leonard, and Virginia Woolf. *Two Stories*. London: Hogarth Press, 1917.

Woolf, Virginia. *A Room of One's Own*. In *A Room of One's Own and Three Guineas*, ed. Michèle Barrett. London: Penguin, 2000.

——. "The Artist and Politics." 1936. Reprinted in *The Moment and Other Essays*, 225–28. New York: Harcourt Brace and Jovanovich, 1948.

——. Letter to Jacques Raverat. 8 June, 1924. In *The Letters of Virginia Woolf*, vol. 3: 1923–1928, ed. Nigel Nicolson, 115. London: Hogarth, 1977.

——. "The Mark on the Wall." 1917. In *The Complete Shorter Fiction of Virginia Woolf*, 2nd ed., ed. Susan Dick, 83–89. New York; London: Harcourt Brace & Company, 1989.

——. "Modern Fiction." 1925. In *The Common Reader*, ed. Andrew McNiellie, 146–54. New York: Harcourt Brace, 1984.

——. "Mr Bennett and Mrs Brown." 1924. In *The Captain's Death Bed and Other Essays*, 94–119. New York: Harcourt, 1978.

——. *Mrs. Dalloway*. 1925. Reprint, New York: Harcourt, 1981.

——. "Thoughts on Peace in an Air Raid." In *The Death of the Moth and Other Essays*, 244–47. New York: Harcourt Brace, 1942.

——. *Three Guineas*. 1938. In *A Room of One's Own and Three Guineas*, ed. Michèle Barrett. London: Penguin, 2000.

——. *The Years*. 1938. Ed. Hermione Lee. Oxford: Oxford University Press, 1992.

Young, Robert J. C. *Colonial Desire: Hybridity in Theory, Culture, and Race*. London: Routledge, 1995.

Zabus, Chantal. "Language, Orality, and Literature." In *New National and Post-Colonial Literatures*, ed. Bruce King, 129–44. Oxford: Oxford University Press, 1996.

Žižek, Slavoj. "How the Non-Duped Err." *Qui Parle* 4, no. 1 (Fall 1990): 1–20.

Zwerdling, Alex. *Improvised Europeans: American Literary Expatriates in London*. New York: Basic Books, 1998.

——. *Virginia Woolf and the Real World*. Berkeley: University of California Press, 1986.